A PROPHETIC VISION FOR THE 21ST CENTURY

A Prophetic Vision for the 21st Century

A SPIRITUAL MAP TO HELP YOU NAVIGATE INTO THE FUTURE

Rick Joyner

A JANET THOMA BOOK

THOMAS NELSON PUBLISHERS
Nashville

Published in Nashville, Tennessee, by Thomas Nelson, Inc.

Unless otherwise noted, Scripture quotations are from the NEW AMERICAN STANDARD BIBLE®, © Copyright The Lockman Foundation 1960, 1962, 1963, 1968, 1971, 1972, 1973, 1975, 1977, 1995. Used by permission.

Scripture quotations noted AMPLIFIED are from THE AMPLIFIED BIBLE: Old Testament. © 1962, 1964 by Zondervan Publishing House (used by permission); and THE AMPLIFIED NEW TESTAMENT. Copyright © 1958 by The Lockman Foundation (used by permission).

Scripture quotations noted KJV are from the KING JAMES VERSION.

Scripture quotations noted NKJV are from THE NEW KING JAMES VERSION. Copyright © 1979, 1980, 1982, Thomas Nelson, Inc., Publishers.

Scripture quotations noted RSV are from the REVISED STANDARD VERSION of the Bible. Copyright © 1946, 1952, 1971, 1973 by the Division of Christian Education of the National Council of the Churches of Christ in the U.S.A. Used by permission.

ISBN 0-7394-0663-9
Printed in the United States of America

DEDICATION

I would like to dedicate this book to the generation of my parents, my generation, and the generation of my children. The sacrifice and vision of my parents' spiritual generation laid the foundation for the ultimate and glorious triumph of truth. My generation has continued the good fight and helped prepare the map for the future. It will be the generation of my children that will probably fight the last battle for truth. God is "the God of Abraham, Isaac, and Jacob"—the God of every generation. In each of these generations His ways are wonderfully revealed.

CONTENTS

Acknowledgments ix

PART 1: HOW SHALL WE THEN LIVE?

1. The Call 3

PART 2: THE CHRISTIAN AND THE 21ST CENTURY

A Vision: Field of Dreams or Nightmares? 19

2. The Mark of God or the Mark of the Beast? 25

3. Accusers of the Brethren 34

4. Storms in the Coming Years 47

5. Know Your Calling and Be an Achiever 57

6. Recognizing God's Voice 74

7. The Many Faces of Racism 94

8. Let the Battle Begin 105

9. Birth Pangs and Earthquakes 122

10. The Religious Spirit 135

PART 3: THE CHURCH AND THE 21ST CENTURY

11. The New Age and the Kingdom of God 157

A Vision: War and Glory 168

12. Civil War in the Church 178

A Vision: *The Next Wave Is upon Us* 192

13. Catching the Next Wave 194

A Vision: *A Bridge to Revival* 205

14. Why Revival Tarries for America 209

15. Prophecy for the 21st Century 226

Notes 247

ACKNOWLEDGMENTS

This book is mostly the result of Janet Thoma's vision and hard work. She pieced together an anthology from my writings that captures the heart of my messages over the last decade in order to present a summary of my prophetic perspective for the future. I think she did a better job than I could have done.

PART 1

HOW SHALL
WE THEN LIVE???

---

1 THE CALL

An important prophecy is given in Acts 2:17–18:

> "And it shall be in the last days," God says,
> "That I will pour forth of My Spirit upon all mankind;
> And your sons and your daughters shall prophesy,
> And your young men shall see visions,
> And your old men shall dream dreams;
> Even upon My bondslaves, both men and women,
> I will in those days pour forth of My Spirit
> And they shall prophesy."

In the last days, the Lord will pour forth of His Spirit on all mankind, and the result will be that prophecy will flow through all of His servants. This will include both men and women, old and young. However, this pouring out of the Spirit and prophecy will be not just for our entertainment but also because we will need it to accomplish the last-day mandate of the church.

I have experienced a considerable amount of prophecy in my own life. After my conversion in 1971, I have had, at times, an ability to foresee certain future events accurately, but usually in a very general sense. I could also occasionally look at people and know details about them, such as problems they were having or spiritual callings on their life. I understood this ability to be the biblical gifts of a word of knowledge and prophecy. Though I understood the usefulness of these gifts in ministry to people, I did not have much interest in the biblical prophecies of end-time events. For the next eighteen years, I did not seek visions, revelations, or the knowledge to understand these end times and remained mostly ignorant of many of the popular end-time scenarios taught within the church. I have actually been much more oriented toward church history than seeking to know impending events.

After several years in the full-time ministry, I was convicted that I was shallow in my personal relationship with the Lord, and, therefore, in my ministry as well. I felt like a real Martha, busy doing so many things for Him that I never really got to know Him. My lack of intimacy with the Lord caused me to lean more on formulas and procedures than the anointing that is essential to giving life to truth.

In 1980, I determined to leave the ministry until I had recovered the simplicity of devotion to Christ. I was a pilot by profession, so I took a job flying corporate aircraft. This gave me a lot of free time for study and prayer. I found a church where I could sit on the back row and just enjoy the fellowship of the people. I was not involved in ministry for the next seven years. Nor did I receive any prophetic revelation or operate in the gifts of the Spirit during that time.

In 1982, I received a specific call to return to the ministry. At the same time, a business opportunity opened. I still felt inadequate and shallow about my ministry. I also had just received the worse personal attack I had ever experienced from the enemy. That attack made me feel even more unprepared for ministry, so I took the business opportunity. Though I did not fall into carnality or what might be considered overt sins, I certainly drifted from the Lord for the next five years as I became consumed with building my business.

In 1987, the Lord again called me back into ministry with the word that my commission would be given to another if I did not return at that time. I did not really know what my "commission" was, but I knew I did not want to lose it, so I responded immediately to this call.

I was quite sure I was not supposed to pastor again, but I really did not know what I was going to do. I had not read a single Christian magazine or watched Christian television for more than seven years. I had little knowledge of what was even going on in the church at large. However, I had written *There Were Two Trees in the Garden* a few years before, and its popularity had brought me some invitations to speak. I called a few pastors I knew and others who had contacted me because of the book and let them know I was available for ministry.

A month or so later, I returned home after my first ministry trip in more than seven years, feeling as empty and inadequate as ever—and quite out of step with the churches I had visited. Yet, I was feeling much closer to the Lord; my desire to serve Him in ministry had returned.

The next morning I went into my office to catch up on some paperwork and to pray for insight on what I was to do in the ministry. I felt an overwhelming presence of the Lord. Then, after seven years with no prophetic revelation, I had a three-day prophetic experience in which I felt the Lord tried to catch me up on all I had missed. At this time I wrote *The Harvest*, which was about the present state of the church and impending events.

Since then, I have had other visions and revelations that were published in books like *The Final Quest* and *The Call*. Some of the revelations came in open visions. These were visible, external visions that were like watching a cinema screen. Others were gentle, internal visions that were like having the "eyes of your heart" opened. I usually relate the word *vision* to the prophetic event of seeing pictures, either internally or externally. I consider *revelation* to be the receiving of knowledge or understanding beyond our natural ability to attain.

I now have visions and dreams filled with symbolism that requires interpretation, as do most biblical visions. Some of what is shared in this book did not come in vision form but came as a massive anointing with the gift of the word of knowledge. All of a sudden, I knew many details about future events, as though they had been poured into me. In all of this, I have been trying to determine God's call on my life and His purpose for His church.

Understanding that prophecy is still "seeing through a glass darkly," and understanding that we only know "in part" (1 Cor. 13:12 KJV), I am aware that what I am sharing must be put together with what others are seeing to be a complete picture. I have tried to share exactly what I have been given to see or understand, but because the canon of Scripture is complete, I do not believe that any prophetic gift today is of the quality of those who wrote Scripture. I believe that this is why we are told in 1 Corinthians 14:29 to "let two or three prophets speak, and let the others pass judgment." I do not believe that anyone alive today is infallible. We must judge prophecy regardless of who is speaking. I offer this book to be weighed and prayerfully considered. I believe that His sheep will know His voice, be able to discern that which is from Him, and disregard the rest.

One of the most significant visions for me and for my understanding of the church occurred in 1998 and was published in *The Call*.

THE CALL

In this vision, I was standing on a high mountain overlooking a great plain. Before me, an army was marching on a wide front. There were twelve divisions in the vanguard that stood out sharply from the great multitude of soldiers who followed behind them. These divisions were further divided into what I assumed to be regiments, battalions, companies, and squads. The divisions were distinguished by their banners, and the regiments were distinguished by their different-colored uniforms.

Then I was close enough to see their faces—male and female, old and young, from every race. There was fierce resolution on their faces, yet they did not seem tense. War was in the air, but in the ranks I could sense a profound peace. I knew that not a single soldier feared the approaching battle. The spiritual atmosphere I felt when close to them was as awesome as their appearance.

I looked at their uniforms. The colors were brilliant. Every soldier also wore rank insignias and medals. The generals and other officers marched in the ranks with the soldiers. Although it was obvious that those with higher rank were in charge, no one seemed overly sensitive to his rank. From the highest officer to the lowest, they all seemed to be close friends. It was an army of unprecedented discipline, yet it also seemed to be just one big family.

As I studied them, they seemed selfless—not because they lacked identity, but because they were all so sure of who they were and what they were doing. They were not consumed with themselves or seeking recognition. I could not detect ambition or pride anywhere in the ranks. It was stunning to see so many who were so unique; yet, they were in such harmony and marched in perfect step. I was sure that an army like this had never existed on earth.

Then I was behind the front divisions, looking at a much larger group that was composed of hundreds of divisions. Each of these was a different size, with the smallest numbering about two thousand and the largest in the hundreds of thousands. Although this group was not as sharp and colorful as the first one, it was an awesome army simply because of its size. This group had banners, but they were not nearly as large and impressive as those of the first group. They all had uniforms and ranks, but I was surprised that many of these did not even have on a full set of armor, and many did not have weapons. The armor and weapons that they did have were not nearly as polished and bright as those of the first group.

As I looked more closely at these ranks, I could see that they were all determined and had purpose, but they lacked the focus of the first group. These soldiers seemed much more aware of their own rank and the rank of those around them. I felt that this was a distraction, hindering their focus. I could also sense ambition and jealousy in the ranks, which unquestionably was a further distraction. Even so, I felt that this second division still had a higher level of devotion and purpose than any army on earth did. This, too, was a very powerful force.

Behind this second army was a third one that marched so far behind the first two armies, I was not sure they could even see the other two groups ahead of them. This group was many times larger than the first and second armies combined, seemingly composed of millions and millions. As I watched from a distance, this army would move in different directions like a great flock of birds, sweeping first one way and then another, never moving in a straight direction for long. Because of this erratic movement, it drifted farther and farther from the first two groups.

As I came closer, I saw that these soldiers had on tattered, dull gray uniforms that were neither pressed nor clean. Almost everyone was bloody and wounded. A few were attempting to march, but most just walked in the general direction in which the others were headed.

Fights broke out constantly in the ranks, causing many of the wounds. Some of the soldiers were trying to stay close to the frayed banners scattered throughout their ranks. Even so, not even those near the banners had a clear identity because they were constantly drifting from one banner to another.

In this third army, I was surprised that there were only two ranks—generals and privates. Only a few had on a piece of armor, and I did not see any weapons except dummy weapons carried by the generals. The generals flaunted these weapons as if having them made the officers special, but even those in the ranks could tell that the weapons were not real. This was sad, because it was obvious that those in the ranks desperately wanted to find someone who was real to follow.

There did not seem to be any ambition except among the generals. This was not because of selflessness as in the first army, but because there was so little caring. I thought that at least the ambition present in the second group would be much better than the confusion that prevailed in this group. The generals here seemed to be more intent on talking about themselves and fighting one another, which the little groups around the banners were constantly doing. I could then see that the battles within the ranks caused the great sweeping, erratic changes of directions this group made from time to time.

As I looked at the millions in the last group, I felt that even with their great numbers, they did not actually add strength to the army but instead weakened it. In a real battle, they would be much more of a liability than an asset. Just sustaining them with food and protection would cost more in resources than any value they could add to the army's fighting ability. A private in the first or second group would be worth more than many generals from the third. I could not understand why the first groups even allowed this group to tag along behind them. They obviously were not true soldiers.

Later, I was standing in the Hall of Judgment before the judgment seat. The Lord appeared as Wisdom, but I had never seen Him more fierce nor His words come with more weight.

"You have already seen this army in your heart many times. The leaders I am commissioning now will lead this army. I am sending you to many of these leaders. What will you say to them?"

"Lord, this is a great army, but I am still grieved about the condition of the third group. I do not understand why they are even allowed to pretend to be a part of Your army. I would like to say that before they go any farther, the first and second armies should turn and drive away this third group. They are really little more than a huge mob."

"What you saw today is still in the future. The ministries I am about to release will gather this army and equip them to be all that you saw. At this time, almost My entire army is in the condition of the third group. How can I let them be driven away?"

This stunned me, although I knew I had never seen any of the Lord's people who were in as good shape as even the second group of this army.

"Lord, I know I felt Your anger at this group. If almost Your entire army is now in that condition, I am just thankful that You have not destroyed all of us. When I was looking at this third group, I felt that their deplorable condition was due to a lack of training, equipping, and vision, as well as a failure to embrace the cross that circumcises the heart."

Sometime later, I was no longer before the judgment seat, but on the mountain overlooking the army again. Wisdom was standing beside me. He was resolute, but I no longer felt the pain and anger that I had felt before.

"I have allowed you to see a little into the future," Wisdom began. "I am sending you to those who are called to prepare My army and lead it. These are the ones who have been fighting the battle on the mountain. These are the ones who have met the army of the accuser and remained faithful. These are the ones who have watched over My people and protected them at the risk of their own lives. They are called to be leaders in My army who will fight in the great battle at the end and will stand without fear against all the powers of darkness.

"As you can see, this army is marching, but there will be times when it camps. The camping is as important as the marching. It is the time for planning, training, and sharpening skills and weapons. It is also time for those in the first group to walk among the second, and for the leaders of the second group to walk among the third group, finding those who can be called to the next level. Do this while you can, for the time is near when Revelation 11:1–2 will be fulfilled, and those who want to be called by My name but do not walk in My ways will be trodden underfoot. Before the last great battle, My army will be holy, even as I am holy. I will remove those who are not circumcised of heart and the leaders who do not uphold My righteousness. When the last battle is fought, there will be no third group as you see here.

"Until now when My army has camped, most of the time has been wasted. Just as I only lead My people forward with a clear objective, so it is that when I call My army to camp, there is a purpose. The strength of the army that marches will be determined by the quality of its camp. When it is time to stop and camp for a season, it is to teach My people My ways. An army is an army whether it is in battle or at peace. You must learn how to camp, how to march, and how to fight. You will not do any one of these well unless you do them all well.

"You will come to a time in the future when you see My army exactly as it is now. At that time, you will feel My burning anger. Know that I will no longer abide those who remain in the condition of the third group. Then I will stop the march of the entire army until those in this group have been disciplined either to become soldiers or be dispersed. I will discipline those in the second group to cast off their evil ambitions and live for Me and My truth. Then My army will march forth, not to destroy but to give life. I will be in the midst of them to tread My enemies under this army's feet. I am coming to be the Captain of the Host!"

THE ARMY OF THE TWENTY-FIRST CENTURY

I believe that every Christian will march in one of these three armies in the twenty-first century. One of the factors that will determine where each of us belongs is how well we have been trained for service. Now is the time to camp. Now is the time for planning, training, and sharpening skills and weapons. This book is the result of the last ten years of hearing from the Lord both in visions and revelations. I hope that it can serve as something of a training manual for those who seek to answer God's call to know the Lord and serve Him in the coming perilous days.

Satan's ultimate goal is to populate hell. His greatest ally for accomplishing this goal is death, and his most effective means for bringing about death is war. Instigating war in any form, between anyone he can get to fight, is one of his most basic strategies. He views every war as a victory, and the most destructive ones as some of his greatest achievements. Just as Jesus is the Prince of Peace, Satan is the prince of war.

Some "righteous wars" are fought for righteous causes. Even so, the church should view every war as a significant defeat, even if the side of righteousness prevails. They are defeats because the Lord has invested an authority in the church for waging spiritual warfare, which, if exercised properly, can accomplish the goals of righteous causes without the destruction of war. Just as Jesus was sent to destroy the works of the devil, we have been sent into the world with this same commission.

The ultimate conflict between life and death is about to enter its last and greatest battle. It will rage from one end of the earth to the other, in every city and town, on every social, philosophical, and political front. A time is coming when every debate, every political campaign, and every social movement will be seen as a battle line between these ultimate spiritual forces. There will be no neutral ground, no truces, and no peace in this war. This will be both the most dangerous and the most opportune time for Christianity since the beginning.

THE BATTLEFIELD

Every warrior in this battle is given positions to defend and positions to take from the enemy. We must defend our families, our congregations, and our places of work against the words of death. At the same time, we must work each day to extend the kingdom's domain.

Our battle maps are our prayer lists. We must have specific targets. We must "box in such a way, as not beating the air" (1 Cor. 9:26), but knowing what we are hitting. As we gain dominion over the smaller assignments, we will be given more authority to go after bigger strongholds. For instance, those who take spiritual dominion over their families will then be given their neighbors and their families. Those who take their neighborhoods will then be given their cities. Joel described the army of the Lord:

> They run like mighty men;
> They climb the wall like soldiers;
> And they each march in line,
> Nor do they deviate from their paths.
> They do not crowd each other;
> They march everyone in his path.
> When they burst through the defenses,
> They do not break ranks. (Joel 2:7–8)

Christians must view every encounter with others as an opportunity to sow life. This does not mean that we must declare the plan of salvation to every checkout clerk or waitress, but we must take a stand for God's kingdom by resolutely maintaining our position in Christ. This position is always demonstrated by the fruit of the Spirit (Gal. 5:22). Whenever we can endure the often trying and unfair encounters of life without compromising our position in love, joy, peace, patience, kindness, goodness, faithfulness, gentleness, and self-control, we are extending the limits of the kingdom of God.

One of the greatest demonstrations of the Spirit I have ever witnessed was not a miracle, but a situation in an airline ticket line.

A DEMONSTRATION OF THE KINGDOM

Because of problems with incoming flights and other delays, the line to one connection had grown to many more people than could be processed in the short time before the flight was to depart. Strife and impatience were rising to the point where I seriously thought the situation was going to get out of control.

At the worst possible moment, just after more bad news had been announced, two large, boisterous women, each carrying two huge suitcases, started pushing their way through the line, demanding to go to the front. I do not recall ever witnessing more obnoxious attitudes. Even though they were women, I was fully expecting someone to deck them both. Then, to my dismay, they headed right toward my friend who was in line for the flight.

As others were actually beginning to jostle the two women, my friend instinctively raced to their assistance, asking if he could help them with their bags and offering them his own position near the front of the line. This action was so contrary to the prevailing spirit that everyone was stunned. A great quiet came over the entire scene. As my friend picked up his own bags and moved to the back of the line, every eye was on him. The two women were also undone by the unexpected, undeserved kindness.

The agents, who had also witnessed the scene, suddenly became agreeable and somehow the flight was delayed enough to get everyone on it. I have witnessed many miracles of biblical stature, but that airport scene still stands out to me as a profound demonstration of the kingdom. As hell was fast gaining control of a volatile situation, moving it toward potentially serious strife, Satan brought in two of his biggest guns and aimed them right at the Christian, who quickly disarmed the enemy and his entire host with one genuine act of kindness.

We have been given this same power in every situation. When strife arises in our family or at the office, we can join the side of the enemy or the side of the Prince of Peace. Our choice will almost certainly determine the outcome. If we are the only one who joins with the Lord, the result will still be the same: Evil will be overcome by good. One person plus the Lord always make a majority. This book is an attempt to help Christians make this choice in the new millennium.

The Direction

I have divided the book into three main sections. Part 1, which you are reading now, asks the question: How shall we then live? Part 2 is a guide for individual Christians in the twenty-first century. It contains many of the practical tools we will need to fulfill our commission in the days ahead. I begin with a vision, "Field of Dreams or Nightmares?" which predicts economic turmoil in the coming years. In this section we consider our personal responsibility in our finances, our relationship with other Christians, and our continuous battle against the enemy. We cannot serve in God's army if we are not living in His righteousness. We will also look at ways to deal with the storms that lie ahead, how to know God's call for our lives, and how to hear His voice amid the cacophony in our world today.

Part 3 is a guide for each Christian as a member of the entire army of God: the church. What is the church's call in the days ahead? And why has she seemed to miss her call in the twentieth century? We will look at the devil's strategy to blind the world through the New Age movement, and why he has advanced so far in the twentieth century. Next I will share a vision, "War and Glory," that depicts civil war in the church. Like the American Civil War, this war will ultimately lead to a more perfect union. Then we will look at the next wave of change in the church. This understanding was also inspired by a vision, "The Next Wave Is upon Us." We will ask and answer the question, Why has revival tarried for America? and look at a vision, "A Bridge to Revival," that I had in 1997. Finally, we will look at how the church can put on spiritual binoculars so that she can see into the twenty-first century.

The ultimate goal of the church is to populate heaven. Our weapon is the gospel of salvation, the words of everlasting life. The knowledge of salvation is the most precious gift anyone can have, and we, the church, have been entrusted with it. The church is about to be given the words of life with greatly increased power. These words will be spiritual bombs and hand grenades with the power to destroy even the most effective strongholds of the enemy. Individual statements spoken by Christians to nonbelievers will be able to unravel the intricate webs of deception the enemy has taken years to weave. Public statements by Christians will undo the enemy's propaganda, which has been built on thousands of books, articles, and public statements throughout the twentieth century.

This power in words will not be gained cheaply. Those who are given this authority will have faithfully waged wars against their own tongues and their own wayward thoughts, bringing them into submission to the Holy Spirit. Pure waters must come from pure wells. The degree to which our own lives are pure will be the degree to which the waters of life can flow through us: "Watch over your heart with all diligence, for from it flow the springs of life" (Prov. 4:23).

At the end of the vision in *The Call*, I saw the glory of all ages in a single moment. I saw the earth and the heavens as one. I saw myriads of angels and myriads of people who were more glorious than any angel I had yet seen. These were all serving in the Lord's house. That is our quest, to see the glory of the Lord revealed through His people.

It is my prayer that through this book you will better know the call that is on the life of every believer and especially understand how it relates to our own times. Biblical prophecy is clear about one thing: Before the end comes, the church will become the glorious bride she is called to be, one worthy of our great Savior. A generation is going to fulfill the prophecy of Isaiah 60:1–5. Why not this one?

> Arise, shine; for your light has come,
> And the glory of the LORD has risen upon you.
> For behold, darkness will cover the earth,
> And deep darkness the peoples;
> But the LORD will rise upon you,
> And His glory will appear upon you.
> And nations will come to your light,
> And kings to the brightness of your rising.
> Lift up your eyes round about, and see;
> They all gather together, they come to you.
> Your sons will come from afar,
> And your daughters will be carried in the arms.
> Then you will see and be radiant,
> And your heart will thrill and rejoice;
> Because the abundance of the sea will be turned to you,
> The wealth of the nations will come to you.

PART 2

THE CHRISTIAN AND
THE 21ST CENTURY

A Vision

FIELD OF DREAMS OR NIGHTMARES?

While praying in August 1995, I saw a field in a vision. The end of the field was covered in fog. Not far into the fog there was a very steep cliff. In the middle of the cliff there was a narrow, twisting, steep path that appeared like a descending bridge. It had the same green grass on it that the field did, and this grass went all the way to the bottom.

Most of those who walked into the fog missed the little path and fell over the cliff. Some of these died, but there were nets below the cliff that caught many of them. However, these nets were not there to save the people but to trap them. Others entered the fog carefully, dropping to their knees and searching for the path, which they seemed intuitively to know was there. Most of these people were able to find the path, and they carefully started down on their knees. A very few people had parachutes, and they jumped off the cliff into the fog.

At the bottom of the cliff was a sea with four kinds of ships in the harbor—slave ships, warships, luxury liners, and hospital ships. Most of the ships were slavers. The next greatest number were warships. Only five were hospital ships, all of which were on clean, well-kept docks right in the middle of the harbor. The two luxury liners were docked at each end of the harbor. There was an abundance of supplies on the luxury liners' docks, but both the docks and ships looked filthy and poorly maintained. No warships were docked; they all kept moving about in the harbor.

The people who fell into the nets were put on the slave ships. Most of those who made it down the steep paths headed for the hospital ships, but many headed for the luxury liners. Of those who headed for the luxury liners, some were captured and made to board a slave ship. The luxury liners were closely guarded and were obviously under the control of the warships. The warships occasionally took people from the slave ships and luxury liners, and they took whomever they wanted; they could not be resisted.

Those from the hospital ships also took people from the other ships, but they took only those who were the weakest or who were so sick or wounded that they were not expected to live. The crewmen of the hospital ships were shown respect because they wore brilliant armor that seemed to confound everyone else. Those who were jumping off the cliff with the parachutes were all landing on the hospital ships or their docks.

When a slave ship would fill up, it would depart, making frequent turns as if it really did not know where it was going. The warships were also making so many turns, that it seemed impossible to tell which way they would go next. Any ship that happened to be in the way of a warship when it turned was blasted and sunk. If the warships turned toward each other, they started shooting at each other until one was sunk.

Because of the fog many ships collided with other ships and sank. The water was filled with sharks that quickly devoured those who fell into it. The confusion, despair, and fear over the harbor were as thick as the fog. When the fog became even thicker, these fears intensified. Then as the fog subsided, hope began to rise in the people. Once the fog lifted enough that the open sea could be seen, the ships began heading for it.

The hospital ships were the only ones that sailed as if they knew where they were going. They could sail right through the chaos in the harbor and into the open sea at will. One or two of them were constantly going out to sea, disappearing for a time and then returning. Then another would go and do the same.

As I followed one of these ships to the open sea, suddenly it was as if I were standing on the bridge of the ship. The farther out we went, the more the sky cleared. Soon it became bluer than I had ever seen it, except when flying in a high altitude jet. I was so intrigued by the sky that I had not been watching the sea. When I looked back at it, I saw that we actually were flying at a very high altitude.

I thought that we were going out into space, but soon we descended toward what appeared to be a whole new world. It was composed of islands, each with a different culture of people on it. The wounded on our hospital ship were placed on several of the different islands, so that each wounded person was with those from his or her own culture.

These islands were at perfect peace, and beautiful white bridges connected them to one another, with a constant flow of people across the bridges. On each island vast foundations were being laid for great cities.

Even though each island was very different, and all of them were different from any place I had ever seen, I felt immediately at home on each one. They were each like paradise, and though they seemed to be on a different world, I knew that they were somehow very close to the one I had just left.

THE INTERPRETATION

In this vision, I realized that the end of the field indicated that the end of our economic prosperity is now in sight. What I saw at the end was much more catastrophic than I had ever thought. Some very dark times are ahead, but at the same time, a whole new world is being built right in our midst that is more wonderful than we can even imagine. The time we have been given until that happens is for the purpose of preparation. Let us build our hope and trust on the kingdom, which alone cannot be shaken.

Those people who kept walking into the fog, just as they had been walking in the open field, not discerning or acknowledging the change, either perished or fell into slavery. Those who immediately fell to their knees were able to find a safe way down, but the path still went down. They had to stay on their knees all the way; no one could have stood up on that slope because it was too steep and narrow. Falling to our knees speaks of prayer. As soon as we see the fog or confusion, we must pray for every step we take thereafter.

That no one ascended, but all went down to the bottom of the cliff, spoke to me that the economy of the whole world was going down. Many will survive what is coming, but not at their current level. Much of our present standard of living has been built upon credit, borrowing from the future, and the future is now here. We are fast approaching the time when the bills will have to be paid, and that will cause a drastic reduction of our present lifestyles.

I felt that the slave ships were banks. During the Great Depression, banks were so overextended that most of them failed. Somehow, they have now positioned themselves not only to survive another economic collapse, but also actually to be in a place to enslave those who are in debt to them.

The warships were all different sizes, and I felt they represented different powers. Their efforts were not coordinated, but they all seemed to be in as much confusion as everyone else, and all seemed to be at war with one another. They lived by plundering the other ships and each other. I believe that in the times ahead, small wars will be flashing up almost everywhere and without reason. Anyone who gets in the way of those with some power will be in trouble.

The luxury ships were so filthy that being on them was only slightly better than being on a slave or warship. It was obvious that the luxury of the future will not be as we know it today. Also, the warships were constantly plundering the luxury ships, making them almost an intolerable place to be. Even a hint of luxury in the future may serve only to make us targets.

I knew that the hospital ships were the church. They were glistening white with red crosses on them. They were so bright and clean, they stood out dramatically in my vision. White speaks of purity, and the red crosses told me they were bearing the cross. Red is also the color of sacrifice. These ships were so beautiful that anyone would have wanted to be on them. The church will become the most desirable place in the world to be, and the church will become the pure vessel she is called to be when she takes up the cross, committing herself to the life of sacrifice. In the times ahead, the life of sacrifice and service to others will be the most desirable life in the world.

The people on the hospital ships each wore brilliant silver armor. They, too, stood out dramatically whenever they appeared, and this caused everyone to show them great respect, even the warships. This told me that when believers learn to wear their armor, they are going to command the whole world's respect, and they will have authority because of it.

The docks of the hospital ships were also spotless and were overflowing with supplies. There was far more wealth on them than on the luxury ships, but the wealth was being used for service, not luxury. Because the individuals with the armor and the hospital ships commanded such respect, no one was trying to plunder their great stocks of supplies, even though they were obvious to everyone.

When a hospital ship pulled between two warships that were fighting, they would stop fighting and give them their wounded. It seemed that this was one of the primary purposes of these ships—simply to stop the fighting whenever they could.

In the midst of the chaos of this place, the dignity, resolve, and purpose with which the Christians and their ships moved was stunning. The greatest feeling of freedom came over me when I stood on the bridge of the ship leaving for the open sea. As soon as we entered the open sea and were out of the fog, we ascended into the heavenly places. When we came back down, it was to a seemingly new earth, even though I knew somehow that it was right in the middle of what I had left.

That I entered this extraordinary freedom on a hospital ship speaks of finding our true peace when we take up our crosses to serve others. And if we do that, we will begin to dwell in the heavenly places. Then we will see the earth very differently; we will see what God is doing. I really felt that those paradise islands were already right in our midst, but we just could not see them yet.

In prophetic language, the sea often represents mass humanity. That the sea at the bottom of the cliff was in the most terrible chaos represents what the kingdoms of this world are headed for. The islands represent the Lord's laying a foundation for His kingdom, right in our midst, at this same time. That I knew these islands were close to the sea of confusion spoke to me that what the Lord is about to build on the earth is also very close at hand.

At the very time when the world descends into a terrible chaos, which will probably begin with economic chaos, God is building bridges between peoples that will be the foundation of a glorious future. The end of this age is the beginning of the one over which Christ will reign. In Revelation 17:15, we are told, "The waters which you saw where the harlot sits, are peoples and multitudes and nations and tongues."

The bridges are right now being built between peoples. The bridges were for interchange, and it was obvious to me that each island was building something wonderful, as if it were the very best from their culture, in order to share it with the other islands. That new foundations for cities were being laid represented a whole new beginning for the earth. What is now being built for the Lord, for the sake of His kingdom, will remain and be a foundation for the age to come.

2 The Mark of God or the Mark of the Beast?

Many wonder if we will watch the book of Revelation unfold before our eyes in the twenty-first century. Will the Antichrist come upon the earth and perform great signs, deceiving those who live here? Will he make all the people take a mark on their foreheads and right hands so that they can buy, sell, and trade?

Many Christians spend considerable time trying to figure out what this mark of the beast will be like so that they will not be fooled by it. Yet almost no attention has been given to how we receive the mark of God, which is mentioned in Revelation 7:1–3. If we are truly in the end times, then God will send four angels to hold back the four winds of the earth until He marks the foreheads of His bond slaves.

Choosing God's Mark or the Beast's Mark

The only way we will be able to resist the mark of the beast is to take the mark of God, which is given to bond servants. The key to understanding this seal of God is to understand the meaning of the words *bond servant*.

In Scripture, Hebrew bond servants were able to go free after six years of service, but if they loved their master and chose to be slaves for the rest of their life, they were permanently marked (Ex. 21:5–6). Bond servants, then, are those who are in the service of the Lord because they specifically choose to be. Not all professing Christians are bond servants. Many claim to have given their lives to the Lord but still go on living for themselves.

Bond servants do not have any money of their own; therefore, they cannot freely spend what has been entrusted to them because it is not theirs. Their time and even their families belong to their master.

The commitment to be a bond servant is not just an intellectual agreement with certain biblical principles; it is the commitment to a radical lifestyle of obedience. A bond servant no longer lives for himself but for the Lord. To voluntarily become a slave is the ultimate commitment that can be made in this world, and only a fool would do it without carefully considering what it implies.

To understand the mark of the beast, which is an economic mark, we must understand what it means to "worship the beast." Even if we do not love money, we often put our trust in it. The love of money, or the trust in money, releases some of the ultimate evils in the human heart. At the end of the age, we will either be delivered from this or become totally enslaved by it. We will either be God's slave or the devil's.

Even though we understand both the mark of God and the mark of the beast, we will still have to choose between them. We may think that this will be easy if we recognize the significance of the choice, but we will not choose correctly unless our hearts are right.

And there can be no heartfelt obedience unless we have the freedom to disobey. God put the Tree of Knowledge in the Garden to give people the freedom to choose whom they would serve. This was not to cause us to fall, as some might think, but rather so that we could prove our devotion. If all the Lord had wanted was obedience, He would have done better to have created computers and programmed them to worship Him. Would this kind of worship be acceptable to anyone, much less to our glorious Creator? No, true worship from the heart involves freedom. Likewise, those in the service of the Lord must be those who choose to be.

THE YOKE OF THE BEAST

Probably the number one reason Christians are not free today to respond to the call of God in their lives is financial debt. When there is a call to do anything—from entering full-time ministry to going on a mission trip—our first consideration is usually, "Can I afford it?" This is a clear indication that we may be taking on the mark of the beast.

People in our culture have reconciled themselves to the idea that their parents lived with debt, so they must accept the reality of debt. Yet what does the Bible say about this? Paul warned against such thinking:

Do not be conformed to this world—this age, fashioned after and adapted to its external, superficial customs. But be transformed (changed) by the [entire] renewal of your mind—by its new ideals and its new attitude—so that you may prove for yourselves what is the good and acceptable and perfect will of God, even the thing which is good and acceptable and perfect [in His sight for you]. (Rom. 12:2 AMPLIFIED)

Debt is a yoke of slavery that victimizes most Americans. Almost every door you walk through today has a charge card emblem on it. Believe it or not, a bank in Denver, Colorado, once announced a plan to issue credit cards to children as young as twelve years old!

In less than twenty years, America went from being the largest creditor nation in the world to the largest debtor nation. (In other words, we went from having other nations owe us more than any other nation on the planet to the exact opposite: owing other nations more than any other country.) There has never been a greater or faster shift in wealth in the history of the world.

Because the borrower is servant to the lender (Prov. 22:7), our country is now in slavery to our lenders, and the yokes are becoming stronger every day! Since the church is called to be "the light of the world" and "the salt of the earth," we have a responsibility to speak out against this great transgression. Yet, how can we speak out when we are as mired in debt as everyone else, both as individuals and as churches and ministries?

The expression "Money talks" is very true. More than any other single factor, money reveals commitment. By looking at a man's check stubs, you can write his biography. You can easily distinguish between his likes and his loves (between what he's interested in and what he is really committed to). Jesus put it this way: "Where your treasure is, there will your heart be also" (Matt. 6:21 KJV).

THE GOAL

The Bible does not contend that it is wrong to have money. Actually, money can be one of God's gifts to us, as is stated in 1 Timothy 6:17 (NKJV): "God, who gives us richly all things to enjoy." But the perennial question is this: Why are we always short of money? We are given the answer in Haggai 1:5–6 (AMPLIFIED):

Now therefore, thus says the Lord of hosts, "Consider your ways [and set your mind on what has come to you]. You have sown much, but you have reaped little; you eat, but you do not have enough; you drink, but you do not have your fill; you clothe yourselves, but no one is warm; and he who earns wages has earned them to put them in a bag with holes in it."

This Scripture vividly describes the way most people live week after week, rushing to the bank right after work on Friday to cover checks written the day before. If you consistently find you don't have enough money, consider the following questions:

- Have I misused or abused what God has given me?
- Do I really "need more" or "greed more"?
- Have I violated the biblical principles concerning my stewardship of that with which I have been entrusted?
- Have I, like those in the book of Haggai, cared more for building my own house than the house of God?

If any of the above are true, our response must be repentance. Repentance is more than just feeling sorry for our failures; it is changing our ways. As C. S. Lewis once pointed out, once we miss a turn and start down the wrong road, it will never become the right road. The only way we can get back on the right road is to go back to where we missed that original turn.

The biblical definition of financial independence is not necessarily being wealthy. The goal is to never have to make a decision based on financial considerations but simply on God's will. This should be the financial goal for every one of us.

We usually think that the way out of our situation is to make more money. However, that is almost never the answer and can sometimes make matters worse. God's plan does not require you to make any more money than you do now—and that is not because He is going to give you a revelation so that you can win the lottery!

Scripture gives clear procedure for getting out of debt, staying out of debt, and becoming financially independent. Regardless of how bad your present financial condition is, you have a simple way of escape—obedience. This is your heritage as a son or daughter of the King.

THE OBEDIENCE PRINCIPLE

The first principle to getting out of your present financial situation is to experience financial healing.

EXPERIENCE FINANCIAL HEALING

The first step toward experiencing financial healing is to give, not to get. If you cringed at that statement, it is evidence that you have a wound that must be healed. Have you withheld your money from the Lord? Unfortunately, the church has been financially raped by hype, manipulation, and at times the spirit of control.

The way out of the clutches of the world's yoke is to enter the kingdom. We do this by first submitting to the King in everything and by living according to His Word. Our first consideration in making any major decision must be to determine our Master's will. An important biblical text for the church today is found in Malachi:

> "Will a man rob God? Yet you are robbing Me! But you say, 'How have we robbed Thee?' In tithes and offerings. You are cursed with a curse, for you are robbing Me, the whole nation of you! Bring the whole tithe into the storehouse, so that there may be food in My house, and test Me now in this," says the LORD of

hosts, "if I will not open for you the windows of heaven and pour out for you a blessing until it overflows." (Mal. 3:8–12)

Are you so financially blessed that it overflows? Then bring the "whole tithe" into the storehouse. That means the before-taxes tithe (tithing is giving the first 10 percent of our entire income to the Lord). After all, He promises a blessing so great, you cannot contain it!

Many Christians think that they cannot afford to tithe, but we cannot afford *not to*. Most of us do not need to increase our income as much as we need to have the devourer rebuked. The Lord promises not only to rebuke the devourer but also to open the windows of heaven. This is the only place in Scripture where He actually tells us to test Him. Try Him in this. I have never known anyone who started tithing faithfully who did not experience the Lord's faithfulness to His word.

I have seen some continue to sink financially because they said, "I'm going to set aside my tithes until the Lord tells me where to give them." This sounds noble, but if the money is still in our account, then we have not given it. Sometimes it is wise to set aside money in special accounts to wait for the time and place to give it, but this should only be done from our offerings, which are over and above the tithe, not our tithes.

The Word is clear about where to put the tithe—in His storehouse, which is the church.

Some do not feel they can trust church leaders to use this money wisely, but if we cannot trust our leaders to handle money, we are certainly foolish to trust them with our souls (Heb. 13:17). Our responsibility is to obey and let the Lord deal with those who may be irresponsible. However, if a church's leadership exhibits serious financial irresponsibility, we should consider that they would not watch over our souls well either.

I have heard others say, "I do not tithe because everything I have is the Lord's." That is another tragic delusion. If everything they have is the Lord's, they would obey His word to tithe. He is not fooled by that kind of flawed reasoning. We must understand that God does not need our money. The whole world is His. Tithing is for us, not Him. Our excuses are only hurting us.

The same truths apply to our churches and ministries.

CHURCHES ALSO SHOULD TITHE

Since a church is the storehouse of God, does that mean that our churches should also tithe? Yes, giving is fundamental Christianity. Again, He calls us to do this for our sakes, not His. God is looking for faithful people whom He can trust to be His conduits of supply. We are not seeking prosperity for ourselves; we are trying to be faithful servants like those in the parable of the talents, who invested well what they were entrusted with, and then their employer trusted them with even more.

When we started our congregation, the MorningStar Fellowship in Charlotte, North Carolina, we carelessly forgot to begin tithing from the church's income. We suffered significant losses until we started to tithe, and immediately our finances turned around. We could count this as coincidence, but we would have to be spiritually brain-dead to do so.

When we give a biblical tithe, which is to take the "first fruits" and give it to Him, we are making a statement that we trust Him, not ourselves or our jobs, as our Source. This is important for individuals, churches, and parachurch ministries.

Once you have pledged to tithe your money, you should ask yourself if you are succumbing to one of the enemy's three traps to keep you in bondage to the world's system.

The second principle to getting out of a bad financial situation is to free yourself from three traps of financial bondage.

THREE TRAPS OF FINANCIAL BONDAGE

To what degree do these traps influence or dominate you?

1. Impulse Buying

Everything we see in newspapers and on TV pushes us to "go for it." Get all the money you can! Yet Ecclesiastes 4:8 (KJV) reminds us that the eye is never "satisfied with riches." Ecclesiastes 5:10 (KJV) further explains, "He that loveth silver shall not be satisfied with silver; nor he that loveth abundance with increase." Impulse buying is a symptom of what Solomon is describing in these verses.

2. Dissatisfaction

Dissatisfaction is the disease of never having enough: enough clothes or the right clothes, enough furniture or matching furniture. It's an insatiable hunger to possess more and more. Ecclesiastes 5:11 (AMPLIFIED) puts it this way: "When goods increase, they who eat them increase also; and what gain is there to their owner except to see them with his eyes?"

I've heard people say, "I want to be a millionaire so I can give it to the Lord." You don't have to make millions for the Lord. The Lord is not poor. Be careful not to disguise your desires with such statements. The Lord said, "Seek ye first the kingdom of God, and his righteousness; and all these things shall be added unto you" (Matt. 6:33 KJV).

3. Laziness

Maybe you never have enough money because you're lazy. Solomon advised the sluggard to consider the ways of the ant:

> Go to the ant, thou sluggard; consider her ways, and be wise: which having no guide, overseer, or ruler, provideth her meat in the summer, and gathereth her food in the harvest. How long wilt thou sleep, O sluggard? when wilt thou arise out of thy sleep? Yet a little sleep, a little slumber, a little folding of the hands to sleep: so shall thy poverty come as one that travelleth, and thy want as an armed man. (Prov. 6:6–11 KJV)

Verse 7 in this text is most interesting: "Which having no guide, overseer, or ruler." The word *guide* here is the Hebrew word for *commander*. In this sense, that ant is a representation of the born-again believer. Ants instinctively know what to do, and so should Christians; such a person does not need an outside source of motivation since he is motivated from within. At times a believer may need counsel, but our goal must always be to have the Word and ways of God established in our hearts.

Also notice what Solomon says about sleep. We all have the tendency to reach over and turn off the alarm clock for just a few more minutes of sleep. This verse warns against the addictive nature of this habit. When it's time to get up, get up! God will not drop prosperity on you while you're lying in bed. If we are bond servants, our time is also His.

THE LAW OF PHYSICS AND WEALTH

A law of physics states that energy is never destroyed; it simply changes form. The same is true of wealth: It is never destroyed, but it often changes hands. Even during the Great Depression, wealth was not actually lost; it was just transferred to those who were in a position to take advantage of the times. And those who benefited were those who were not in debt and had cash readily available. Businesses were bought for as little as 10 percent of their value. Land was bought for as little as a dollar an acre—from those who had overextended themselves with debt.

We are heading toward an even greater economic upheaval than the Great Depression. Those who are not prepared for it will be devastated. The Lord wants His people prepared for these times, not just so they can endure them or become wealthy, but for the sake of the gospel. As the Scriptures promise, the wealth of the nations will be brought to the people who serve the Lord.

The Lord is right now preparing His people for what is about to come. He has been warning His church for more than twenty-five years to get out of debt. That's given us plenty of time to do it. Yet, because these catastrophic economic problems have taken so long to come, many have disregarded these warnings. There is still time to repent and get our houses in order, but there is no more time to delay!

3 ACCUSERS OF THE BRETHREN

In the spring of 1995, Bob Jones, a prophetic friend, told a number of us that the Atlanta Braves baseball team was going to win the World Series that year as a message for the church in America. This prophecy was fulfilled, and there indeed was a message in it.

For years the Atlanta Braves have been called "America's Team." America is called "the home of the brave." Braves are courageous warriors, and true warriors will fight until they win. After years of futility, the Atlanta Braves finally made it to the World Series in 1992 and 1993, but they failed to win the championship. They did not quit, and in 1995 they won the World Series, just as Bob Jones had prophesied.

Likewise, the church in America has been struggling for a number of years. God has raised up great movements and ministries in America to bless the world. Even though we have had many great years, it has been a very long time since the church as a whole has truly had a world-class breakthrough or victory.

As I was expecting Atlanta to win in 1995 because of Bob's word, I was also keen to understand the message in it. It was curious to me that the Braves' victory came in the year of the O. J. Simpson saga, which was perhaps the most controversial trial in American judicial history, as well as the year when the burning of churches and the Million Man March became front-page news. Just when it seemed that justice was under its greatest assault in America, David Justice hit the winning home run to give "America's Team" the victory.

I think it was also significant that it was David Justice who hit that home run. He is a black man, and I do expect young, black "Davids" to arise and slay the spiritual Goliaths who have been intimidating and holding back the armies of God in America. I also believe that these great champions are going to come in the name of justice. They are not going to just demand justice for themselves, but they will also win it for others.

None of us want justice in relation to our sins; rather, we want mercy and grace. That's understood. However, God's justice is more than this. The Lord obviously cares a great deal about equity and fairness in human dealings. Scripture makes it clear that "righteousness and justice are the foundation of His throne" (Ps. 97:2) and "to do righteousness and justice is desired by the LORD rather than sacrifice" (Prov. 21:3).

If justice is so important that it is one of the two pillars on which God established His own throne, justice needs to be given a much higher priority. As the Lord spoke through Jeremiah:

> For if you truly amend your ways and your deeds, if you truly practice justice between a man and his neighbor, if you do not oppress the alien, the orphan, or the widow, and do not shed innocent blood in this place, nor walk after other gods to your own ruin, then I will let you dwell in this place, in the land that I gave to your fathers forever and ever. (Jer. 7:5–7)

I have traveled quite extensively around the world, and the more I do, the more thankful I am to live in America. I also believe that we have the best system of justice to be found in the world today, but it is not as good as it could be. There is not justice for everyone. And there is an increasing assault upon justice throughout our entire social fabric, from economic empowerment to educational opportunities. Even more frightening than that is the almost complete lack of either a vision or a system of justice within the church.

As Paul wrote to the Corinthians: "I say this to your shame. Is it so, that there is not among you one wise man who will be able to decide between his brethren?" (1 Cor. 6:5).

We can trace much of the shame that has come on the body of Christ in recent times to not having a true system of justice in the church so that we can judge ourselves "lest we be judged." When the Israelites lost their sense of justice, they quickly fell into apostasy because justice is a foundation of the Lord's throne in our midst. The Lord had to use the heathen nations around Israel to discipline them until they returned to Him. Likewise, the Lord has had to use the secular press and other "heathens" to discipline the church. However, the Lord did not appoint journalists or investigators to judge His church. The Lord gave that authority to the elders of the church. The vacuum of authority created by a lack of true judges will continue to be filled by those who are not called, and who will make a mess of it, until the true elders of the church take the authority God has given them.

The Fall from Grace

In the spring of 1996, Bob Jones received a word that the Braves would not win the World Series again that year and that this would be a message. When I was offered tickets to go to Game Five of the 1996 World Series in Atlanta, I knew that the Lord was going to show me something important. I was not disappointed.

As Bobby Conner, Mike Dean, and I walked to the stadium, Mike told us how the first time the Braves went to the Series, an unprecedented excitement spread throughout the city. More than a hundred thousand people came to the stadium, even though they knew they could not get inside, just to stand outside and give their support to the team. As I listened to him describe this, I was surprised by the contrast that night. People were not standing outside to support the team. Those entering the stadium did not even seem enthusiastic.

This was the very pinnacle of baseball, the World Series. It was being played by one of history's most popular teams, the Braves, against one of history's most storied teams, the New York Yankees. Even so, I have felt more energy in the fans at Little League games than I did in Fulton County Stadium that night. Instead I felt an attitude of arrogance that made me very uncomfortable.

During the game, when the Atlanta fans began to do their famous "tomahawk chop," which had previously been an awesome war cry to strike fear into the hearts of their opponents, that night it was so sub-dued, it was more like a bellyache than a war cry. I was stunned by the heaviness in the air. I was even more surprised by the fans' shouts of criticism when the Braves failed to get a hit or did not make a play that would have been almost miraculous if they had been able to pull it off.

The Braves lost that pivotal game because a player dropped a ball he should have caught. It seemed fitting. The heaviness that night was so great, I expected an error on almost every play. What had changed this city from one where people stood outside the stadium in support of their team to one that almost seemed angry at them?

Could it be pride? Sportswriters had favored the Braves to win the Series again before play began the spring of 1996. This prediction was not necessarily bad, but combined with their victory the year before, the players and fans became overly haughty and proud. And when people become critical of anything that falls short of their expectations of perfection, it does not inspire; it adds a pressure on the players that will sooner or later cause them to "drop the ball."

The next morning, I could hardly believe the outrageous things the Atlanta commentators said about the Braves. These talk show hosts had probably never played in a professional baseball game, much less experienced the pressure of a World Series. The venom directed at the player who made the error was shocking. Even the people who called in with comments came across as if they were experts who knew more than the team's managers knew. It was no surprise to me that the Braves were not able to win a single World Series game at home that year. It was obviously easier for them to play on the road, for they did win two games in New York.

I believe this same attitude is what causes many churches, min-istries, and individuals to fall after just one victory. When we experi-ence a victory, it is good for us to press forward and even expect to keep winning. However, when the expectations of the people become tainted with arrogance, so that anything short of those expectations starts to draw criticism rather than intercession, a defeat is sure to follow. Solomon realized this long ago when he wrote, "Pride goes before destruction, and a haughty spirit before stumbling" (Prov. 16:18).

It is hard for anyone who has not played sports to imagine just how much the fans affect a game, which is why there is such a definite home field advantage. If the fans are cheering you on, it inspires you to play beyond your usual abilities. But when they are not supportive, it's as if the players are dragging a heavy weight around. The same is true in our churches. When the leadership feels the support of their people, they will rise to new heights. When they are weighed down with criticism, it will be hard to function at all.

A primary reason why many leaders lack God's anointing is because their people are not hungry for God. A second reason is the unrealistic expectations we often put on them. We Americans have become extremely demanding. When anyone tries to lead us, we so attack them that it makes one wonder why anyone would ever want to be either a pastor or a president in the United States.

Just as the critics and commentators on the radio in Atlanta that morning were composed mostly of those who had never played a game of professional baseball (much less played in the World Series), most of the critics of the church have never either led a church or built anything of significance. It is amazing that anyone would listen to these commentators, and it is even more amazing that mature Christians will listen to those who have set themselves up as judges over the church.

All of us have the option to choose how we will relate to our leaders; we can become a part of either one of two ministries that exist before the throne of God.

The Two Ministries

Two ministries go on continually before God's throne: One is the ministry of *intercession*, the other is *accusation*. Jesus lives to intercede for His people. To the degree that we abide in Him, Jesus will use us to intercede for the church and for others and ourselves. His church is to be a "house of prayer for all the peoples" (Isa. 56:7).

Satan, however, is called "the accuser of our brethren," and we are told that his ministry goes on "day and night" before the throne of God (Rev. 12:10).

THE MINISTRY OF ACCUSATION

How can Satan continue to accuse the saints before God if he has been thrown out of heaven and no longer has access to the throne? The answer: Satan uses the saints, who do have access to the throne, to do this diabolical work for him. He is called by many titles, but certainly his most effective guise has been "the accuser of the brethren," because of his effectiveness in getting brother to turn against brother. Division is his specialty.

Unity in the church is the greatest threat to Satan's domain. The devil knows very well the authority Jesus has given any two Christians who will agree: The Father will give them what they ask. Unity does not just increase our spiritual authority—it multiplies it. One Christian can put a thousand demons to flight, but two of them together can put ten thousand to flight.

Ironically, the accuser's access to most of us is often through our insecurity, which drives us to become territorial. If we are insecure, we are threatened by anything we cannot control. We may cite doctrines or a feigned noble determination, but few divisions in the church are ever caused by anything but territorial preservation, which ultimately results in our losing the very thing we are trying so desperately to preserve. It is an incontrovertible law of the spirit: If you seek to save your life, you will lose it; if you lose your life for Christ's sake, you will find it (Matt. 16:25).

Isaiah addressed this issue most succinctly:

> Then your light will break out like the dawn,
> And your recovery will speedily spring forth;
> And your righteousness will go before you;
> The glory of the LORD will be your rear guard.
> Then you will call, and the LORD will answer;
> You will cry, and He will say, "Here I am."
> *If* you remove the yoke from your midst,
> The pointing of the finger, and speaking wickedness.
> (Isa. 58:8–9, emphasis added)

Do you need more light in your life? Do you call to the Lord, but He does not answer? The reason is almost always the same: You have a yoke in your midst called "the pointing of the finger, and speaking wickedness" (Isa. 58:9). That is a critical spirit. God promises that your life will radically change if you remove this yoke.

The critical person is usually critical of everyone but himself. As the Lord stated, he is so busy looking for specks in the eyes of his brothers, he cannot see the big log in his own eye, which is the reason for his blindness.

When we criticize someone else's children, who will take offense? The parents! This is no less true with God. When we judge one of His people, we are really judging Him. When we judge one of His leaders, we are really judging His leadership—we are saying that God does not know what He is doing with the leadership He is providing. When we criticize another brother or sister, we are actually saying that God's workmanship does not meet our standards. Yet, which one of us can change ourselves into what we should be? If we cannot improve ourselves, how can we have an effect on someone else?

Criticism is one of the ultimate manifestations of pride because it assumes superiority. Pride brings something any rational human being should fear most—God's resistance. Scripture says, "God resists the proud, but gives grace to the humble" (James 4:6 NKJV). Personally, I'd rather have all the demons in hell against me than God.

Look at what happened to the children of Israel. God allowed the first generation out of Egypt to spend their entire lives wandering in the wilderness because of their grumbling and complaining. This is the chief reason why so many Christians do not walk in the promises of God; instead, they spend their lives in dry places, going around the same mountains—the same old problems and weaknesses—over and over again. As James warned us:

> Do not speak evil of one another, brethren. He who speaks evil of a brother and judges his brother, speaks evil of the law and judges the law. But if you judge the law, you are not a doer of the law but a judge. There is one Lawgiver, who is able to save and to destroy.

[When we judge the law, we judge the Lawgiver.] Who are you to judge another? (James 4:11–12 NKJV)

I once visited one of the poorest states in this country. That had always been a curiosity to me, since this state was rich in natural resources and beauty. When visiting there, I immediately noticed a fundamental characteristic of the people. They scorned and criticized the wealthy or anyone who was just doing well. This seemed to be a universal obsession with everyone from waiters to church leaders. I knew that this was the primary reason for their poverty. When we are guilty of "pointing of the finger" like this, we yoke ourselves to that same criticism. As the Lord warned: "Judge not, that you be not judged. For with what judgment you judge, you will be judged; and with the measure you use, it will be measured back to you" (Matt. 7:1–2 NKJV).

Some of the pastors in this state had actually yoked themselves and their congregations to poverty by criticizing how other men of God raised money, so these pastors could not even receive a biblical offering without feeling guilty. Still other men of God should have had national or international influence in the church because of their spiritual authority, but they had spent their lives ministering with little fruit to shrinking churches. I admit that sometimes our crowds will shrink because we are doing the right thing, just as the Lord's own did when He preached truths that were hard for people to receive, but this was not the case with these men. They had criticized the ministries of others who were gaining influence, and therefore God could not give them a platform equal to their anointing.

Please understand, our criticisms can be rooted in true discernment. The ones we criticize may well be in error. Sometimes these pastors were criticizing others who *had* raised money through manipulation, hype, and outright deception. The apostle Paul expected the Corinthian church to be discerning. He told them to make others accountable for their actions when he asked, "Do you not judge those who are within the church?" (1 Cor. 5:12). *The issue here is how we deal with what we discern. Are we going to use it to accuse our brethren or to intercede on their behalf?*

In Matthew 18:6 Jesus warned that if anyone caused one of His little ones to sin, it would be better for that person to have a rock tied around his neck and be thrown into the sea. In this same conversation, He gave us clear instructions about how we were to deal with a brother who is in sin. First, we should go to him *in private*. If he rejects our counsel, we should go to him with another brother. Only after he has rejected both these options should we take the issue to the rest of the church. If we do not follow this pattern, we will be in jeopardy of becoming the last thing we ever want to become—a person who has caused a Christian, for whom the Lord died, to stumble.

I have heard numerous excuses for not following Matthew 18. A popular one is: "I knew he would not listen to me." I have also heard the excuse, "If he has a public ministry, I have a right to expose him publicly." This is preposterous because every ministry is public, at least to some degree. The Lord gave no such conditions. Those who take such liberties with the clear commandments of Jesus are claiming to have authority to add to the Word of God.

If a man has a large ministry and we are not able to contact him directly, we must not bring judgment. If the Lord felt we were the ones to bring this judgment, He would make a way for us to do so. If He does not, trust Him to do it in His own time. Do not accuse; instead, intercede. Following this order will protect us from coming under a judgment that is more severe than that of our wayward brother.

If we have not followed the Lord's prescribed manner for dealing with an errant brother, we have absolutely no right to talk about it to anyone else. What we may call getting someone else's opinion, God calls gossip. He is not fooled, and we will pay the price for such indiscretions. His commandment was to go first to the person in private. Only after we have done that should we talk to another person, and then only for the purpose of going together to help the one in sin. Our goal must always be to save the brother from his sin, not to expose him. As Paul warned, "Brethren, if a man is overtaken in any trespass, you who are spiritual restore such a one in a spirit of gentleness, *considering yourself lest you also be tempted*" (Gal. 6:1 NKJV, emphasis added).

Let us not become petty with the presumed sin of another. Remember, "Love covers a multitude of sins" (1 Peter 4:8). The majority of us still have a few hundred things wrong in our lives, and the Lord is usually dealing with one or two of them at a time because that is all we can handle. (Often Satan's strategy is to try to distract us into dealing with the other three hundred problems as well, which results in frustration and defeat.)

Of course, the Lord Jesus Himself is our perfect model. When He corrected the seven churches in Revelation, He first praised each church, highlighting what they were doing right. Then He straightforwardly addressed their problems. Incredibly, He even gave the wicked queen Jezebel an opportunity to repent! Finally, He gave each church a wonderful promise of reward for overcoming their weaknesses. The Lord never changes. When He brings correction today, it always comes wrapped in encouragement and hope. Matthew 18 was not given to us to use as a club to let our brother know how he offended us. We must use this Scripture, and indeed all Scripture, in love, not out of self-preservation or retaliation.

The "accuser of the brethren" is trying to bring correction to the church by methods and goals that are obviously quite different from the Lord's. Jesus encourages us and gives us hope; Satan condemns us and tries to make us feel hopeless. Jesus builds us up so we can handle the correction; Satan tears us down, trying to get us to quit. Jesus loves us and wants to bring us to the highest place; Satan's goal is to destroy us.

One of the more remarkable phenomena of the Pentecostal and Charismatic movements has been the inability of those with spiritual gifts and experiences to discern the spirits, especially the most deadly enemy spirit of all—the accuser of the brethren! Could it be that our judgments against those who do not have the baptism, or other spiritual experiences like ours, have yoked us with an inability to discern the spirits? Much of what has been paraded as discernment is nothing less than suspicion, a shallow pseudo-spiritual disguise used to mask territorial preservation. Even without the spiritual gift of discernment, James gave us clear guidelines for discerning the source of wisdom, which if heeded would have preserved the church from some of her most humiliating failures:

> Who is wise and understanding among you? Let him show by good conduct that his works are done in the meekness of wisdom. . . . This wisdom does not descend from above, but is earthly, sensual, demonic. . . . But the wisdom that is from above is first pure, then peaceable, gentle, willing to yield, full of mercy and good fruits, without partiality and without hypocrisy. (James 3:13–17 NKJV)

We are saved by grace, and we need all the grace we can get to make it through this life. If we want to receive grace, we had better learn to give grace, because we are going to reap what we sow. If we expect to receive mercy, we had better start sowing mercy, because most of us are going to need all the mercy we can get. We do not want to come before the Lord with our brother's blood on our hands. He warned:

> You have heard that it was said to those of old, "You shall not murder, and whoever murders will be in danger of the judgment." But I say to you that whoever is angry with his brother without a cause shall be in danger of the judgment. And whoever says to his brother, "Empty head! [author's trans.]" shall be in danger of the council. But whoever says, "You fool!" shall be in danger of hell fire. Therefore if you bring your gift to the altar, and there remember that your brother has something against you, leave your gift there before the altar, and go your way. First be reconciled to your brother, and then come and offer your gift. Agree with your adversary quickly, while you are on the way with him, lest your adversary deliver you to the judge, the judge hand you over to the officer, and you be thrown into prison [bondage]. Assuredly, I say to you, you will by no means get out of there till you have paid the last penny. (Matt. 5:21–26 NKJV)

If we have been guilty of slandering a brother or sister, we should forget about our offerings to the Lord until we reconcile with our brother.

Unfortunately, we often think our sacrifices and offerings can compensate for such sins, but they never will.

The Lord said that when He returned He was going to judge between the sheep and the goats (Matt. 25:31–46). Those who are judged to be "sheep" inherit the kingdom and eternal life. Those who are designated "goats" are sent to eternal judgment. The separation is determined by how each person has treated the Lord, which is determined by how he or she treated His people.

As John stated:

If someone says, "I love God," and hates his brother, he is a liar; for the one who does not love his brother whom he has seen, cannot love God whom he has not seen. (1 John 4:20)

Everyone who hates his brother is a murderer; and you know that no murderer has eternal life abiding in him. We know love by this, that He laid down His life for us; and we ought to lay down our lives for the brethren. (1 John 3:15–16)

If we really have Christ's Spirit, we will also have His nature. If you or I knew that our best friends, whom we had loved and instructed for three and a half years, were about to desert us, would we "earnestly desire" to have one last meal with them? Our Lord's love for His disciples was never conditional. Even though He knew they were about to deny Him, He loved them to the end—He even gave His life for them. He has commanded us to love with that same love.

How much greater would our leadership be if we started praying for our leaders instead of just criticizing them? The single change that would probably have the greatest positive effect on the churches in America would be to turn our criticism into intercession. When those who are involved in any kind of ministry receive the support of others, it helps greatly, because it really is a powerful form of intercession.

Of course, not all churches in America are critical of their leaders. There are some that are overly supportive, not questioning things that *should be* questioned. There are also leaders who want to take all the credit for victories, but refuse to take any of the blame for failures, choosing instead to blame the people. Overall, however, the scales are tipped overwhelmingly toward our having become far too critical of our leaders.

I felt sorry for the player who cost the Braves that game in 1996. He made a mistake, but he had also made dozens of outstanding plays throughout that year. No one except his fellow teammates seemed to remember his dozens of home runs or his usually great fielding. They only remembered one dropped ball. Is that *justice*? Is it not also the way the church has treated many of her leaders? That is not God's justice, and if we are going to represent Him to the world, we must learn from the righteous Judge.

We are very close to experiencing a great move of God in America that may ultimately exceed anything we have experienced. However, this revival is not coming because the church in America is so righteous; rather, it is a last call to turn around before we receive a devastating judgment.

Our ability to be the generation that prepares the way for the Lord and His ultimate purposes will be determined by which of the two ministries we choose—accusation or intercession. Let us remove the terrible yoke of "pointing the finger" from our midst and turn our criticisms into intercession.

4 STORMS IN THE COMING YEARS

For the last few years, we have taken our staff to a little island on the North Carolina coast with which we have fallen in love. We were on this island when Hurricane Fran set a course directly toward us. That night the intercessors and many of the children marched around the island to pray for its protection from the storm. As the hurricane approached, it suddenly jogged to the east, just bypassing our island, and then it turned back to the west and went up the Cape Fear River. Hurricane-force winds brushed our island, but we did not even lose power; little or no damage was done to the island. The beaches just north of us were devastated, as well as cities and towns all the way to Raleigh, well over a hundred miles inland. We have no doubt that our little island was spared because we prayed. God really does hear our prayers, and He will answer those that are offered in faith.

Storms in our lives can be of natural causes, like Hurricane Fran, or of man-made causes, like the Y2K problem at the end of the century. By the time some of you read this book, we will probably know how extensive the Y2K problem really was, but whether it meets expectations or not, we can reach some spiritual conclusions from an impending difficulty like this. The first should be to comply with Philippians 4:6–7: "Be anxious for nothing, but in everything by prayer and supplication with thanksgiving let your requests be made known to God. And the peace of God, which surpasses all comprehension, will guard your hearts and your minds in Christ Jesus."

Y2K and the Year 2000

The Y2K problem is the computer glitch that will cause many computers to malfunction when their internal clocks turn to the new century on New Year's Day 2000.

In the 1950s when many of the computers were created, programmers were at a shortage for disk space. Therefore they registered dates with just two digits: 1955 became 55; 1970 became 70. No one then realized that these computers would still be functioning at the turn of the century.

Now when computer clocks go to "00" at midnight on December 31, 1999, many will read this as "1900" instead of "2000," making the data stored in them inaccessible. Some fear that banks will not know how much money they have—or how much money you have in them. It is expected that factory inventories will be lost and many manufacturing plants will shut down. Airline reservations may be erased, and worse than that, air traffic control computers may malfunction. Federal, state, and local governments may lose all or much of their data, crippling Social Security, the IRS, and even local water and sewer systems. Experts differ in their predictions about the effect this problem will have on civilization; some see it as a bump in the road, others as the end of the modern world.

One of the potentially devastating problems can come from the dependence on "Just In Time" (JIT) inventory control, which has been almost universally adopted by Western industry. For example, most products are made from a combination of parts, each of which is manufactured by smaller vendors. A car, for instance, may be built from several hundred parts, all made by different companies. To save the expense of storing large inventories of these parts, most industries have instituted JIT, which means they have the parts delivered to the assembly plant "just in time" to be used. Of course, all of this must be computerized. Even if most of the smaller vendors solve the problem, the assembly plant will still be shut down, and production will grind to a halt if just a few vendors don't, and possibly if even one doesn't.

Most companies have already reprogrammed their computers, but many have not, and it seems that they are not going to make it on time. For those who have figured out their own computer problems, another potential problem has arisen. Many resolved the Y2K problem by writing new software, but now they are not sure that the software programs will be able to talk to their other vendors, assembly plants, or agencies, creating a modern, technological Tower of Babel that some say can never be resolved.

Even though I have a fairly good understanding of the technical and commercial issues Y2K can cause, I wanted to hear from the Lord about it. For more than a year I prayed about this concern, but He said nothing to me. When He finally did begin to speak, I was surprised by what He said.

DO NOT BE SHAKEN

The first thing the Lord said to me about this was that He is not sitting in the heavens, wringing His hands and worrying about Y2K—and neither is anyone who is abiding in Him. This is not going to be the end of the modern world, but it is going to cause some problems, which we need to be aware of. The most severe difficulties will come from the panic generated by the situation, not actual computer glitches themselves. The Lord warned me, "My people should neither be controlled by this fear nor contribute to it."

If we are beset with such fears, we need to examine the foundations on which we have built our lives. If we have built our houses on the Rock by hearing and doing the Word of the Lord, the floods can come, but our "houses" will stand (Matt. 7:24–29). The Word of God is greater than any flood, even the flood of problems from Y2K and a recession or depression.

This does not mean that we should neglect to make some changes and preparations, but we must do all that we do in faith, following the Lord and not the world.

The whole world and all of its systems are extremely shaky and vulnerable, and Y2K is not by any means the worst problem now facing us. The meltdown of the Russian economy, North Korea, terrorism, and the rising tension between India and Pakistan are all going to be far worse problems than Y2K. The world is tottering at the edge of many different precipices. Only God's grace has kept us until now, and only God's grace will keep us in the future. As we discussed in Chapter 2, we are in the period of time spoken of in Revelation 7:1–3:

> After this I saw four angels standing at the four corners of the earth, holding back the four winds of the earth, so that no wind should blow on the earth or on the sea or on any tree. And I saw another angel ascending from the rising of the sun, having the seal of the living God; and he cried out with a loud voice to the four angels to whom it was granted to harm the earth and the sea, saying, "Do not harm the earth or the sea or the trees, until we have sealed the bond-servants of our God on their foreheads."

God can and will restrain the effects of Y2K and other forces that are trying to break forth across the earth until He is finished sealing His bond servants.

As we discussed before, the true bond servant is a slave. He does not own anything, but everything that he has belongs to his master. Even his time is not his own. Many claim this position, but few truly live it. A true bond servant cannot lose anything in the stock market, or in any other business, because he does not own anything. He may be a steward of much, but it is not his, and he does not treat anything as if it were his. Those who have become true bond servants have built their lives on the kingdom that cannot be shaken by Y2K, an economic collapse, or any other disaster. Those who are true bond servants are being sealed in this hour, and they are protected. But Christians who have claimed this position and have gone on living their lives for themselves will fall with the kingdom of this world.

We still have time to get our houses in order. It does not matter how entangled we are with the ways of this world—true repentance will bring us under the Lord's care. Though we are His slaves, we could have no greater Master, and He will care for us much better than we can care for ourselves. This does not mean that we will not suffer any loss. Those who have built their lives on the ways of this world will lose much in what is coming. Even those who have done their best to live as bond servants of the Lord may lose some of that which is entrusted to them. We do live in the world even if we are not of it. However, those who are living as bond servants will soon be entrusted with much more to steward than what they have lost. We are coming to the time that the prophet wrote about:

> The wealth of the nations will come to you. . .
> Foreigners will build up your walls,
> And their kings will minister to you;
> For in My wrath I struck you,
> And in My favor I have had compassion on you.
> Your gates will be open continually;
> They will not be closed day or night,
> So that men may bring to you the wealth of the nations,
> With their kings led in procession.
> For the nation and the kingdom which will not serve
>   you will perish,
> And the nations will be utterly ruined. (Isa. 60:5, 10–12)

During the time of darkness, the nations will bring their wealth to God's people. That is why God's people have nothing to fear when they do not take the mark of the beast that will allow them to buy, sell, or trade. A greater provision of God will be coming to those who are faithful. Even so, it will still require a test of our faith to remain faithful, putting more trust in the economy of the kingdom than the economies of this present world.

Those who have truly submitted to the lordship of Jesus are soon to be rulers themselves. If you are moved in your heart to repent, begin by reading, studying, and obeying the following:

It is for discipline that you endure; God deals with you as with sons; for what son is there whom his father does not discipline? But if you are without discipline, of which all have become partakers, then you are illegitimate children and not sons. Furthermore, we had earthly fathers to discipline us, and we respected them; shall we not much rather be subject to the Father of spirits, and live? For they disciplined us for a short time as seemed best to them, but He disciplines us for our good, that we may share His holiness. All discipline for the moment seems not to be joyful, but sorrowful; yet to those who have been trained by it, afterwards it yields the peaceful fruit of righteousness. (Heb. 12:7–11)

We are approaching Judgment Day. We will not be able to get away with the things that God may have overlooked in the past. As He promised, those who call Him "Lord, Lord," but do not do what He says, will pay a terrible price (Matt. 7:21–23). We must get rid of the roots of bitterness and forgive others as He has forgiven us. Excuses will not stand up when we are before His judgment seat.

Now is the time when all true bond servants will be revealed, and they are the ones who truly do all things for the sake of His gospel. The Lord also showed me the spiritual parallels of Y2K.

Spiritual Parallels of Y2K

The Lord told me to observe the problems that Y2K will cause in the natural world as a reflection of the problems we have in the body of Christ.

For example, possibly the most severe problem will be caused by the corporate trend toward downsizing, JIT, and other such solutions to cutting costs. These have worked well to a degree, but as Suzanne deTreville, a world-class business professor and corporate consultant, recently related to me, this has resulted in what is now being called "corporate anorexia." The system is so lean and mean, there are no reserves. Not only can this be devastating when a problem like Y2K comes along, but there are also few reserves for taking advantage of new possibilities.

How does this relate to the church? Many churches have adapted and promoted a system that lives hand to mouth, without building reserves. Of course, many have done this seeking to comply with the

Lord's admonition to "not be anxious about tomorrow" (Matt. 6:34 RSV) and instead to trust that He will take care of them just as He does the birds of the air. I think that this would be good if we had *really* complied with it, but many have to live hand to mouth because they have accumulated so much debt. This is borrowing against our future to pay for today. For those who have done this, let me ask you a question: If you are trusting the Lord to take care of you each day by supplying all your needs, why did you go to the bank and borrow?

There is a biblical place for setting up reserves, and some are feeling called to help prepare "Joseph's storehouses." One thing we are *not* to do is hoard. Everything we do we are to do with our neighbors in mind. It may be wise to store some things that we believe there will be a shortage of, but we should not do this as a survival community, but as a mission base. How could Christians hoard anything if their neighbors were starving? If we establish a storehouse, our aim should be to help as many people as possible through future difficulties, whether or not it is the Great Tribulation. We should seek the Lord for a specific understanding of the coming troubles, but we are doing this out of love, not fear.

We all need to question our own motives. While I do believe in the calling for some to establish "storehouses" for the future, I have noticed that many of those who feel called to do so are doing very little to help people in need now—and may do even less when the really pressing needs come. Fear, rather than love, drives them. Those who trust in the Lord to take care of them like the birds of the air will be much better off during the times ahead.

When Agabus prophesied that a famine was about to come upon the whole earth, the first-century church did not respond to this word by beginning to hoard; instead they took up an offering for the relief of the brethren in Judea (Acts 11:28–30). Their "Joseph's storehouse" was built in heaven, where it is secure, and where there is ample supply for any need. It is also noteworthy that they gave to the brethren in Judea. They obviously understood that the famine was a curse coming upon the world, and that those who blessed Israel would be blessed, and those who cursed Israel would be cursed. Read on in Isaiah 60 and see what God promises:

Instead of bronze I will bring gold,
And instead of iron I will bring silver,
And instead of wood, bronze,
And instead of stones, iron.
And I will make peace your administrators,
And righteousness your overseers.
Violence will not be heard again in your land,
Nor devastation or destruction within your borders;
But you will call your walls salvation, and your gates praise.
No longer will you have the sun for light by day,
Nor for brightness will the moon give you light;
But you will have the LORD for an everlasting light,
And your God for your glory. (Isa. 60:17–19)

All of this should make even the coming darkness of the end times a great encouragement to those who know the Lord. As He said, we should look up because our redemption draws near (Luke 21:28).

We can also see from the text above, as well as from the entirety of Scripture, that our goal should be to seek the glory of the Lord, not to stash provisions. The glory of the Lord is what will attract the provision of the Lord in these times. In the coming darkness, the glory will stand out more than ever, and even the kings of the earth and the nations will turn to those who have it.

BUILDING FOR THE STORMS

Storms can be demonic, but they can also represent moves of the Holy Spirit. For example, the Lord answered Job out of a whirlwind (Job 38). Wind often represents the Holy Spirit, and rain sometimes represents teaching (Deut. 32:2). Hurricanes will uproot trees that do not have deep roots, and they can destroy anything that is not well built.

Last year, we were directed to a cottage on our favorite beach, which I spoke of in the first paragraph of this chapter. This cottage was for sale at an extraordinary value. We purchased it as a place at the ocean where our staff could go to seek the Lord. We had been encouraged by how it had been protected from Hurricane Fran. Then came Hurricane Bonnie. A huge and powerful storm, it was aimed right at our little island just as Fran had been. We prayed for it to go around the island as Fran had done. The storm did turn that Wednesday, but only enough to make our little island "ground zero" for the hurricane to make landfall. Because the greatest damage from hurricanes comes from the seawall they create, the worst nightmare is for them to come ashore during high tide. Hurricane Bonnie not only came at high tide, but then nearly stopped so that it continued to pound our island with some of its strongest winds through a second high tide. The hurricane also dropped nearly twelve inches of rain.

The Saturday after Bonnie came ashore, we had planned a beach retreat for our staff. I did not think there would be much left on the whole island, but even if there were, I figured it would take weeks to restore power, and probably months to repair the damage so that the cottage could be used. Twice that morning the Lord told me, "Watch My miracle." I told my wife and others, "Somehow we are going to witness a miracle from the Lord in this, but it will probably mean that we will get a good insurance settlement and be able to build a bigger, better place."

I prepared to cancel the beach retreat, but several people, including my wife, felt we should go anyway. I thought they were out of their minds, but I agreed to wait until I had a chance to fly down and check the damage, or until we heard from the real estate company concerning the damage.

I was shocked when the Realtor informed us that not only had the island survived, there really was not any damage; residents had not even lost power through the entire storm! Only a few shingles had been blown off some homes, along with some window screens. Several times I have witnessed the devastation hurricanes can do, and I thought this was a miracle of biblical proportions. All around our island, this storm had caused millions of dollars worth of damage, and we should have gotten the worst of it. The police said that the storm surge actually parted and went around both sides of our island, but did not touch it. The Lord had directed us to buy our beach retreat, and He was going to protect it. I confess that I did not have the faith that He was going to protect it that much! However, I now have much more faith for the storms that are coming. God stretched out the heavens like a tent curtain, and He is quite able to take care of us through anything that is coming on the earth.

For months, the Lord has been speaking to many of our prophetic people about living in Goshen. Goshen is no longer a place; it is a state of abiding in the will of the Lord. The darkness that is coming will come on the whole earth. The plague of darkness recorded in the book of Exodus even came on Goshen, but the Israelites had lights in their dwellings (Ex. 10:21–23). As the Lord promised in Matthew 7:24–27:

> Therefore everyone who hears these words of Mine, and acts upon them, may be compared to a wise man, who built his house upon the rock. And the rain descended, and the floods came, and the winds blew, and burst against that house; and yet it did not fall, for it had been founded upon the rock. And everyone who hears these words of Mine, and does not act upon them, will be like a foolish man, who built his house upon the sand. And the rain descended, and the floods came, and the winds blew, and burst against that house; and it fell, and great was its fall.

Difficult times are coming to the whole world. In fact, most of the world has been in them for some time. However, we need not be fearful. As Isaiah 60:1–2 suggests, the darker it becomes, the greater the glory will be for those who abide in the Lord. We need not fear the storms if our houses are built on the Rock. If you have fear, do not complain about what is happening. Instead, repent for the way you have lived for yourself, and then choose to become a bond servant of the Master who is quite capable of taking care of His people.

5 KNOW YOUR CALLING AND BE AN ACHIEVER

In the winter of 1996, I sat in Reggie White's den, listening to him and a teammate from the Green Bay Packers discuss their football careers. Reggie has been called the best defensive lineman ever to play the game. He has been an All-Pro for ten straight years and was recently named to the All-Time NFL Team, which is composed of the best players over the seventy-five-year history of the league. His teammate was also one of the outstanding players at his position over the last decade. During this conversation these two athletes commented, "There are probably many young men in every city who have the potential to be the very best players and dream about doing it, but never will."

What is true of those who have the potential to be great athletes is probably true of every position in life. Many potentially great musicians will spend their lives listening to others perform. Many persons who could be gifted businessmen, artists, scientists, statesmen, doctors, lawyers, writers, or ministers will probably spend their lives doing something they are bored with rather than fulfilling their talents. This is tragic, but an even greater tragedy is Christians who are not fulfilling their callings in the body of Christ. Even so, before the end of this age, the body of Christ will arise to become the most unified and powerful force the world has ever known. If we are going to be a part of it, we must understand some basic principles of achievement.

We can be sure we will be frustrated if we do not fulfill our natural talents. That frustration is even greater, however, if we do not fulfill our spiritual destiny. Such frustration could be at the root of many divisions in churches, denominations, and even our families. In fact, frustration is a major problem in the church, but the latter stages of such frustration—boredom and lukewarmness—can be even more devastating.

Being angry is not good, but it does show that one still has the ability to care. I see more hope for a congregation that has tensions in it than one that is asleep. However, if those in ministry are doing their primary job, which is to equip the saints to do the work of ministry (Eph. 4:12), much of the energy that is now manifested in these tensions will be used to produce fruit. And that is a primary reason we are in this world:

> By this is My Father glorified, that you bear much fruit, and so prove to be My disciples. . . . You did not choose Me, but I chose you, and appointed you, that you should go and bear fruit, and that your fruit should remain, that whatever you ask of the Father in My name, He may give to you. (John 15:8, 16)

According to the Lord, our primary purpose is to bear fruit that will remain, which involves more than just growing personally in the fruits of the Spirit. The Lord is implying that we are called to *do* or *be* something of such consequence that our lives will continue to impact this world even after we have departed.

Every Christian has a ministry, a purpose he or she has been given in this life. The Scriptures state that we were foreknown and called by God before the foundation of the world. Yet, the Scriptures also teach that "many are called, but few are chosen [or go beyond calling to commissioning]" (Matt. 22:14). Most people today are like the Israelites, who were called to go to the promised land but spent their lives wandering in circles in the wilderness.

God does not want us to live in the perpetual frustration or boredom that comes from not walking in our true purpose. He wants us to have the indescribable pleasure of knowing we have accomplished all that He put us on this earth to do. Our first step to getting out of our wilderness is believing that He has something better for us—and that He is able to bring us into it.

How many Christians do you know who are fulfilling their potential? How many churches? Few indeed. Yet that is why the Lord placed in our hearts the desire to do something significant.

Five basic characteristics can be seen in the lives of those who have accomplished notable achievements.

FIVE CHARACTERISTICS OF ACHIEVERS

These five same characteristics can be found throughout the Scriptures in the biographies of those who fulfilled God's purpose in their generation:

1. They have a clear vision of their purpose.

2. They stay focused on their goal.

3. They have the wisdom and resolve to gather the necessary resources or training to accomplish their purpose.

4. They do not associate with "problem-oriented people" but with "solution-oriented people."

5. They refuse to let obstacles or opposition stop them; they stay resolutely on the course to fulfilling their purpose, regardless of setbacks and disappointments.

Let's look at each of these in more depth, as well as the stumbling blocks that keep us from accomplishing our purpose in life.

FACTOR ONE: HAVE A CLEAR VISION OF YOUR PURPOSE

I often ask audiences, "How many of you know what your calling is?" Usually less than 10 percent raise their hands. Then I ask, "How many of you are walking in your calling?" Most hands go down. Usually only 1 percent of the entire audience acknowledge that they know their calling *and* are walking in it.

How much could each of us accomplish if only 1 percent of our body were functioning? This is a major reason for the general weakness and ineffectiveness of the church today. Each of us needs to have a clear vision of our purpose.

Scripture tells us, "Thy word is a lamp to my feet, and a light to my path" (Ps. 119:105), which means that we are supposed to be able to see where we are going. However, most of the time our vision will be general at first, and then get more specific as we proceed toward the goal. Solomon observed: "But the path of the righteous is like the light of dawn, that shines brighter and brighter until the full day" (Prov. 4:18). This means that our path should become clearer as we proceed. If it is not, something is probably wrong with our walk.

Every Christian's overall purpose is to be like Jesus, who was the composite of the entire new covenant ministry in one person. He was *the* Apostle, *the* Prophet, *the* Evangelist, *the* Shepherd, and *the* Teacher. When He ascended, He gave gifts to men (Eph. 4:8–12), and now we have individuals who are apostles, prophets, evangelists, pastors, or teachers. It takes all of the ministries together to fully manifest Christ. That is why Paul did not say, "I have the mind of Christ," but rather "We have the mind of Christ" (1 Cor. 2:16).

In the Scriptures, we can see that the Lord always reveals people's calling to them before He expects them to accomplish it. Yet many of us do care enough to seek the Lord for this understanding. He has ordained that we must ask, seek, and knock before we will receive. You may reply that the Lord showed the apostle Paul his calling when he became a Christian, but by Paul's own confession he spent many years defining that calling, much of that time alone in the wilderness. Our calling is possibly our most precious treasure, and what makes treasure valuable is that it is either rare or hard to find. Those who receive treasure too easily will not understand its true value.

When you seek the Lord, get specific. *Those who have goals that are too general rarely accomplish them*. Those who want to "go into business for themselves" almost never do. Those who want to "be a musician" or "go into the ministry" almost never do, or if they do, they quickly fail. However, those who go into business because they love a certain product or service are much more likely to succeed. Those who fall in love with a certain musical instrument, like the violin, and devote themselves to being as good a violinist as they can be, are much more likely to succeed. Those who go into the ministry because they have a heart for reaching a certain people group with the gospel, or a desire to plant churches or reach teenagers, are also much more likely to succeed.

Actually, the answer to what we are called to be is usually found in our own hearts, because living waters can only come out of the "innermost being." However, many people have a hard time knowing the deepest desire of their hearts because they wear so many veils and defense mechanisms. These veils are most often the facades that we wear in order to meet human expectations (or even perceived human expectations) and therefore avoid rejection. It is sometimes a major undertaking to strip these away so that we can know what is in our own hearts.

Yet, to be changed into the image of the Lord, we must behold His glory *with an unveiled face* (2 Cor. 3:18), which is the result of a heart that has been unshackled from self-centeredness and fear—sins that are the results of the Fall. These primary obstacles keep us from seeing God's glory and being changed into His image.

We are not called to be conformed to the image of another person or even another ministry. This delusion tries to creep into every church and movement, especially those headed by a dynamic leader. Soon the members begin to take on the appearance and nature of that leader instead of Christ. What would you think if you were a husband whose children looked like your best friend? Maybe that mirrors the way the Lord feels when His children look more like His people here on earth than Him.

When we try to become like others, we are still seeing the Lord through the thick veil of another earthen vessel. We must look directly to Him if we are to be changed by His glory. That is why the Shulamite maid, who represents the bride of Christ in the Song of Solomon, asked: "Tell me, O you whom my soul loves, where do you pasture your flock, where do you make it lie down at noon? *For why should I be like one who veils herself beside the flocks of your companions?*" (Song 1:7, emphasis added).

This does not mean that we should never submit to the shepherds and teachers the Lord has provided for His church or seek to be equipped by them, but we must not seek to conform ourselves into the image of another person.

To know and fulfill our ministry, we must first fall in love with the Lord. Then we will become drawn to the specific aspect(s) of His ministry to which we are called. If we are called as shepherds, we will see the Lord's shepherd heart in almost everything He does in the Gospels. Likewise, if we are called as teachers, we will see Jesus the Teacher in almost all that He does. Sometimes we may also look for further confirmation.

Confirming Our Calling

The gift of prophecy is sometimes used for confirming gifts and ministries, just as we see in 2 Timothy 1:6. However, we must be careful in how we use this gift. If I prophetically perceive a person's calling, I seldom share what I see until I know that he has begun to see it himself. When vision comes prematurely or too easily, it will bring forth a superficial ministry at best.

One of the primary purposes of New Testament prophetic ministry is to encourage the members of the body to fulfill their callings. Even so, it is a misuse of this ministry to use prophets as gurus or soothsayers, or as a cheap source of supernatural knowledge. Members of the body will be stronger if they receive most of the revelation directly from God, and the prophets are used to confirm it.

I first heard every one of the most fruitful aspects of my ministry from the Lord, but I did not launch out into them until I received a word from a prophetic friend. (I just did not have the faith or courage that I needed to go forward.) I am not saying that this is best, as one of these prophets rebuked me each time for not having the faith to believe the word of the Lord to me directly, but I thank the Lord for helping me in my unbelief.

Even David, one of the greatest prophets of all time, often called for other prophets when he wanted to inquire of the Lord. There are times when we need the help of prophets, and there are times when we are better off to seek Him for ourselves.

To achieve God's plan for our lives, we must first ask for a clear vision of our purpose, then we must stay focused on that goal.

FACTOR TWO: STAY FOCUSED ON YOUR GOAL

A lack of focus keeps many from the ranks of achievers. Some of us cannot see past the obstacles to attaining our goals, so we seek easier ones.

Others are diverted by successes in lesser purposes. Harry Truman once remarked, "Most people are defeated by secondary successes."

One of the hardest tests we must pass if we are going to fulfill our ultimate calling is not to be distracted by all the other things God is doing. It is often difficult to resist joining another successful move of God, especially when well-meaning people suggest that we are missing God if we do not join that movement. We must learn to give ourselves only to what God has called us. When we get before His judgment seat, the Lord is not going to ask us how many successful churches or movements we were a part of. He is going to ask us if we did His will.

It is even harder to pass up being a part of other movements when God is calling you just to wait on Him before He leads you into your ultimate purpose. Abraham could not wait for the Lord to bring forth His promised child; instead he listened to Sarah's suggestion that they help God out, which led to the birth of Ishmael by Sarah's handmaiden, Haggar. Even then, God blessed Ishmael and made him a great nation, which may be confusing to us. Very often He will also bless our "Ishmaels," which are conceived in our own minds and wills. *But they will never become God's real purpose for our lives*. Abraham only had one Ishmael; most of us have many! Even so, if we are going to have Isaac, there is a time to drive Ishmael out of the house. Ishmael(s) cannot be an heir with Isaac.

When we have a clear vision of our purpose, and the resolve to stay focused on it, we are much more likely to see all that will be required to fulfill our goal.

FACTOR THREE: HAVE THE WISDOM AND RESOLVE TO GATHER THE NECESSARY RESOURCES OR TRAINING TO ACCOMPLISH YOUR PURPOSE

Between the time God reveals the calling, and the actual commissioning of our ministry, there will always be a time of education and training. Yet the inability to use this time between our calling and our commission has caused the failure of many. Albert Einstein once said, "Premature responsibility breeds superficiality." Martyn Lloyd-Jones, the well-known theologian, thought that premature success was one of the most dangerous things that could happen to a person.

Paul was called as an apostle somewhere from eleven to thirteen years before he was commissioned to that ministry at Antioch. He did not just sit back and wait; he spent much of this time in the wilderness seeking his own revelation of God's purpose in his life as well as a deeper understanding of the gospel he was to preach (Gal. 1). Instead of being impatient, we should be thankful for all of the time we are given to get ready for our calling, and we should use every bit of it wisely.

Possibly the greatest difference between the star athletes, musicians, artists, or great professionals in any field, and those who have the talents but are sitting on the sidelines, is this devotion to training, practice, and preparation. The ballplayer who wins the World Series with a single swing of the bat thrills us. It seems to happen so quickly—and so easily. Yet, this batter probably spent thousands of hours swinging his bat in practice, enduring the heat, the boredom, and the blisters day after day, week after week, and year after year just to be able to do this. Athletes train for "a perishable wreath." How much more should we give ourselves for that which is eternal?

Many years ago the Lord told me that some of His greatest leaders in the last-day church were going to come out of professional sports. Sports is their seminary, He said. They are being taught principles in their seminary that are not being taught in our seminaries, and these characteristics will be crucial to the church in the end times. This got my attention. Since then, every time I have been around professional athletes I have tried to learn all I can from them.

I was once asked to speak to the Denver Broncos before a Monday night game. The focus, resolution, and determination on the faces of those players as they waited for the game was greater than I had ever witnessed in an audience. As I pondered this, the Lord spoke to me. "When I see the same kind of focus and resolution in My people," He said, "then the beginning of the last-day ministry is at hand." Where would the church be today if we all devoted ourselves to preparing for a place on God's team as these athletes prepared themselves? There probably would not be such a consuming devotion to sports because the church would be so exciting, people would not have time for such mundane things as being spectators at a game.

This kind of heartfelt resolution will lead all of us to develop a thoughtful plan that gathers the necessary resources to achieve our purpose.

Last year I was speaking to the New Orleans Saints in their team chapel just before a game, and the Lord again used the players to challenge me to a higher level of commitment. Afterward I was asked to have dinner with the team. While eating I asked some of the players what they had done to reach such a pinnacle of their profession. They almost all began as children to have a dream of playing professional football, and then they devoted hours of their lives every day practicing, building their strength and speed, and studying others who were successful at their position. I could not help but wonder what kind of transformation there would be in the church if Christians gave that kind of devotion to fulfilling their calling in Christ! How much more worthy is our calling in the Lord than even being the greatest athlete? Yet, very few Christians will even spend one hour a day preparing themselves for their purpose in the Lord. This must change.

Those Who Fail to Plan, Plan to Fail

A subtle delusion that says planning is not spiritual has crept into large sections of the body of Christ. Many actually infer that if you know what you are going to do ahead of time, God cannot be in it. This is amazing because we are supposed to be taking on the nature of God, and a lack of planning is profoundly contrary to His basic nature. Revealing *His* plan is one of the most glorious revelations of His character. Jesus was crucified before the foundation of the world, and we were called to Him before the world began. That's planning!

If we are becoming like Him, planning should be one of our greatest skills. It can even be argued that the level of one's ability to plan will be a major factor in determining the significance of his or her accomplishments. It is during the time of your preparation that you will be able to lay the best plans for your life and ministry. There is much truth to the ancient proverb that "those who fail to plan, plan to fail."

As a pilot, I learned that the safety of every flight was determined by the quality of my preflight planning. Often I had to make changes to these plans during the flight, but because preflight planning included reviewing my options—such as alternate airports in case of an emergency—I made changes much more easily. During my flying career, I had to make a couple of such emergency landings, and with one of those the emergency was demanding so much of my attention, I could not take the time to get out my charts to find an alternate airport. I had to know where it was and put the plane down immediately. There is no doubt that the average person's life would be much more fruitful, not to mention easier and safer, if he or she would develop planning skills.

What are athletes so focused on before the game? The game plan. A good coach will know his team's strengths and weaknesses right down to who has a sore foot. He will then seek to know the opposing team the same way. The coach formulates a plan to highlight his own team's strengths and compensate for its weaknesses, at the same time that he tries to neutralize the opposing team's strengths and exploit its weaknesses. Finally, the team practices that plan until every member knows his part and can execute it with the highest efficiency and precision.

Coaches and players know that they will probably have to make adjustments to that game plan. Even so, the plan is crucial because it gives them some parameters. The most successful coaches are usually the ones who can formulate the best plans before the game and can also make decisive changes when they are needed on the field. The same is true of pilots and anyone else in a leadership position.

Even though I was in naval aviation, I was once assigned to a ground defense force and had to go through the infantry training taught by the marines. We were taught many different battle plans and maneuvers. We practiced them over and over. Then we were told that no battle ever goes as planned. "The only thing that you can count on during a battle is confusion," our commander said. "The side that can best cope with this confusion—which is usually the result of plans not going as planned—is usually the one that wins. And the way to cope with confusion is to make new and effective plans in the midst of it."

Because my primary calling is to equip believers for their ministry, I have tried to do my best to understand people. In doing so, I have found that probably 90 percent of us are subject to a high degree of confusion in our lives. It has also become obvious to me that this confusion is directly linked either to how well people understand their calling, or if they are not believers, how well they define their goals. It is also obvious that the ability to formulate a clear, effective plan is a rare human quality that almost always separates those who are leaders from those who will always be followers.

We should have strategic objectives that lead step-by-step toward the goal, while avoiding the trap of overplanning. Over the years, I have watched some of the most noble visions lead only to frustration, discouragement, and failure because those with the vision were either weak planners or overplanners, whose plans became so complex no one could follow them. As the saying goes, "There is a ditch on both sides of the path that leads to life."

Achievers have a clear vision of their purpose, they stay focused on their goals, they have the wisdom and resolve to gather the necessary resources to accomplish their purpose, and they surround themselves with "solution-oriented people."

FACTOR FOUR: SURROUND YOURSELF WITH SOLUTION-ORIENTED PEOPLE

One of the first steps that successful leaders implement when assuming a leadership position is to get rid of everyone who spends more time talking about problems than solutions. Could this be why the Lord Jesus Himself spent so much time developing the faith of those who would be His future leaders? Maybe this is also why it is not possible to please Him without faith (Heb. 11:6). Solution-oriented people have faith.

The Essential Factor

A primary factor that separates those who will accomplish their goals from those who will not is faith. In talking about goals, I am not just talking about faith in God, but faith in general. Everyone has faith; everyone believes *something*. Some principles of faith will work for anyone who uses them, whether they believe in God or not.

If we have faith in our natural talents, we will probably use them. But if we have more faith in our weaknesses than in our gifts, the weaknesses will prevail in our life, and we will be perpetual failures. Likewise, if we have more faith in the obstacles before us than in our talents, those obstacles will dictate our course. What we believe in will determine the quality of what we accomplish. If we truly believe in God, we will accomplish what He has given us to do. The degree of our faith will determine the quantity of what we accomplish.

The Faith Test

The apostle Paul exhorted: "Test yourselves to see if you are in the faith; examine yourselves! Or do you not recognize this about yourselves, that Jesus Christ is in you—unless indeed you fail the test?" (2 Cor. 13:5).

True faith is not a faith in ourselves, or a faith in our faith, but a faith in the Lord and who He is. The only way we will accomplish our purpose in this life is to keep our focus on Him. Even Jesus did not focus on Himself when He walked the earth; He kept His attention on the Father. He said that He did not do anything of Himself, but He only did what He saw the Father doing. We must walk the same way.

As Christians, we not only personally know the Creator, but we also have Him living within us: "Abide in Me, and I in you. As the branch cannot bear fruit of itself, unless it abides in the vine, so neither can you, unless you abide in Me. I am the vine, you are the branches; he who abides in Me, and I in him, he bears much fruit; for apart from Me you can do nothing" (John 15:4–5).

We can test our faith by asking ourselves, "How fruitful am I?" The degree of our fruitfulness will always depend on the strength of our union with the Vine. The Lord loves to use the ordinary to do the extraordinary. He took men who would probably make anyone's "least likely to succeed" list and transformed them into people who turned the world upside down. Our God has not changed. He still delights in using the foolish to confound the wise and the weak to confound the strong. Therefore, being weak and foolish can be one of our qualifications for being used by God. However, this does not mean that we remain weak or foolish, but that we learn to walk by His strength and His wisdom.

We will never fulfill our callings if we are focused on our own inadequacy. When Moses was told of his calling at the burning bush, he immediately began to protest that he was not adequate for such a task. The Lord did not commend him for this humility. Scripture says that "the anger of the LORD burned against Moses" (Ex. 4:14). Such a mentality is not true humility. It is the devastating sin of self-centeredness and is actually a profound pride. By this, Moses inferred that his inadequacy was greater than God's adequacy. God does not call us because of our abilities or our inabilities but often because of our *availability*.

Solution-oriented people have faith that God has chosen them. If we are going to accomplish God's purpose for our lives, we must surround ourselves with people who talk about solutions rather than being bogged down by problems and fears.

When General Grant took over the Union army during the Civil War, the Union had already suffered many defeats at the hands of General Lee and the Confederate army. The officers and men had become so conditioned to defeat that members of Grant's own command team prophesied his doom when he first marched against Lee. Grant promptly dismissed these men. Then, in his first engagement with Lee at the Battle of the Wilderness, reports came in from every division of his army that they were beaten. All day long his officers begged Grant to flee back north to the safety of Washington before Lee cut them off from their path of retreat. Finally, when it was obvious even to Grant that they were beaten in that engagement, he astonished everyone by giving orders to turn south and advance on to Richmond!

Grant's generals begged him to reconsider, assuring him that Lee would cut off their retreat, so Grant dismissed them and retreated to the solitude of his own tent. As he thought about their argument, Grant realized that if Lee did try to cut off his retreat, it would actually enable him to do something every other Union general had tried to do and failed. He could position his army between Lee and Richmond so that he could advance on the Southern capital. As Union troops started marching south, a great cheer went up from the entire army. For the first time they had a general who would fight. Grant's "defeat" at the Battle of the Wilderness opened the door for his greatest opportunity, and he seized it. Later, Grant confided to a reporter that he had never been in a battle in which it did not look at some point as if they were doomed. "I believe an opportunity exists in every crisis," he said.

When General Lee heard that Grant had not retreated but had in fact turned his army south, he acknowledged to his generals that the end of the Confederacy was near. Lee won several more battles, but never once did Grant consider retreating. Never once did he pay attention to the doomsayers. He probably never won an outright battle against Lee, but he held his course until he won the war.

One of the basic principles every successful leader understands is this: If you are going to accomplish your goals, you must get rid of the people on your leadership team who are more focused on the problems than solutions. This is the principle of the ten spies at Kadesh-barnea. The evil, negative report of these ten spies cost their entire generation their inheritance. If you cannot change such people, you must remove them, or they will cost you your vision.

Finally, in order to be an achiever, you must refuse to let obstacles or opposition stop you.

FACTOR FIVE: REFUSE TO LET OBSTACLES OR OPPOSITION STOP YOU

Some factors that help individuals attain extraordinary achievements can be controlled, and some cannot. Hard work, defining goals, staying focused on those goals, and attaining the necessary resources for achieving them can be controlled. However, we cannot control—and usually will do everything that we can to avoid—the factor that has the greatest possibility to release a high level of human achievement: *adversity*.

One of the faces of the Lord in Scripture is the face of an eagle. It has been said that all of nature fears storms except for the eagle. Early on eagles learn an important principle: If they face an opposing wind *at the proper angle*, they will be carried higher. They use opposing winds to reach the greatest heights. The same is true of those who learn to soar spiritually. Every opposing wind is an opportunity to go higher, *if you will approach it at the proper angle or with the right attitude*.

Some of us are deluded by the belief that others become achievers because they have favorable circumstances. That excuse is one of the main reasons many fail. The obstacles that confronted Reggie White and almost every other player in the NFL were as great, or greater, than those others faced. These men were not given special breaks. Very few achievers in any field are. In fact, when special breaks are given to those with great ability, it often works to cause them to fall short of their true potential.

Alexander Solzhenitsyn, the famous author and survivor of Russian concentration camps, once said, "Even biology teaches us that perpetual well-being is not good for any creature." Adversity does more for our development than possibly any other single factor. Adversity helps us to focus, to eliminate the nonessentials, and devote ourselves to the essentials. Adversity will cause the truly devoted to work harder, which will cause them to become stronger. If success comes too easily, we will be weaker.

THIS IS NOT MAGIC

I have watched many of my friends who play golf try one new golf club or ball after another, seeking the magic remedy to improve their game. As one famous golfer said in a commercial for a new golf ball, "This ball really can improve your game, if you will hit three hundred of them a day!" When the same golfer was asked about a "lucky shot," he replied, "You know, the more I practice, the luckier I get."

The same is true of our gifts and callings. People frequently ask me to pray for them to have the gift of writing. To me that is almost like one of my student pilots asking me to pray for him to have the "gift of piloting," so he can go out and fly an airplane without going through the proper training. Would you fly with someone who received his or her "gift of piloting" that way? I don't think so. You would want them to have the best training and then thousands of hours of experience.

I do believe in prophetic impartation, but I think that very few people really understand it. Even spiritual gifts are imparted as seeds that must be cultivated and cared for with great patience and devotion.

For me to just pray and impart the "gift of writing" to those who ask for it would only bring judgment on them; if they are not willing to pay the price to develop this gift, they will be judged for burying it. Having gifts or callings does not impress me. Using gifts with wisdom and maturity does.

Do you want to know how I got my gift of writing? When I was a young child, I felt I was destined to be a writer. I did not know any writers and knew no one to turn to for help, so I did the only thing I could think of to develop my writing skills—I began reading. I did not just read a few books; I read thousands of them.

I felt that if I was going to be the best writer I could be, I should read the best books, so I started reading the classics. It was a hard discipline at first, but soon I fell in love with them. I then turned my attention to studying everything from psychology to semantics. For several years after I became a Christian, I spent more than forty hours a week studying the Bible. Then I read church history and the works of the great prophetic voices who shaped that history. For more than thirty-five years I have read at least one book a week, and sometimes more.

I planned to go to journalism school, but when it became clear that I couldn't because I was about to be drafted during the Vietnam War, I did not give up. I determined that I would teach myself the mechanics of writing, so I studied it on my own. (I have had to learn almost everything that I know about anything, except flying, in this way.) I knew that my writing skills were rough from the lack of formal education, but I did not let that stop me. Instead I determined to do the best I could with what I had available.

It has been, and continues to be, a difficult struggle. I'm sure that others with more training could do the writing that I do in much less time and with much less effort, but I am thankful to be doing what I have been called to do. Even so, it is hard to be patient with those who ask me to impart the gift of writing to them, as if I could just say a simple prayer and they could have what I have. (I would also love to be able to pray for people to "be mature!" but I cannot find that miracle anywhere in the Scriptures.)

If you want an important gift, you will have to value it enough to develop it to that level. I have had many friends who are smarter than I am and more gifted, naturally and spiritually. Many of them had a similar calling and would be accomplishing much more than I am now if they had just disciplined themselves and made the necessary preparations for their ministry.

Even though I have not been able to go to journalism school, or even Bible school, in many ways I would not trade my education for anyone's. Like Paul, I can say that what I received I did not receive from men. Even so, I do my best to make the way easier for others if I see them devoted to the discipline, focus, and resolve that all true success takes—and that our calling in Christ Jesus certainly deserves. If we will fulfill our purpose in this life, we must set our faces like a flint "to go to Jerusalem" (Luke 9:51), the place of our destiny.

6 RECOGNIZING GOD'S VOICE

I read about a man visiting the Middle East. While sitting on a hillside, he watched as three shepherds approached a watering hole with their flocks. All three flocks just merged into a single great mass, and the writer was sure it would be impossible for them to ever get the sheep sorted out again. To his amazement, the shepherds seemed completely unconcerned.

After the sheep had finished drinking, each shepherd started walking down a different path, and began singing as he went. A convulsion erupted in the great mixed flock, and then little streams of sheep started following after each shepherd until they had all separated again into their own flocks.

Even though all of the shepherds were singing, the sheep could distinguish their own shepherd from the others. They knew their shepherd's voice because they knew their shepherd so well. They had grown up hearing him sing in the hills and pastures season after season—they had been with him enough to be able to distinguish his voice from that of anyone else.

Scripture gives us this same picture as an example of God's relationship with us:

> When He puts forth all His own, He goes before them, and the sheep follow Him *because they know His voice*. And a stranger they simply will not follow, but will flee from him, because they do not know the voice of strangers . . . *My sheep hear My voice*, and I know them, and they follow Me (John 10:4–5, 27, emphasis added).

In this text the Lord declared that His sheep followed Him *because* they knew His voice. The better we know His voice, the better we will be able to follow Him. The reverse is also true: If we do not know His voice, we will have difficulty following Him.

It is typical of our Western mind-set to want a clear formula for how to get to know the voice of the Lord. There must at least be an obvious "how to" in the Scriptures, we think. Many have attempted to wrestle one out of the Word, but it is not there. The only way we can come to know the voice of the Lord is the same way that the sheep came to know their shepherd's voice—through time spent in His presence.

The single greatest endeavor to help us cultivate this is *to love the Lord.* And the single greatest thing we can do to cultivate that love is to ask for it.

The Lord's Prayer recorded in John 17 is considered by many to be the most important prayer in the Scriptures. The Lord completed this prayer with: "I have made Thy name known to them [His followers], and will make it known; *that the love wherewith Thou didst love Me may be in them, and I in them*" (John 17:26, emphasis added). We know that Jesus was "one with the Father," so we know that this is the Father's will. Ponder this for a few minutes: *It is the Father's will that the same love that He has for His Son would be in us!*

One of the basic characteristics of true love is communication. It is the nature of lovers to share everything. The more we love the Lord, the more we will be drawn to know His voice so that we can follow Him more closely. The first step is to love Him so much that we will seek Him until we find Him. Ask, seek, knock, but do not settle for anything less than a true and holy intimacy with the Lord. As one of my prophetic friends, Paul Cain, once so eloquently stated, "Everyone of us is as close to the Lord as we want to be." Or as the apostle Paul said, "Draw near to God and He will draw near to you" (James 4:8). Is this not the greatest promise in all of Scripture?

Much of the Lord's communication with us is not meant to concern matters of great eternal or strategic gravity, but is simply the communication of a lover. This may be one of the most difficult issues for us to learn. In spite of all our flaws, our mistakes, and our failures, He really loves us and wants to be close to us simply because He *enjoys* us. This kind of true intimacy will produce offspring, and we will bear true spiritual fruit only through abiding in Him. However, if the only reason a husband had relations with his wife was to have children, the marriage would be a very shallow union, and the same is true of our union with Christ.

In the story of Lazarus's death, we have a striking illustration of the power of intimacy.

THE POWER OF INTIMACY

The story unfolds in the eleventh chapter of John. As Jesus approached Bethany, Lazarus's sister Martha ran out first to meet Him. In her grief she reproached Jesus, "Lord, if You had been here, my brother would not have died" (v. 21). He responded by giving her a good teaching about Him as the resurrection. Then Lazarus's sister Mary came out to meet Jesus and reproached Him with the very same words—but with a much different result. The Scriptures tell us that "He was deeply moved in spirit, and was troubled" (v. 33), and "Jesus wept" (v. 35). Jesus then raised Lazarus from the dead. Mary had the ability to move God deeply in spirit; she caused the Lord to weep! She received much more than a good teaching about the resurrection. She got a resurrection!

One of the most touching experiences I have had as a father came after my oldest daughter's third birthday. In two days she had two birthday parties—one at our house and one at my in-laws'. She received more gifts than we should have ever allowed and greatly enjoyed what seemed to be a constant diet of cake and ice cream. She was undoubtedly having the time of her young life. While riding home in the car, I asked her what had been her favorite gift—or the favorite thing that she had done during those days. She pondered the question seriously and then stated matter-of-factly, "Sitting on your lap."

You know what that did to her daddy! It does the same thing to our Father in heaven when, after all of His gifts and all of His great blessings, just being with Him really is our favorite thing.

Almost everything that we define as ministry today involves service to people, but the greatest ministry of all is ministry to the Lord.

Almost every characteristic that we ascribe to spiritual authority concerns the ability to motivate people, but the greatest spiritual authority is the ability to touch and move God's heart. Mary had the ability, the authority, if you will, that is greater than any other. She was so close to the Lord, she could touch His heart. When we can touch God's heart and move Him to action, we have an authority that is greater than any governmental or spiritual office on this earth. The foundation of this greatest of powers is simple intimacy with Him.

Intimacy is directly related to communication, which usually does not come with flashes of lightning or even King James English. The Lord is not nearly as religious as we tend to be. Mary, who was able to move God so profoundly, was just as wrong in her reproach of Him as Martha had been. Always being theologically correct is not nearly as important to the Lord as it may be with some of His people. He does not look at the mind as much as the heart. Of course, if we love the truth, we will want to be theologically correct too, but we must get the most important issue first.

When fruit becomes the basic reason for drawing close to the Lord, we are in jeopardy of succumbing to the "Martha spirit"—the tendency to substitute works for intimacy. Yes, there are times when we do need to work for Him, and the Lord, of course, loved Martha very much. Many churches and ministries could not exist without the "Marthas." But when we become too busy working for Him to recognize just sitting at His feet as the highest priority, we are truly missing the greatest part. It may be unfathomable, but it is nevertheless true that He has chosen us to be His dwelling place.

We cannot expect to know His voice if we do not worship Him. Possibly the most telltale sign of what we truly worship will be found in what we do with our free time. When was the last time we thought of using our day off for prayer and fasting? The answer to that question could explain why we have such difficulty knowing the Lord's voice, or discerning truth from error.

Once we are truly intimate with the Lord, how do we recognize God's voice and His will for us? First through studying His Word in the Bible, but certainly much, much more than that. We will also consider the role of the Holy Spirit, the prompting of another Christian, which often necessitates humility on our part to receive it, and the message of dreams and visions.

FOUR WAYS TO HEAR GOD'S VOICE

Let's begin by looking at God's Word as a path to knowing His presence.

1. GOD'S WORD

The first principle we must understand to know the Scriptures properly is that *every Christian* can discern biblical truth as surely as even the most learned theologian. There has been a diabolical conspiracy since the beginning to try to keep the truth from the common people and to confine it exclusively in the hands of a few professionals. Some say one must attain a certain depth of knowledge or education and understand the science of biblical interpretation before he can properly understand the Scriptures. The Lord Jesus stated the exact opposite: "At that time Jesus answered and said, 'I praise Thee, O Father, Lord of heaven and earth, that Thou didst hide these things from the wise and intelligent and didst reveal them to babes'" (Matt. 11:25).

It was necessary for Saul of Tarsus *literally* to be struck blind in the natural so that he could see in the spiritual, and the same must happen *figuratively* to us. We can only discern spiritual truth by the Spirit, through grace because "God is opposed to the proud, but gives grace to the humble" (James 4:6). No one can properly understand the Scriptures, prophecy, or the will of God unless he or she maintains true humility.

The apostle Paul warned that "knowledge puffs up" (1 Cor. 8:1 NKJV). However, the Scriptures also warn, "My people are destroyed for lack of knowledge" (Hos. 4:6). The Christian walk is a straight and narrow path that must be navigated with great care. We must continually cast ourselves on the grace of God, knowing our dependence on Him. We especially need His grace to remain humble as we pursue and gain biblical knowledge. Otherwise, the very knowledge that would set us free can hasten our downfall by resulting in pride.

For this reason, it is crucial that we learn to abide in the Holy Spirit and the Scriptures. The Holy Spirit is easily grieved or offended by sin, which can be a barometer of our pride. The Scriptures teach that He will depart if we do not walk uprightly, a primary factor of which is to walk humbly before Him. Only when we keep this sensitivity to His presence will we be able to receive biblical knowledge without being puffed up by it. The presence of the Holy Spirit in our lives must be *as important* as biblical truth.

We also need the Holy Spirit's guidance to truly hear God's voice.

2. GUIDANCE FROM THE HOLY SPIRIT

The Bible is the map to God's kingdom, but it is not the kingdom any more than a map of the United States is actually the mountains, valleys, cities, and country towns of America. You may need a map to get to the beach, but having the map will never substitute for being on the beach. We must be utterly committed to knowing the Scriptures, but knowing them will never substitute for knowing the Lord Himself.

The Bible was never meant to supplant the Holy Spirit in our lives, nor was the Holy Spirit meant to take the place of the Bible—they both have *different functions* in leading us to truth and keeping us in the will of God. The Scriptures alone are used for establishing doctrine, while "the voice of the Lord" is used to give us day-to-day guidance as well as revealing the strategic will of the Lord. The Bible does not address some of the most important decisions we must all make—whom we should marry, our choice of professions, where we should live. These decisions can have a fundamental impact on our lives, and we do need the Lord's counsel, and sometimes directives, in each of them.

What kind of marriage would it be if, on your wedding day, your spouse gave you a book that laid out all of his expectations for your relationship—and then you never spoke to each other again? It would be hard to blame someone who was trapped in such a situation for wanting a divorce. Neither has the Lord trapped us in such a lifeless relationship. In fact, He is usually far more interested in communicating with us than we are with Him.

Knowing the Lord is much more than just knowing His works. How many people can you recognize by looking at their hands? With maybe a few exceptions, most people can only recognize others either by their face or by their voice. Yet, how often we devote our attention to seeking the "hand of the Lord" (what we can receive from Him, rather than seeking His face or hearing His voice).

In contrast to the statement made by the Lord Jesus Himself, "My sheep hear My voice, and I know them, and they follow Me" (John 10:27), many Protestant and Reformed theologies not only hinder, but actually prohibit, Christians from knowing God's voice. These theologies can be traced to the extreme interpretation of the prime Reformation motto *sola scriptura*, which means "Scripture alone."

The Reformation's Greatest Weapon

The great motto of the Reformation, *sola scriptura*, was initially penned in reaction to the pope's indiscriminate institution of dogma for the doctrines of the faith, many of which were actually in conflict with the Scriptures. The justification for this was the pope's claim of infallibility; his authority, he said, exceeded that of the Scriptures. This practice led to the greatest spiritual darkness the world has ever known, and this motto could be credited as the primary force that broke that darkness and began the release of every true spiritual advance since.

The motto *sola scriptura* sums up what was by far the most important doctrine of the Reformation: A Christian should never accept a doctrine that is in conflict with the written Word of God. However, this important truth was never intended to imply that we do not also need to know the voice of the Lord for personal guidance. If it was, it too would have been in conflict with the very integrity of the Scriptures.

In John 16:7 the Lord said, "But I tell you the truth, it is to your advantage that I go away; for if I do not go away, the Helper shall not come to you; but if I go, I will send Him to you." The Lord did not say that it was to our advantage that He go away so that He could send us a book. Neither did He say that He was going to send us a Book to lead us into all truth, but rather the Spirit (John 16:13).

The Bible is a most precious gift from the Lord to His people, and it alone should be used to establish or judge doctrine. The Lord Himself continually combated error with the statement "It is written." How much more should we depend on the Bible for the same thing! However, as important as it is to have accurate doctrine, walking in truth means much more than that. Regardless of how accurate our doctrines are, we are deceived if we are not abiding in the will of the Lord.

Christianity is far more than just knowing accurate doctrine—true Christianity is a restored, living relationship with the Lord.

Christianity Is More than a Doctrine

Even under the old covenant of the law, with its hundreds of burdensome commandments, each person was required both to know and obey "the voice of the Lord."

> And He said, *"If you will give earnest heed to the voice of the LORD* your God, and do what is right in His sight, *and* give ear to His commandments, and keep all His statutes, I will put none of the diseases on you which I have put on the Egyptians; for I, the LORD, am your healer." (Ex. 15:26, emphasis added)

> Now then, *if you will indeed obey My voice and* keep My covenant, then you shall be My own possession among all the peoples, for all the earth is Mine; and you shall be to Me a kingdom of priests and a holy nation. (Ex. 19:5–6, emphasis added)

> But from there you will seek the LORD your God, and you will find Him if you search for Him with all your heart and all your soul. When you are in distress and all these things have come upon you, in the latter days, you will return to the LORD your God *and listen to His voice*. (Deut. 4:29–30, emphasis added)

> Like the nations that the LORD makes to perish before you, so you shall perish; because *you would not listen to the voice of the LORD your God*. (Deut. 8:20, emphasis added)

> And when the LORD sent you from Kadesh-barnea, saying, "Go up and possess the land which I have given you," then you rebelled

against the command of the LORD your God; *you neither believed Him nor listened to His voice."* (Deut. 9:23, emphasis added)

Here we see that the first generation perished in the wilderness because they did not believe the Lord *or* listen to His voice. The written Word, even with all the commandments of the old covenant, was never meant to take the place of hearing God's voice. We often attribute the many apostasies of biblical Israel with their inability to keep His commandments, but these Scriptures show us it could be blamed just as easily on their not listening to His voice.

As Jesus told the Sadducees, "You do err, not knowing the scriptures nor the power of God" (Matt. 22:29 KJV). Many who know the Scriptures but do not know the power of God complain that they are considered second-class citizens in the kingdom by Charismatics and Pentecostals who claim to know the power. This charge is justified. However, it is just as true that those who may know the Scriptures, but not the power, consider the Charismatics and Pentecostals second-class citizens in the kingdom because they tend to have less biblical or academic knowledge. The fact is, both are true, and both sides need to repent of their spiritual pride and learn from each other.

If fundamentalists have come to understand the Scriptures, it has only been by the grace of God. If Charismatics have come to know something of the power of God, it has only been by the grace of God. In either case we have nothing to boast about—all that we receive is by grace. Few have come to a depth of biblical knowledge without stumbling because they became puffed up by that knowledge. And few have come to know God's power without stumbling because of pride. Even so, we need much more knowledge and much more power than we now have if we are to follow the Lord fully. Our quest is to attain both without the pride that will cause us to fall from grace.

I have been greatly encouraged the last few years as many on both sides of this issue have humbled themselves to reach out to those of the opposite camp. This was not done for the purpose of converting them to their ways, but to receive from them. Many bridges are now being built between those who know the Scriptures and those who know the power. Both sides need each other, and we will not accomplish our mandate in this hour without one another.

The Reformation accomplished much in recovering biblical truths that were lost during the Middle Ages, but the Reformation is not yet over. It will not be over until the Holy Spirit has again been given His rightful place in the church. God has called the church to sit with Christ in the heavenly places. We must have the proper balance of being established on solid, biblical truth, as well as knowing the voice of the Lord. If not, we are like someone trying to fly an airplane with only one wing. Not only is it impossible for us to get off the ground, we will just keep spinning around in circles until we have the other wing properly joined to us. We need the proper balance.

An Example of the Balance Between God's Word and His Voice

The book of Acts is an example of normal church life. Nothing has changed in the way the Lord relates to His people now from the way He did then. The apostle Paul's knowledge of the Scriptures gave him a profound understanding of Christ and the new covenant, as well as God's general plan to extend His ministry of reconciliation and His plan for Paul to go to the Gentiles with that ministry. However, when the Lord wanted Paul to go to Macedonia, Scripture could not give him that direction; he had to know the voice of the Lord (Acts 16:9–10).

We see this same pattern in Peter's life. He based his message and his ministry on the Scriptures, but when the Lord needed to give him special guidance, such as the commission to go to Cornelius's house to be the first to preach the gospel to Gentiles, the Lord gave him a special vision (Acts 10:9–48). Peter first obeyed the leading of the Holy Spirit, and then went to Jerusalem to confirm what he had done with the elders. Finally they all turned to the Scriptures.

This new, unprecedented action of preaching to the Gentiles would ultimately establish an important new doctrine: Gentiles were also to receive the grace of God through faith in Christ. Giving the Holy Spirit to the Gentiles demonstrated the Lord's power. However, as the Bereans did later (Acts 17:1), the apostles and elders likely did not accept it *until they had searched the Scriptures to verify it*.

This procedure also established an important precedent in the church, which should be a model for all Christian ministry. If an action did not clearly contradict the Scriptures, Christians were free to pursue what they perceived to be the leading of the Holy Spirit. However, even if this action resulted in something significant, it had to be confirmed by the Scriptures before it could be accepted as church doctrine. Each believer had the freedom to follow the Lord at the same time that the young church was protected from accepting just any new action as a new doctrine or practice.

If Peter had not taken the liberty that he did, it is unlikely the Jewish believers ever would have understood the Scriptures concerning the Lord's will to take the gospel to the Gentiles. His action illuminated the Scriptures; the Scriptures verified his actions. Both the foundation of biblical authority and the liberty of the Spirit in the church were established, and we must never allow either to be compromised. We should keep in mind that many of the great missionary endeavors in history were initiated against the counsel of other leaders. Without the liberty of the Spirit, we will often miss God's will. Without the Scriptures, we will drift into error. Both are essential if we are going to stay on the path of life!

We hear God's voice through His Word, through the Holy Spirit, and through the prompting of another Christian.

3. THE PROMPTING OF ANOTHER CHRISTIAN

Often the Lord's voice will come to us through a person, and the Lord will require us to humble ourselves to receive it. Throughout the Scriptures the Lord brought forth His Word in a way that required humility on the part of those who would receive it. Pride caused the fall of man in the first place, and we will not be delivered from the consequences of the Fall until we are delivered from pride.

Jesus is the Word of God personified, and He came in such a way that only those who would not care about appearances would receive Him. Not only was He born in humble circumstances in a humble nation, He was raised in one of the most humble and despised towns in that nation. The Lord of glory came to this world as what later generations would call a peasant. Only those who loved truth above appearances would follow Him, and those were the only disciples He wanted.

We think that if renowned and prestigious men and women acknowledge God, it will help us promote the gospel, but the Lord has clearly stated the opposite:

> For consider your calling, brethren, that there were not many wise according to the flesh, not many mighty, not many noble; but God has chosen the foolish things of the world to shame the wise, and God has chosen the weak things of the world to shame the things which are strong, and the base things of the world and the despised, God has chosen, the things that are not, that He might nullify the things that are, *that no man should boast before God.* (1 Cor. 1:26–29, emphasis added)

The apostle Paul did not entirely omit those who are noble, strong, or wise in this world—God just did not call *many* of them. Had He not called any, we would worship humility, which is obviously not the intent. The Lord who was born in a stable also had one of the most expensive buildings ever constructed as His temple. This extends true humility to *obedience.* The apostle Paul was wise; he learned to be content in whatever circumstances he found himself. At times, he learned to be abased, and this sometimes required that he also learn to abound. The issue is to keep a level head regardless of the state in which the Lord has placed us.

While in this life, we *are* in a humble state. The modern conveniences and lifestyle of the poor today may greatly exceed the conveniences of the wealthy just a century ago. We can regard both poor and rich as relative terms if we look from the perspective of history. When we look at eternity, even the wealthiest people on this earth are very poor—their lives are but a vapor. Compared to eternity, all of the treasures in this world would be less than a grain of sand in the ocean. We are all both very wealthy and very poor. Humility comes by simple dependence on God for everything we are or have, including our next breath.

It is quite easy for one who is in a humble state to display humility, but such meekness is often a facade for pride and pretending. Money can be anyone's god, not just the rich. I have seen those who are poor more consumed with seeking money than many of the wealthy I know. The unknowns who are most offended by the renowned usually have a lust for fame written all over them. Solomon stated, "There is one who pretends to be rich, but has nothing; another pretends to be poor, but has great wealth" (Prov. 13:7).

The highest form of humility will be displayed in the wisdom of those who seemingly have legitimate reasons to be proud if they compare themselves with others, but remain humble because eternity is in their hearts. The fruit of true humility will always be obedience, contentment despite circumstances, and compassion for others in whatever state the Lord has them. You cannot hear God's voice through other people if you're not willing to humble yourself.

Finally, God speaks to us through dreams and visions.

4. THROUGH DREAMS AND VISIONS

From the beginning, the two primary ways the Lord has spoken to His people have been through dreams and visions. According to Joel 2, which Peter quoted on the day of Pentecost, dreams and visions will be significant ways the Lord will speak to His people "in the last days." However, this is probably one of the least understood subjects in the church. As we come to the end of this age, it will become increasingly essential for us to know how to distinguish dreams and visions that are from the Lord from those that are not. We must also know how to interpret them.

The Language of the Spirit

The Lord uses dreams and visions to introduce us to His ways—which are not our ways—and His language—which is not our language. Dreams and visions are the language of the Spirit, and in the language of the Spirit, a picture is worth much more than a thousand words. Dreams and visions usually convey much more than just facts. As we learn to decode these special messages, we will also learn a great deal about God's ways. Paul explained this to the Corinthians: "But a natural man does not accept the things of the Spirit of God; for they are foolishness to him, and he cannot understand them, because they are spiritually appraised. But he who is spiritual appraises all things, yet he himself is appraised by no man" (1 Cor. 2:14–15).

A basic part of human nature is the curiosity that compels us to seek a deeper understanding of God and His creation. The Lord is courting His bride, and He continually seeks to draw us after Him. This is not a carrot-on-the-stick trick to just keep us moving, but a beckoning that lifts us to another realm of perception where we can fathom His mysteries.

When Paul was caught up into heaven, he heard many things he could not utter. He did not use this knowledge to form another sect, such as the Gnostics would later try to do, claiming that their comprehension of secret knowledge elevated them to a higher spiritual plane. However, many spiritual truths simply cannot be limited by human definitions; we do not have the language to express them, or the mental capacity to fully comprehend them. It would be heresy to try to do so.

How do you discern if a dream or vision is truly from the Lord? First, by becoming spiritual people who have the fruit of the Spirit within them.

Distinguishing the Source of Dreams and Visions

One of our primary goals must always be to become spiritual people. Until we become spiritual, the elements of the Spirit, such as dreams and visions, will seem like foolishness to us. When we become spiritual, we will be able to "appraise all things," because we will be led by the Spirit of Truth Himself. This is the primary way we will be able to distinguish whether dreams and visions are from the Lord or whether they are just the result of our own mental processes—or even from the enemy.

First, becoming spiritual means having the fruit of the Spirit. If unrighteous anger or fear and suspicion, rather than love, influence us, we will be open to receive messages that are sent by a spirit of anger or fear—yet we will think they are from the Lord. When we are angry or feel hurt by a particular person, we might have negative dreams about that person if this pain deeply touches our soul. I have learned never to trust any dreams or visions that could be colored by my present state of mind. However, if I have unrighteous anger toward a person and have a dream or vision that changes my perspective toward him so that it is easy for me to forgive him, I can conclude it was probably from the Holy Spirit.

That which is given by the Holy Spirit will always have His nature, and His nature is the fruit of the Spirit—love, joy, peace (Gal. 5:22). The ministry of reconciliation is basic to the work of the Spirit. He always seeks to reconcile us to Him and to each other. Contrary to this, the enemy always seeks to bring and maintain division in the church. Dreams and visions that seek to accomplish this alienation are from him, and we must disregard them.

The second way to discern if a dream or vision is from the Lord is to realize they are never given to us to establish doctrine.

We do not have a single biblical example of the Lord giving any dreams, visions, or other revelations for the purpose of establishing a new doctrine. This is a basic guideline for discernment. Most dreams and visions are given for specific, personal guidance, such as Paul's dream of the Macedonian man (Acts 16:9–10).

However, we do have examples of visions that are given to highlight biblical truths, such as Peter's vision, which instructed him to go to the Gentile, Cornelius. This was not a new truth. It was one the church was not yet walking in and obviously did not understand. Through this vision Peter responded to what Simeon had foretold; His gospel would be a light to the Gentiles (Luke 2:32). This vision did not result in a new doctrine, but rather the illumination of a biblical truth.

We all would like to have a basic formula for interpreting dreams, but there simply is none. One of the greatest biblical interpreters of dreams had to learn an important lesson to be prepared for this great calling. Joseph had to learn humility and forgiveness, and so must we. This gift is a great and powerful weapon, and it will only be trusted to those whom God entrusts with His grace—the humble.

Of course, some guidelines will help us, but at best they are guidelines. Joseph had no guidelines for determining that cows and ears of corn represented years—the Holy Spirit had to tell him this. We can learn from biblical examples and then from our own experience; but with every true revelation of the Holy Spirit, He will hold the key to the interpretation, and He must unlock it. Humility simply opens us to grace. We are all utterly dependent on grace, not just for interpretations of dreams and visions but for everything else as well.

Humility and intimacy are keys to hearing God's voice. And often this intimacy requires some secrecy on our part.

The closer two people are, the more intimate their secrets will become. What lover would continue to bare his heart if he knew that everything he was sharing would be broadcast? In this I am not talking about doctrine or the prophecy of Scripture, but rather the personal communication we have with the Lord. Joseph not only got into trouble with his brothers, he was even rebuked by his father, Jacob, for sharing his dreams prematurely.

Amos said, "Surely the LORD God does nothing unless He reveals His *secret counsel* to His servants the prophets" (Amos 3:7, emphasis added). It is difficult for many to understand that most of the secrets the Lord shares with us are meant to be just that—secrets. Much of the power of prophetic ministry is related to proper timing. Learning to keep secrets until He instructs us to share them is crucial if we want to receive the more important revelations from Him.

Developing a secret relationship with the Lord is critical to helping our spiritual life. God looks on the heart, and He speaks to us more through our hearts than through our minds. That is why Paul prayed that "the eyes of your heart [not mind] may be enlightened" (Eph. 1:18). The Lord Jesus instructed us to pray and give alms to the Father in secret, and He would reward us. When we pray and then tell others about how much we have been interceding, we lose our spiritual reward from the Father just to attain the brief, fleeting human recognition. But if we pray, give alms, or do ministry that no one knows about but the Father, we are placing our treasure in heaven with Him. "For where your treasure is, there will your heart be also" (Matt. 6:21).

Spiritual gifts and callings are involved in prophetic ministry, but its true essence is simply friendship with God. One reason the Lord does not do anything without sharing it with His servants the prophets is that He does not want to do anything without sharing it with His close friends. When we become close enough to the Lord, having the wisdom to know how to keep secrets until the proper time to reveal them, He will share everything that He is doing with us.

Some fall into the snare of believing that God only speaks about matters of the gravest nature. Yet, true lovers communicate simply because they want to know and be known by each other, and much of the Lord's personal communication with us is simply for that same reason. First Corinthians 1:9 says, "You were called into fellowship with His Son, Jesus Christ." We cannot have fellowship without communication.

Yet, communication for the sake of fellowship is different from communication for the sake of control. Some Christians are unable to make even the simplest decisions without hearing from the Lord—*sometimes* out of genuine zeal to be obedient to the Lord in all things, but *usually*, out of insecurity. The need to hear from the Lord about the most mundane decisions is not a sign of maturity, but immaturity. My four-year-old son needs far more oversight than my fourteen-year-old daughter. Much of my communication with my young son is "Do this" or "Don't do that." I actually talk much more to my older daughter, but our communication has much less to do with decision making, since she has the ability to make most decisions without my help.

When the Holy Spirit sent out the apostles Paul and Barnabas, they were sent with a general directive: Go to the Gentiles. They made most of their own decisions about where and to whom to go because they were mature and had the mind of Christ. The Scriptures reveal that the Lord then gave them dreams, visions, and prophecies when they needed a course correction. As we mature, we should not continue to be led around by the hand, directed specifically in every little decision; instead, we are *sent*.

Yet, sometimes our vision or dream is only part of God's message for us.

We See in Part

Each significant revelation is like one piece of a puzzle that must be properly fitted with pieces that have been given to others. This is true of both doctrine and prophecy. No single denomination or movement has the whole truth, and no prophet has the whole revelation. Even if we have been given the biggest part, it will still be a small part of the entire truth. That is why the apostle Paul said, "But *we* [not I] have the mind of Christ" (1 Cor. 2:16, emphasis added). We each have but a part of His great mind, which must be properly joined to the rest of the body to compose the true mind of Christ.

In my experience, the Lord has often given the pieces to revelations that I needed to people I disliked the most or who were the most different from me. I have learned that if someone for some reason repels me, he is the one I should pursue, knowing that he probably has something very valuable for me to hear. Inevitably, I find that the distance between us was due to misconceptions anyway, the result of my trying to know this person after the flesh, or externals, rather than after the Spirit.

If two congregations in a locality tend to have a lot of conflict with each other, you can just about count on them being the two who need each other the most. I have never seen this fail. This is true even with nations. There is an extraordinary spiritual destiny between Britain and Germany, which is why the enemy has stirred up such conflict between them.

Now that we know how to hear God's voice, let's look a little closer at how to discern His voice from the enemy's.

RECOGNIZING THE ENEMY'S VOICE

At times the enemy tries to counterfeit the Lord's voice to mislead the saints. He would not do this unless the Lord were speaking to His people. After all, the only reason for counterfeit money is because real money exists. Let's take this analogy one step further. Are we going to say that we will never have anything to do with money again, just because some counterfeit money is out there? Of course not. Just because the enemy sometimes tries to counterfeit the Lord's voice is no reason for our not seeking to know His voice; it is another reason why we should!

So, how do we learn to distinguish the Lord's voice from the enemy's? The answer is obvious if we remember the story of those sheep and shepherds in the Middle East with which I began this chapter—we become more acquainted with God's voice.

Become More Acquainted with God's Voice

After twenty-some years of marriage I can now recognize my wife's voice, regardless of whether she whispers or shouts. She can be in a crowd of women who are all talking, but I can still distinguish her voice instantly. I can do this because we have been together so much. We must come to know the Lord's voice in this same way. No other formulas or shortcuts can be substituted for just being with Him.

I heard of a blind man whose job was handling money for the Treasury Department in Washington, D.C. He became so sensitive to the feel of money that if someone handed him a counterfeit bill, he could recognize it instantly. His discernment came from knowing true money so well, not the false; he probably would never have been able to recognize real money had he spent his time trying to get to know the feel of the many different counterfeit bills out there.

Likewise, the best way to tell the enemy's voice from the Lord's is to know the Lord's voice so well that we will instantly be able to distinguish it from any other voice. Those who spend more time studying the enemy—how he works, speaks, and deceives—may eventually be able to recognize the enemy very well, but they usually cannot recognize God's voice. I have learned not to trust the discernment of anyone who majors in understanding the enemy's deceptions.

Nor can we expect to distinguish accurately God's voice from the enemy's just because we know those who do.

No Second-Class Citizens in the Kingdom

None of us are saved by knowing someone who knows the Lord. Neither will we be used for miracles because we know someone who has the faith for miracles. Nor will any of us be able to distinguish the voice of the Lord just because we sit in the congregation of someone who does or because we read their books or watch their programs. The Lord has no grandchildren. Every one of us is called to be His own child.

However, we should be careful not to expect new believers to rely on their own discernment. I have watched many new Christians strive to hear the voice of the Lord prematurely, only to be misled by either the enemy or their own thoughts. This has sometimes devastated them so much that they have become spiritual cripples. The Lord said, "My *sheep* hear My voice" (John 10:27), not My lambs.

Young lambs do not follow the shepherd as much as they follow other sheep. Young Christians need to follow other Christians until they mature enough to know God's voice. In this sense it is wise to stay close to those who know Him better, but we can never settle for that as our ultimate goal—we must know the Lord for ourselves.

Even though Joshua was the closest associate of one of the greatest men of God of all time, Joshua was not satisfied with that. It was certainly wonderful to be Moses' servant, and Joshua obviously learned a lot from Moses, but he had to know the Lord for himself. When Moses departed from the tabernacle, Joshua stayed there, developing his own relationship with the Lord (Ex. 33:11).

The goal of every Christian should be to know the Lord and His voice so well that he can easily distinguish it from all of the other voices in the world. Someone once said, "A goal is a dream with a deadline." I do not know that we can determine to know the voice of the Lord by a specific time, but if we do not establish a goal, the probability of accomplishing anything diminishes greatly. God promises to go before us if we know His voice—leading us through the valley of the shadow of death into eternal life.

7 THE MANY FACES OF RACISM

One of the most remarkable stories in the New Testament is that of two men on the road to Emmaus. The resurrected Jesus joined them and expounded the Scriptures concerning Himself. Here we have Christ preaching Christ! It just does not get any more anointed than that, but they still could not recognize Him! Why? Mark 16:12 reveals the answer: "He appeared [to them] in *a different form*" (emphasis added).

It seems that most of the Lord's appearances after His resurrection came in a different form from what His disciples were accustomed to. This was obviously done for a reason, and we must understand this if we are to recognize the Lord when He draws near to us. *If we are going to know the living Christ, we must know Him by the Spirit and not by appearances.*

How many times do we fail to recognize the Lord because He comes to us in a form we are not used to? If we become comfortable with the Pentecostal form, we will not recognize the Lord if He tries to come to us through a Baptist form. If we become used to the Charismatic form, we will not recognize Him if He tries to come to us as a Pentecostal. The reason for this is spiritual *racism*. Racism is not just between physical races but against people groups who are different from us, whether the differences are based on actual race, religion, culture, geography, or other factors that make people different.

If you go to Los Angeles, you should visit the Museum of Tolerance. It's a fascinating place run by rabbis, and it's filled with exhibits showing hate crimes from the beginning of history right up to the present day. As you enter the museum, there are two doors. One is marked

"Prejudiced," the other is marked "Not Prejudiced." If you stand and watch, you'll notice that practically everyone who goes into the Museum of Tolerance tries to enter through the "Not Prejudiced" door. Surprise! It's locked. You can't go through that door, because everybody has some kind of prejudice. I have mine, and so do you.

God wants us to admit what we are. He wants us to go through the door marked "Prejudiced." Only by admitting the truth about ourselves can we be set free.

This is far more than a Pentecostal-Baptist or a black-white or a Jew-Gentile issue. This is one of the most base forms of pride—pride in the flesh or in externals. Racism promotes bondage to the familiar that can rob us of our closest encounters with our Lord.

When the Lord lamented over Jerusalem for killing the prophets and those who were sent to the city, He declared that its house was being left desolate and that they would not see Him again until they said, "Blessed is He who comes in the name of the Lord" (Matt. 23:39). What was true for Jerusalem is also true for the church. We will not see the Lord until we learn to bless those who come in His name. The God who stretched out the heavens like a tent curtain is too big to dwell exclusively in our insignificant little denomination, regardless of how big it may be. He is too big to be found exclusively in our snappy new or progressive form of worship. That which is truly Christ is still being birthed in the least likely places.

The Lord promised to separate those who are of the nature of goats from those with the nature of sheep when He returns. One of the distinguishing characteristics of the sheep was—"I was a *foreigner* and you took Me in" (Matt. 25:35, author's trans.). A *foreigner* is someone different from us, someone from a different place who may speak a different language, or one who may even be from a different denomination. In other words, *one of the primary factors that will distinguish us as either sheep or goats is our openness to those who are different.*

The Israelites were commanded to "show your love for the alien, for you were aliens in the land of Egypt" (Deut. 10:19). This implies that the Lord allowed Israelites to be held captive in a foreign land so that they would have compassion for foreigners. Another important reason for Israel's compassion for the foreigner is stated in Deuteronomy 31:12 (emphasis added): "Assemble the people, the men and the women and children and the alien [foreigner] who is in your town, *in order that they may hear and learn and fear the* LORD *your God*, and be careful to observe all the words of this law."

True spiritual authority is founded on compassion. Because Jesus felt compassion for the sheep that were without a shepherd, He became our Shepherd. We cannot have compassion on those we scorn, belittle, or reject because they are different. We will never have the true authority to correct the doctrines of another movement or denomination until we have God's love for them.

To a certain degree it seems that regardless of wrong doctrines, or how antiquated a church's form of worship is, if they love the poor, the orphans, the widows, and the foreigners, God will bless and take care of them, *because they love and care for the ones He wants to care for*. This is the primary reason God has blessed America—our doors have been open to foreigners and the oppressed more than possibly any other nation in history. (We have not always treated them well after they have arrived, but we have received them.)

Because of this, we have a unique potential for demonstrating harmony and tolerance among those from different cultures and people groups.

A HOUSE OF ALL NATIONS

The Lord has called His church to be a "house of prayer for all the nations" (Mark 11:17). The word *nations* is translated from the Greek *ethnos*, or "ethnic." In a similar way, America truly is a house for all nations. While it is the Lord's intention to use America because of this, the enemy's intention is to have a meltdown of the racial situation here to sow even more discord and distrust between racial groups throughout the world.

The enemy planned to use South Africa in this same way during its last election. His strategy was thwarted by the worldwide prayer offered up for that country. Yet, when Satan is thwarted in this way, he looks for somewhere else to unleash his wrath. When he met a dead end in

South Africa, he turned with a vengeance on the closest opening he could find—Rwanda.

What happened in Rwanda was a spiritual attack of the magnitude Satan intended to release in South Africa. Missionaries called these people "the most peaceful in Africa." Yet they awoke one morning to a cruel insanity. Neighbors who had good-naturedly waved good night to each other just hours before were suddenly beating down doors to kill entire families. After the carnage abated, some who had been involved in this ruthless slaughter said they had been in something like a trance, and could hardly even remember what they had done. Others seemed to genuinely disbelieve they had committed such atrocities, but they had. This cannot be explained in the natural because it was a spiritual assault.

Rwanda was considered the most "Christian" nation in Africa. Almost 90 percent of the population claimed to be members of the faith. However, the popular definition of what it means to be a Christian is far from the biblical one. Those who claim to be Christians, but do not have the Spirit of God, can be the most vulnerable to the powerful onslaughts of darkness. Nominal Christians have proved to be the most dangerous people on earth; they are still under Satan's domain, and Satan sees in them a unique opportunity to tarnish the name of Jesus Christ.

Germany claimed to be a Christian nation before both world wars. Hitler claimed to be resurrecting the Holy Roman Empire to establish its one-thousand-year reign on the earth. The majority of the "Christians" in Germany were swept up by this deceit, even though ruthless murder and oppression established the Third Reich.

Likewise, America claims to be a Christian nation. Almost 85 percent of the population claim to be Christians, and more than half claim to be born again. But where is the fruit? It is likely that the rolls in heaven actually contain but a small percentage of the total population of America (just as the greatest evangelists acknowledge that fewer than 10 percent of the people who make decisions for Christ in their crusades go on to become members of a church).

When Jesus was asked what signs would signal the end of the age, one of those He mentioned was, "Nation will rise against nation, and kingdom against kingdom" (Luke 21:10). The Greek word translated "nation" here is *ethnos*, the same word we saw before in Mark 11:17. Jesus was not so much talking about *countries* fighting each other as He was referring to the increase of *ethnic conflict*.

Nearly every major conflict in the world today is fundamentally an ethnic conflict rather than a political one. Amid the great onslaught of racially motivated destruction that will come at the end of the age, the church is called to be a house of prayer for all *ethnos*, or ethnic groups. I believe that churches that do not confront and overcome the stronghold of racism will *be overcome* in the times ahead.

The "gates of hell" (Matt. 16:18 KJV) are the enemy's doorways into the world, and racism is possibly the biggest gate the enemy will use at the end of the age. Satan will release some of his greatest power to thwart our calling as a house of prayer for all nationalities. If he can, he will use America as an instrument for sending forth death and destruction on an unprecedented level.

THE CULTURES WITHIN OUR LAND

America does not need to go to the nations to reach the nations. One of the great missionaries of our time, Bob Weiner, has spent most of his adult life trying to get the church to understand that almost every major nation is represented in the student body of our universities. At one count, sixty of the world's political leaders had been educated in the United States. Many foreign students are lonely, far from family, friends, and culture, and they are wide open to the gospel. In one poll of foreign students, one of their greatest desires (second only to an education) was for an American friend.

Both the man who planned the Japanese attack on Pearl Harbor and the man who commanded the Japanese forces during that attack were educated at an Ivy League school. Both of these men were offended by the racist treatment they received in the United States. How might history have been changed if they had been treated differently? A significant number of Islamic leaders who now call the U.S. "the great Satan" were also educated here. How might our present world be different if we had loved and befriended them while they were in our country? Our future could be greatly impacted if we would repent of our racism and begin to love the foreigners in our midst as we are commanded to do.

Many foreign students have no place to go during holiday seasons. Because dormitories are sometimes closed, these students are forced into expensive motel rooms or have to seek shelter from charities. Churches and families who have approached universities with the offer of hospitality for these students have usually been wonderfully received. Many of these students come to Christ. They come not because He was forced on them after being held as a captive audience, but because of the love and acceptance they received in these homes.

The little kindness we may show a foreign student by taking them on a weekend excursion to see the countryside can have a greater long-term impact on our foreign relations than the State Department's best programs. Those sent to the United States and other Western nations for their education are usually the brightest future leaders in every sphere of their society; therefore, those who are led to Christ can potentially impact an entire nation for Him.

It is a basic doctrine of Islam to subject the entire world to Allah, either by conversion or by force of arms (Jihad—holy war). Presently Islam is a fast-growing religion. Nations are being added to this camp while they are being lost from ours. Unless we throw off the humanistic yoke that restrains us from sharing our faith with foreigners because it may infringe upon their "rights," we will continue to lose many more to Islam.

One of the most perplexing sociological questions is why children who grow up in the turmoil, fear, and violence from alcoholic parents are so prone to marry alcoholics. For some reason, the pain and fear that inevitably result from their alcoholic spouse are more tolerable than change. This has been called "the tyranny of the familiar." In a similar way, our fear of people groups who are different from us generates hindrances to true spiritual freedom. Instead of fearing them, we could learn much from them.

This same tyranny of the familiar is a primary reason why the world remains in sin and why those bound to the cruelest forms of religion remain devout in their bondage. To fallen human beings, inevitable physical and mental torment is more acceptable than change. Only love can cast out that terrible fear and bring a true conversion of the heart. For this reason, Paul stated that "the kindness of God leads you to repentance" (Rom. 2:4).

At any given time between 200,000 and 300,000 foreign students are in the United States, alone and often isolated. Thousands more live in other Western nations. Even though we strongly believe in foreign missions, it is apparent that the greatest mission field of all has been brought to us, and we seem to be overlooking it. Foreigners who are in our land are far more open to the gospel than those in their own countries. These precious people need our love and acceptance *and then our message.*

Israel was told to love the foreigners *before* they were commanded to teach them God's ways. In Deuteronomy 14:28–29 and 26:12 the tithe was to be given to the Levite *and* aliens, orphans, and widows. With all of our emphasis on tithing, have we been putting it in the right place?

This issue of caring for the foreigners is so important that when Paul listed the qualifications for leadership in the church, one of the qualifications was that the prospective overseer had to be given to hospitality to strangers. (See 1 Tim. 3:2 and Titus 1:8. Note: The Greek word translated "hospitable" in these texts is *philoxenos*, which literally denotes hospitality to strangers or foreigners.)

Usually we who believe that we are free of the spirit of racism only have tolerance and acceptance if the "race" in question becomes like us. The Baptists will gladly accept the Presbyterians, just as soon as they immerse their people. The Pentecostals will gladly accept the Methodists, just as soon as they speak in tongues. The white church loves the blacks, and we want more of them in *our* church, but very few whites want to join a black church. Most of the tearing down of dividing walls is still rooted in the arrogance of having *our* own terms met, and making everyone else like us. This is not to imply that we should in any way compromise the truths that we hold dear, but if we could build bridges of trust with others who do not see things as we do, our friendship and openness to them would win many more to our views than our hostility does.

The church loves to see the Jews converted as long as they become a part of the church, but the "Messianic movement" is an affront. Neither the church nor the Messianic movement is a true reflection of the new creation. The way that I will come into unity with my wife is not by making her a man! Our unity comes when we see how our differences complement one another instead of bringing conflict. Paul wrote that Christ Himself "might make the two into one new man, thus establishing peace, and might reconcile them *both* in one body to God through the cross, by it having put to death the enmity" (Eph. 2:15–16, emphasis added).

The Lutherans, Baptists, Pentecostals, Charismatics, and others have all added truth and life to the church, which are needed for her to accomplish her purpose. With all of our progress during the Reformation, the church's foundation is still more in Rome than Jerusalem. As Paul stated to the Jews: "It is not you [the Gentiles] who supports the root, but the root supports you" (Rom. 11:18). When Israel is grafted back in, she will help the church return to her true roots, which she has not yet been able to do. This is not to be misunderstood as returning to the law or to mere rituals. It is far more profound than that, which even the Messianic movement has not yet comprehended.

However, there is hope. The Lord is going to send another great awakening to America! It will have the potential to make us a fortress against this great darkness, which is coming at the end of the age. This nation that is made up of all nations does stand in a place of unique potential.

LIGHT AMID THE DARKNESS

In preparation for the great move of God that is coming, an increasing number of revivals and renewal movements will break out in different parts of the country. Some will come with such impact that they will make headlines in secular newspapers and become feature stories on television news. Revival among Hispanics will burn like a great prairie fire, spreading to almost every major city. An army of Asian-American missionaries will be sent out from America as one of the great missionary forces in the last days. All of this will help to melt the ice off the cold remnants of European-American Christianity, creating the critical mass that will explode into the greatest awakening ever.

These streams flowing together from different ethnic groups will overflow to bring healing and reconciliation to the Native Americans. Then the entire church will give its attention to the ancient wounds the Jewish people suffered at the hands of historic, institutional Christianity. When we in the church have finally obtained the grace and humility needed to embrace those who are different from us, the truth of the gospel will be set free of the corruption and deception that have perverted it since the first century. Then there will be an outbreak of God's power like the world has not witnessed before. Those will be the days of the "greater works" (John 14:12).

Meanwhile we can do a great deal to heal the racism in our land. In many cities, a growing fellowship of believers is building bridges of understanding, cooperation, and community investment between white Christians and black Christians. The following is one example of this bridge building from Charlotte, North Carolina.

A Loving Sister-Church Relationship

The story began a number of years ago when a black woman named Barbara Brewton lost her husband to a shooting in a crime-ridden Charlotte neighborhood known as Double Oaks—an area the *New York Times* once listed as one of the five most violent "'hoods" in America. Devastated and embittered by her loss, she moved her family away—but over the next few years, God began to work on her heart. As she grew closer to Jesus Christ, she felt God calling her to return to Double Oaks.

Barbara Brewton went back to Double Oaks and started a Friday night ministry for neighborhood children, completely on her own. She not only taught the neighborhood kids about Jesus, but she also helped them learn to read and write. She pulled them off playgrounds and street corners whenever gunfire erupted—which was fairly often. Soon she was ministering not only to kids, but to their parents as well. As a result, the Community Outreach Church was started—and Barbara Brewton was its pastor. They met in a house, placing speakers in the windows so the music and preaching could be heard out on the street. Drug dealers, gang members, and addicts began showing up and getting saved.

Barbara's church was soon moved to a brick building that had previously served many other functions—including being a community center and a house of ill repute. The building housed Sunday school rooms, offices, and a sanctuary. The church grew so fast, worshipers would spill onto the stairs and out onto the sidewalk. The reason the church was attracting so many people was because people could see it was a church that truly cared. The church was improving the lives of children and adults in Double Oaks, and increasing the safety and security of the neighborhood by getting the city to barricade traffic on certain streets (which led to less drug traffic) and increase policing.

Meanwhile, across town in the wealthy south end of Charlotte, another woman, Mary Lance Sisk, felt God calling her to become involved with the pain of the inner city. Mary has an international ministry teaching people how to pray that has taken her all over the world. She is also very involved in the affluent, mostly white, Forest Hill Evangelical Presbyterian Church. She contacted Pastor Barbara and met her for lunch. That meeting began a partnership that has grown into a beautiful example of what God can do to bring *ethnos* and *ethnos* together. Mary and Barbara were two women from different worlds—white and black, suburban and inner city—yet they came together.

As an outgrowth of Mary and Barbara's friendship, their churches embarked on an incredible sister-church relationship. One of their first projects was to clean up the Double Oaks area. A partnership was formed between the churches, the city, and civic groups. This partnership went into Double Oaks, bought up run-down or burned-out houses from the slum lords, renovated them, and sold them to responsible, carefully screened low-income applicants on low-interest loans. The renovated section was renamed Genesis Park. *Genesis* means "beginning," and this place truly represented a new beginning for the old neighborhood. Even many of the streets, which had become synonymous with murder, drugs, and prostitution, got new names like Rush Wind Drive and Peaceful Way Drive. Streets that had been so dangerous that even police cars and ambulances refused to drive through them suddenly became zones of hope and pride.

Seeing that the Community Outreach Church was quickly outgrowing its facilities, Mary Lance Sisk of the Forest Hill Church sparked a drive to help this bold church in the tough part of town begin building a larger worship center. A committee was formed that took the proposal to the church board of Forest Hill Church, and the church board did an amazing thing. Even though the church leadership had been wanting for some time to build a new and expanded ministry facility for *itself*, these leaders responded to God's call and made a decision to spearhead a drive to raise $150,000 to give to this black sister-church.

In May 1996, a banquet was held to kick off the fund-raising drive, but they were too late! The $150,000 goal had already been reached! By word of mouth alone, the people had responded and met the goal. So the "kickoff" banquet became a celebration banquet instead—and by the end of the banquet, the amount of pledges toward the goal had more than doubled, to about $320,000! Even more important than the money, however, was the fact that members of the two churches were visiting back and forth, getting involved in each other's ministries and worship services, sharing Communion, praying together, asking forgiveness for past prejudice, and building unity and understanding. A powerful two-way partnership was emerging as Forest Hill members began to learn more and more about ministry in the inner city.

Through this experience, hope has come to the city of Charlotte, North Carolina. The spirit of racism is being tarred and feathered and run out of town on a rail. It can happen in your church and your community as well. All it takes is one person—someone like you—who is willing to make himself or herself available to God.

We must remember that all true relationships are built on bridges of trust. The stronger the bridge, the more weight that can be carried across it. We all need to ask ourselves what we can do to help build these bridges for true and lasting racial reconciliation. The alternative is, as the Lord warned, that "nation (*ethnos*) will rise against nation (*ethnos*)."

8 Let the Battle Begin

On February 16, 1995, I was given a dream in which I saw a demonic army so large, it stretched as far as I could see. It was separated into divisions, with each carrying a different banner. The foremost and most powerful divisions were Pride, Self-righteousness, Respectability, Selfish Ambition, and Unrighteous Judgment, but the largest of all was Jealousy. The leader of this vast army was the Accuser of the Brethren himself. I knew that there were many more evil divisions beyond my scope of vision, but these were the vanguard of this terrible horde from hell that was now being released against the church.

The weapons this horde carried had names on them: The swords were named Intimidation; the spears were named Treachery; and their arrows were named Accusations, Gossip, Slander, and Faultfinding. Scouts and smaller companies of demons with such names as Rejection, Bitterness, Impatience, Unforgiveness, and Lust were sent in advance of this army to prepare for the main attack. I knew in my heart that the church had never faced anything like this before.

The main assignment of this army was to cause division. It was sent to attack every level of relationship—churches with each other, congregations with their pastors, husbands and wives, children and parents, and even children with each other. The scouts were sent to locate the openings in churches, families, or individuals of rejection, bitterness, and lust that the enemy could exploit, making a larger breach for the divisions that were coming.

The most shocking part of this vision was that this horde was not riding on horses, but on Christians! Most of them were well dressed, respectable, and had the appearance of being refined and educated. These were believers who had opened themselves to the powers of darkness to such a degree that the enemy could use them and they would think God was using them. The accuser knows that a house divided cannot stand, and this army represented his ultimate attempt to bring such complete division to the church that she would completely fall from grace.

This vision was combined with many others over a period of a year and released in a book entitled *The Final Quest*. This prophecy is a warning to the church about the spiritual battles that lie ahead in the twenty-first century. But it was not the first warning the Lord gave me.

On December 31, 1990, I had seen storm clouds in the spirit from which there could be no escape. As the storm had been about to break, a voice said, "Psalm 91 is for 1991." I realized that even though we may not be able to escape this onslaught of the evil one, we do have shelter in the midst of our struggles.

The storm clouds that are happening in the natural realm are but a reflection of what is happening in the spirit. The "prince of Persia" (Dan. 10:20), one of the strongest principalities on earth, is determined to assert its authority and ultimately take dominion of the whole earth. Even though this conflict is reflected in earthly battles, the real battle is in heaven. We will not have a breakthrough until the body of Christ prays and fasts with Daniel's zeal and focused vision for the restoration of God's temple (which is not made of brick and mortar but of human beings) and the heavenly Jerusalem, whose restoration will be reflected by the engrafting of the earthly Jerusalem.

The body of Christ must prepare for this war spiritually as an army would prepare for battle. We must get rid of our excess baggage. Paul told his disciple, Timothy, "No soldier in active service entangles himself in the affairs of everyday life, so that he may please the one who enlisted him as a soldier" (2 Tim. 2:4). We must:

- Get rid of the sin and spiritual pollution in our life.
- Get rid of those "good" things that distract us from our spiritual calling.

- Get out of debt and make no major purchases without a clear leading from the Lord, as I suggested in Chapter 2. (Read and heed 1 Tim. 6:3–19.)

Then we will be ready to fight in a spiritual war. During the past ten years, much has been written on the subject of spiritual warfare. Yet, beyond the theories and the war cries, many believers still find themselves wondering: *What does it take to wage war successfully against the enemy of our souls?*

In my own life, I have discovered the effectiveness of eight scriptural principles in combating the forces of darkness.

EIGHT KEYS TO SUCCESSFUL SPIRITUAL WARFARE

The first key to spiritual warfare is: We must be lovers first, then warriors.

1. WE MUST BE LOVERS FIRST, THEN WARRIORS

One of the most sobering rebukes the Lord made to any of the seven churches in Revelation was telling the church of Ephesus: If you do not return to your first love, your candlestick will be removed (Rev. 2:4–5). This was, in effect, saying they would cease to be a church. Love is first, and the foremost commandment of all is to love the Lord Himself. Many more Scriptures call us to love the Lord than call us to fight the enemy. Without question, our life should be devoted more to drawing near to the Lord than to fighting the darkness.

The foundation of everything we are called to be and do is found in Christ. He has already won the victory. Abiding in intimacy with the Lord is the very first principle of spiritual warfare. Once we commit ourselves to this first principle—loving and worshiping the Lord—we must remember that we are in a war with an enemy whose intent is our destruction. Therefore, we must be committed to the fight.

2. WE MUST BE COMMITTED TO THE FIGHT

We are in a war every day, whether we want to fight or not. In fact, if we choose not to fight—disobeying the biblical exhortations to fight the good fight and to put on the whole armor of God—we will become a casualty.

Immediately after His resurrection the Lord had the legal right to bind or destroy Satan and reclaim this earth. Why did He not do it? For our sake! This whole age is a test. The entire church age is for the bride to prove her devotion and faithfulness by overcoming an evil world and to learn the responsibility that will enable her to reign with Christ. God does not test us so we can fail, but so He can see where to place each of us in the authority of His eternal kingdom.

There is a moment in a battle when real issues, even life and death, are decided, and the essence of who we are surfaces. Will we selfishly hide our salvation, or will we fight for righteousness? Will we lead others into the life of the Son of God, or will we give way to sin and rebellion when we are under pressure and drag others down with us? Now, at the beginning of a new millennium, when the deepest darkness of all is coming on the earth, the greatest conflict between good and evil will come. We may die fighting for the kingdom, or we may be caught up in the air, but let us die or be caught up while attacking the darkness of our times with unyielding resolution and using our shields of faith for the protection of the weak or immature.

No Time-Outs in Battle

Paul's exhortation to the Ephesians as they prepared to battle the evil of their age is to put on the "full" armor (Eph. 6:11). If we leave off part of our protection, the enemy will very likely find our weak spot, and he will hit us there. There are no truces in this conflict—we cannot just say, "I am tired and do not want to fight anymore for a while." We cannot say, "Don't hit me in that place." Our enemy will not play by our rules, and he will not play fair! He is looking for anything he can use to exploit us.

The Scriptures are full of examples of people who left a small opening in their lives only to have the enemy come flooding through the gap. King David's great sin is an obvious example. In the spring, "when kings go out to battle" (2 Sam. 11:1), he stayed home. The result? He fell into adultery and committed murder to cover it up in one of the most tragic falls from grace in the Scriptures. The Lord forgave him, but the sword did not depart from his house until tragedy struck some of his own family. The Lord will forgive our sins, but there will still be consequences for them—we will reap what we sow, and those entrusted to our care will suffer.

As David learned, when it is time to fight, one of the most dangerous places to be is in the rear. When the enemy sees us dropping back or letting up, he will hit us even harder. Never forget that our enemy has no mercy or compassion, and he is determined to destroy us. However, he has no power against us as long as we submit to the Lord, draw closer to Him, and resist the devil. We must do all three.

We must keep in mind that "the Son of God appeared for this purpose, that He might destroy the works of the devil" (1 John 3:8). We, too, have been sent into the world to destroy the works of the devil. Jesus prayed the night before His crucifixion, "As Thou didst send Me into the world, I also have sent them into the world" (John 17:18). The world may now lie in the power of the evil one, but, ultimately, "the earth is the LORD'S, and all it contains" (Ps. 24:1). We are here to reclaim the earth and break the enemy's power over it.

In Luke 10:17–19 the Lord made a remarkable statement about our warfare:

> And the seventy returned with joy, saying, "Lord, even the demons are subject to us in Your name." And He said to them, "I was watching Satan fall from heaven like lightning. Behold, I have given you authority to tread upon serpents and scorpions, and over all the power of the enemy, and nothing shall injure you."

If the Lord has given us authority over all the power of the enemy as this Scripture says, why can't we just bind him, cast him out, and be done with this war? The answer is found in the first verse of this chapter. The seventy did not go out on their own initiative, but the Lord *sent them out*, and they only went to "every city and place *where He Himself was going to come*" (Luke 10:1, emphasis added).

Our Mandate

Often good principles for spiritual battles can be found by observing modern wars, such as the Persian Gulf War. In this conflict, the Allies did not begin the battle against Iraq without a mandate from the United Nations. Neither did the Allies attack Yugoslavia for their genocide of the Albanians without a mandate from the North Atlantic Treaty Organization. Of course, the church does not get her mandate from the United Nations or NATO, but we do need a mandate from the Lord.

The church has the general commission to "go therefore and make disciples of all the nations" (Matt. 28:19). But this general commission does not give us the liberty to just go anywhere we want at any time. The Lord gives specific commissions. What He has not addressed specifically in His Word, we are to receive directly from His Spirit. That is the biblical procedure (such as when Paul and Barnabas were sent out and when Paul was directed to Macedonia).

We have authority only to the degree that we are under His authority. It is foolish to attack the enemy's strongholds without a mandate, but when we get the commission we cannot be timid. If the time to fight comes, and we do not fight, the "paralysis of analysis" will quickly set in. Then we will be defeated by our own indecision. As the Allies in the Persian Gulf War demonstrated, when we get a mandate or commission, we must go after the enemy's strongholds with everything we've got, determined not to compromise on a single point.

We are told that "the gates of hell shall not prevail" against the church (Matt. 16:18 KJV). These gates of hell are the enemy's access points into our lives, our congregations, our cities, and our nations. The church has the authority to shut those gates—they *cannot* prevail against us.

The church is presently made up of many "nations"—denominations and movements. If the United States leadership can get unanimous approval of the UN resolutions, and then forge a coalition of such diverse nations to fight the battle, why can't we unite our forces to win against the schemes of our enemy? Remember, we are told that "the gates of hell shall not prevail against it [*the church*]" (Matt. 16:18 KJV, emphasis added).

Notice that the Lord did not say "churches" (plural), but "church" (singular). The church has the authority to shut these gates—they *cannot* prevail against the church, singular, but they will continue to prevail against churches for as long as we are divided. If the Syrians, Egyptians, Saudi Arabians, Americans, French, British, and others could join under one command to fight Iraq, then certainly the Baptists, Methodists, Lutherans, Pentecostals, Charismatics, and others should be able to get together to fight Satan.

During the Persian Gulf War, the Allied Coalition did not require the Syrians to become Americans or British, or to give up their sovereignty in any way. I am certainly not advocating that the church come under one permanent organization either. History has resoundingly testified to the terrible fallacy of the church coming under any head but Jesus, *the only Head of the church*. But we do have common purposes that we must support together. The different camps within the church have become so afraid of losing their domain that we have been giving territory to the enemy in order to keep our brothers from getting too much! To escape excessive authority we have often chosen anarchy, which is an even worse enemy, since one of the great evils of the last days is lawlessness.

A congregation will not prevail against the gates of hell until unity exists among the different members. Similarly, the church in a city will not be able to prevail against the gates of hell in that city until unity exists among the different congregations. Likewise, it is going to take apostles, prophets, evangelists, pastors, and teachers who are able to work together in harmony for the church to be properly equipped. No single movement or denomination is complete and will be truly effective in its commission until it learns to interchange with and function in harmony with the others. Each has its specific purpose, but if each one is not coordinating with the other, each is at best falling far short of its purpose. And at worst we might continue attacking and bombing each other. Presently we have far more casualties from "friendly fire" than from the enemy.

If the church is to have victory in what is now pressing on us, we must learn to join coalitions that confront specific issues, with specific objectives, until those objectives are fully accomplished. We must lay aside the fears that compel meetings of pastors and leaders to be so ambiguous nothing is accomplished. At the risk of offending other world leaders and powers, the United States took the initiative, the authority, and the leadership to get the job done in Iraq. Instead of bringing division, that initiative and resolve brought the most improbable coalition into a unity that accomplished an astonishingly one-sided victory.

The church's mandate comes from God alone. We only have true spiritual authority to the degree that we abide in the King. He has already defeated Satan and seen him fall from heaven. We have everything going for us that should cause us to be bold in our confrontation with the strongholds of the enemy.

In a scene in the movie *The Bear*, a large cougar was chasing a little bear cub. Finally, the cub was trapped and had no choice but to turn and face his enemy. To the cub's astonishment, the cougar began to back off in terror. Amazed and thrilled at his newfound authority, the cub did not realize that the cougar was not retreating because of him. Unbeknownst to the cub, his large bear friend had come up behind him to protect him. The cougar backed off because he saw the one who was standing behind the cub. The same is true of us.

When the enemy starts fleeing from us, he flees not because of who we are; he flees because of the One who is with us. If we are wise, we will stay close to Jesus, our Big Brother. This is why, after the Lord told the seventy of the authority given to them, He continued by saying: "Nevertheless do not rejoice in this, that the spirits are subject to you, but rejoice that your names are recorded in heaven" (Luke 10:20). We only have authority because our names are written in His Book of Life. We must know the authority that we have in Christ, but we must also understand that it is in Christ, not in ourselves.

3. WE MUST HAVE THE WISDOM TO KNOW OUR OWN IGNORANCE

We are fighting a foe that is far wiser and more powerful than we are. Our enemy has thousands of years of experience doing what he's doing. While we were made "*lower* than the angels" (Heb. 2:7), Satan began as a highly positioned angel with much more intelligence and cunning than we can ever hope to have. We will never win with our own intelligence, strength, goodness, or determination. That is why the verses on overcoming the enemy are often surrounded by exhortations to remain humble: "But He gives a greater grace. Therefore it says, 'God is opposed to the proud, but gives grace to the humble.' Submit therefore to God. Resist the devil and he will flee from you. Draw near to God and He will draw near to you" (James 4:6–8, emphasis added).

Here we see that the exhortation to resist the devil is sandwiched between the exhortations to submit to God and to draw near to Him. To be successful, we must both submit to the Lord and draw near to Him.

In this text we also see that humility enables us to receive the grace of God, and the grace of God is a power much greater than that of any enemy. Those who walk in humility, which is submission to God, will see the devils fleeing from them. We are an easy prey for them when we depart from His grace by walking in pride, which is basically taking our stand on our own strength or wisdom.

The enemy himself fell when he became prideful, and he knows very well that the first step in getting us to fall is to make us proud. "Therefore let him who thinks he stands take heed lest he fall" (1 Cor. 10:12). When we think we are the ones who are standing, we will be in jeopardy of a fall. But when we take our stand on God's grace and the victory of Jesus Christ, all the hordes of hell will not be able to bring us down. True humility is to stand on the finished work of Christ alone!

In order to win spiritual battles, we must be lovers first, we must be committed to the fight, we must have the wisdom to know our own ignorance, and we must also know when not to fight.

4. WE MUST KNOW WHEN NOT TO FIGHT

In most wars the young men do the fighting. Children and older men are usually exempt from combat duty except in extreme cases. It seems that this is often true in spiritual warfare as well. In John's statements to the children, young men, and fathers, the young men were the ones who had "overcome the evil one" (1 John 2:12–13).

Peter also exhorted young men:

You younger men, likewise, be subject to your elders; and all of you, clothe yourselves with humility toward one another, for God is opposed to the proud, but gives grace to the humble. . . . Be of sober spirit, be on the alert. Your adversary, the devil, prowls about like a roaring lion, seeking someone to devour. But resist him, firm in your faith, knowing that the same experiences of suffering are being accomplished by your brethren who are in the world. (1 Peter 5:5, 8–9)

New believers should not be thrust into the thick of spiritual warfare. They usually have all they can handle just learning to stand and walk on their own. And the "fathers" also should refrain from heavy involvement, simply because their ability to disciple and raise up others is a much more fruitful use of their time than service in the trenches.

5. WE MUST KNOW OUR WEAPONS WELL

The enemy's spiritual strongholds are basically patterns of thought that conflict with the Lord and His ways. If we understand this, we will not be surprised that the gospel of the kingdom was the primary weapon the Lord gave to the seventy when He sent them into the world.

Paul described the weapons for fighting the good fight in Ephesians 6:10–20. He told the Ephesians to "put on the full armor of God," not once but twice in these eleven verses (vv. 10, 13). When God repeats something, it is to emphasize the seriousness of the matter. This is so we might "resist in the evil day."

We need to look carefully at these weapons in our arsenal.

First, we must put on the breastplate of truth. Paul told the Ephesians: "Stand firm therefore, having girded your loins with truth, and having put on the breastplate of righteousness" (Eph. 6:14).

Truth is not only an offensive weapon—when used as the sword of the Spirit—but it is also our protection. Truth may have seeming setbacks, but it will always prevail. As Mahesh Chavda (senior pastor of All Nations Church in Charlotte, North Carolina) said, "For seventy years the communists declared that God was dead. Then one day the

Lord declared that communism was dead! Now, all of the places where the communists declared their doctrine from hell, there is the greatest hunger for the Word of God!"

In calling us to represent Him as His ambassadors, the Lord does not just want us to be able to talk about Him—He wants us to be *like Him*. One of His basic characteristics is that He is true to His Word. If we are going to be like Him, we, too, must learn to be true to our word. Our word should be our bond, stronger than any contract. Not only must we know and keep the *Lord's* Word, we need to keep our *own* word.

Along with the greater release of darkness into the world in recent years is a greater erosion of honor and integrity. This is not only true in the world, but in the church as well. A main reason for much of the defeat in the body of Christ is our tendency to break our commitments both to the Lord and to each other.

Second, we must put on the gospel of peace. "Having shod your feet with the preparation of the gospel of peace" (Eph. 6:15). We walk with our feet, and if we have properly put on the armor of God, we will walk in peace. That peace of God is not only effective protection against the enemy, it is also a powerful offensive weapon as we use our feet to crush the serpent's head. Paul reminded the Roman Christians that the "Lord of Hosts" or "Lord of Armies" does not crush the enemy; rather it is the "God of peace" (Rom. 16:20). We must be careful not to let anything steal our peace, or we will be deprived of a most important protection.

Third, we must take up the shield of faith. "In addition to all, taking up the shield of faith with which you will be able to extinguish all the flaming missiles of the evil one" (Eph. 6:16). Everyone in the fight is going to have flaming missiles thrown at him. The issue is, are we going to be hit with them, or are we going to be able to extinguish them? Faith does not keep the enemy from attacking us, but it helps to extinguish what the enemy throws at us. If we get wounded, we can be sure we have dropped our faith. Pick up the shield!

Fourth, we must put on the helmet of salvation. "And take the helmet of salvation" (Eph. 6:17). The helmet of salvation protects our minds.

Unfortunately, it is easy to relax and take off our helmets, letting the pollution of the world attack our minds from TV, magazines, or the confusion of daily life. We must always guard our minds, or we will open ourselves to potentially fatal head wounds intended to rob us of our salvation. The helmet is our salvation, and we must wear it continually.

Finally, we must take up the sword of the spirit. "And take . . . the sword of the Spirit, which is the word of God" (Eph. 6:17). Notice that most of the battle gear Paul listed is defensive in nature, such as the shield of faith. The main offensive weapon he mentioned is the sword of the Spirit. Yet, this sword can also be a defensive weapon. When the devil attacked Jesus, He used the Word of God to drive the devil off. How much more should Christians learn to use this most powerful weapon! The more knowledge we have of God's Word, the more skillful we will be in spiritual warfare, and the more effective we will be in attacking the enemy's strongholds.

Unfortunately, the most powerful weapon the world will ever know sits gathering dust on the shelves of many Christian homes. Charles Spurgeon once said that he could find ten men who would die for the Bible for every one who would read it! This may be one of the primary reasons for the church's ineffectiveness in confronting the unfolding darkness of our times.

A study made by *Leadership*, one of the most popular and respected magazines for evangelical Christian leaders, found that less than 1 percent of its articles contained even one reference to Scripture! Ironically, this poor degree of scriptural content was found in a magazine targeted to conservative evangelicals, the segment of Christianity that most prides itself in its devotion to Scripture! Perhaps we, too, should examine our message to ascertain its biblical content and soundness.

There are times, of course, when just quoting a Bible verse will not suffice. On such occasions, we need to take authority over the demonic powers and cast them out, as shown by numerous examples in Scripture.

Once we know our weapons, we must know our battle plan.

6. WE MUST KNOW OUR BATTLE PLAN

The seventy disciples who discovered their authority over demons had not been specifically sent to cast out demons. They had simply been told to heal the sick and proclaim the message of the kingdom (Luke 10:9). Yet, some scholars have estimated that as much as one-third of the Lord's ministry on earth was casting out demons. Still, He only briefly mentioned this ministry as something we are supposed to do. Casting out demons is, in fact, only a small part of spiritual warfare. If we cast out demons without tearing down the strongholds they have been inhabiting in people, the demons will just return and bring back seven more demons that are even worse (Luke 11:26). On the other hand, demons that come out because their stronghold is demolished will have nowhere to return to.

One of the most common strategic mistakes in historical wars has been the tendency for leaders to spread their lines too thin, trying to fight on multiple fronts at the same time. I hold dear many truths that I believe are worth fighting for, but the Lord has warned me, "They are not truths I have called *you* to fight for." I need to stick to the battle plan He has laid out specifically for me, since He has called others to fight for those truths.

When others try to drag us into their battles, we must resist. "No!" is one of the most important words for Christians to learn if they are going to stay on course. To overcome the forces of darkness, we must know our battle plan and we must know our enemy.

7. WE MUST KNOW OUR ENEMY

As my friend Francis Frangipane likes to say, "With new levels come new devils." The more spiritual authority we have, and the more of a threat we are to the enemy, the more of a target we will be. The enemy did not just send a principality to tempt Jesus or to sift Peter; he trusted them to no one but himself. The more spiritual authority we have, the greater our opposition will be. Conversely, the greater our opposition, the greater the evil that will flee from us if we effectively resist.

If our ministry is mostly to individuals, we will often confront demons that must be cast out. However, if we are given spiritual authority over cities or regions, we will have to deal with greater powers of darkness. These are referred to in Scripture as principalities, because these demons do not inhabit people but regions.

You can cast out demons, but you must wrestle with principalities. Wrestling, which involves a struggle for position and dominance, is the closest and most exhausting form of combat. Dealing with demons that we do not have authority over can leave us wounded and naked (Acts 19:13–16), but confronting principalities that we have no authority over can be even more dangerous. Even so, the greatest revivals in all of church history have been the result of the church effectively engaging in this level of spiritual warfare.

Before we engage a principality, we must know we are going where the Lord has sent us. Unfortunately, the devil uses flattery to lure us beyond what God has called us to do or to try to accomplish what He has called us to do prematurely or in our own strength. If the enemy can get us to go beyond the sphere of authority presently appointed to us, he knows we will lack the grace needed to defeat him (2 Cor. 10:12–16).

As we can see from 2 Corinthians 10:5—"We are destroying speculations and every lofty thing raised up against the knowledge of God, and we are taking every thought captive to the obedience of Christ"—the primary battlefield in spiritual warfare is for people's minds.

One of the most powerful strongholds exalting itself against the knowledge of God today is the *theory* of evolution. We are to confront speculations like this because they are usually the root power behind the great deceptions that keep people in bondage to the powers of darkness. With no credible evidence to support it, this theory is riddled with speculation and reasoning bordering on insanity. For example, the theory of evolution basically says that the intricate harmony and interdependence of nature just happened by chance. As one professor stated when looking at the evidence: "There is a greater chance that a tornado could hit a junkyard and leave behind a perfectly built Boeing 747 than to have all of the factors that came together to form the basis of life just happen without the guidance of a Supreme Being."

If the earth deviated from its orbit by the equivalent of one-eighth of an inch over a one-hundred-mile distance, we would either freeze or fry. To keep the earth in this tiny little slice of space that is the exact distance from the sun to support life, it takes the gravitational pull of all the planets, aligned exactly as they are, as well as the wobble, and tilt, that causes the changing of the seasons. Could anyone in his right mind believe that all of that just happened by chance?

Add to this the perfect balance of the gases found in our atmosphere, the balance of minerals in the earth, and then the contribution of all the plants and animals, without which none of this would have been possible! To date we still do not even have a computer that can compute the odds that all of this could have just happened by chance. It makes one wonder if some of the "scientists" who believe such foolishness maybe did descend from the apes, and in fact did not descend very far!

However, millions hold to this theory as if it were fact, rejecting the evidence for creation and surmising that all this unfathomable diversity and harmony in nature just happened by chance! The widespread acceptance of evolution is one of the greatest proofs that deception does not have to make sense for people to believe it. Millions are, in fact, basing even their eternal destiny on this flimsy theory. Logic, therefore, is not an adequate weapon against such delusions.

Sound biblical truth—not human logic—sets people free. When Satan tempted Jesus, He answered Satan with Scripture (Luke 4:1–13). If the Son of God, who is the Word and the Truth, used Scripture as His weapon against the enemy, how much more should we?

If we build our houses on the stronghold of the Word of God, no storm or attack will ever prevail against us. Knowing the Lord's Word, and keeping it, is fundamental to abiding in Him. Jesus said, "If you abide in Me, and My words abide in you, ask whatever you wish, and it shall be done for you" (John 15:7).

Finally, to overcome the forces of evil, we must keep focused to the end.

8. WE MUST KEEP FOCUSED TO THE END

Many fall because they begin to relax their vigilance once their spiritual authority increases. This is one reason so many tragically fall at the end of their lives. It does not matter how many souls we have led to salvation or how many devils we have cast out; if we do not continue to submit to God, draw near to Him, and resist the devil, we will be in jeopardy.

Satan himself accuses the saints before the throne of God; therefore, the closer we get to the throne, the higher the level of accusation. The

Lord could stop Satan at any time, but He allows it for our maturity—and also for bringing down the higher levels of evil principalities. Remember how the evil spirit answered the Jewish exorcists: "Jesus I know, and Paul I know; but who are you?" (Acts 19:15 NKJV). All of hell knew Paul because of his level of authority, which is why he experienced continual opposition to his ministry. But, with each level of opposition, with each new beating, stoning, or persecution, he had the opportunity to drive out higher levels of darkness. This is why Paul said: "In no way alarmed by your opponents—which is a sign of destruction for them, but of salvation for you, and that too, from God. For to you it has been granted for Christ's sake, not only to believe in Him, but also to suffer for His sake" (Phil. 1:28–29).

Opposition is a sign that salvation is coming to that realm or circumstance. It is also a sign of destruction for the enemy in that region. The Lord has allowed us to suffer for His sake *as a form of spiritual warfare*. The greatest act of spiritual warfare, which utterly defeated the enemy and spoiled his camp, was the cross. Righteous suffering disarms Satan.

In the very place the Lord was wounded, He received authority for healing. The same is true for us. In the very place the enemy wounds us, we will receive authority for healing in that same area. For example, a person who has suffered abuse will be sensitive to others who have been abused and have authority for bringing healing to them.

Spiritual warfare is an inevitable fact of life for every Christian. Some of us are more aware of this than others, but none of us can escape its reality. Not only has God called us to enter the fray, He has called us to be victorious in taking back ground from the enemy. Jesus has already secured our ultimate victory on the cross, and He is calling us increasingly to enforce that victory in our lives today.

I opened this chapter with a part of a dream and series of visions that I had, which was published in *The Final Quest*. In that vision I saw a mountain with different levels. At each level arrows of Truth were scattered about, which I knew were left from those who had fallen from that position. All of the arrows were named after the Truth of that level. Some were reluctant to pick up these arrows, but I knew we needed all that we could find to destroy the great horde below. I picked one up, shot it, and so easily hit a demon that the others started picking them up and shooting them. We began to decimate several of the enemy divisions. Because of this, the entire evil army focused its attention on us. For a time it seemed that the more we achieved, the more we were opposed. Though our task seemed endless, it had become exhilarating.

Our swords grew as we reached each level. I almost left mine behind because I did not seem to need it at the higher levels. I finally decided that it had been given to me for a purpose, so I had better keep it. I drove it into the ground and tied myself to it while I shot at the enemy. The voice of the Lord then came to me, saying: "You have used the wisdom that will enable you to keep climbing. Many have fallen because they did not use their sword properly to anchor themselves." No one else seemed to hear this voice, but many saw what I had done and did the same thing.

I wondered why the Lord had not spoken to me before I had made this decision. I then had a sense of knowing that He had already spoken this to me somehow. Then I perceived that my whole life had been training for this hour. I was prepared to the degree that I had listened to the Lord and obeyed Him throughout my life. I also knew that for some reason the wisdom and understanding I now had could not be added to or taken away from while in this battle. I became profoundly thankful for every trial I had experienced in my life, and sorry for not appreciating them more at the time.

9 BIRTH PANGS AND EARTHQUAKES

The barometer of spiritual intensity in the church is rising around the world. We are now well into the early stages of a great spiritual advance. God is pouring out a wonderful anointing, mobilizing the saints to spread the gospel and tear down the strongholds. As walls and barriers between local congregations are being brought down, churches are being energized with fresh zeal for the Lord. This is not a vision or a prophecy but reported fact. Genuine tokens of revival are now breaking out around the world.

Accompanying these spiritual birth pangs are earthquakes, which occur when the geological plates, the foundations of the earth's crust, begin to shift and move in opposite directions. Insurance companies define earthquakes as "acts of God," and they are right. However, God does not act arbitrarily. The Los Angeles earthquake of January 1994 and the continuing aftershocks are both signs and judgment. In one sense, they were the result of the churches in Los Angeles coming into a degree of unity and praying for their city.

Newsweek reported on the destruction of this quake and listed those who suffered major devastation. One listing was: "The studios of virtually every major American producer and distributor of pornographic videos, *an industry that happened to locate itself almost directly atop the fault zone.*" It was no accident that the quake took place at 4:31 A.M. Though the book of Acts is often referred to as "The Acts of the Apostles" it is, in reality, a record of the Acts of God. Acts 4:31 reads: "And when they had prayed, the place where they had gathered together was shaken, and they were all filled with the Holy Spirit, and began to speak the word of God with boldness."

The Los Angeles quake, which took place at *4:31* A.M., was meant to give greater boldness to the saints for preaching the Word, especially the saints in Southern California.

THE ISSUE IS POWER, NOT RATINGS

Southern California has been the seat of one of the most powerful spirits of seduction released in this century. A movie rated PG-13 coming out of Hollywood can have more power to seduce than some R- or X-rated movies produced in other cities. For this reason we must depend on discernment, not ratings, when we determine what movies we will watch or allow our children to watch. It is not the amount of skin that is shown; it is the spiritual power behind a movie that counts.

The Lord can shut down all pornography around the world whenever He so chooses, but He will not do it without the church fulfilling its commission to be the light of the world and the salt of the earth. He is only waiting for us to come into harmony with His will before He moves. Once He determines that it is time for judgment, He wants His church praying for it, just as Elijah did to revive his nation. Effective prayer touched God's heart *for* Southern California, and He responded with this earthquake as a sign, as well as a judgment. Even though the Lord has been showing great mercy to Southern California for the entire twentieth century (beginning with the Azuza Street Revival and continuing with the great movements and ministries He has based there), His strategy is moving toward increasingly serious judgments.

In the new millennium, earthquakes will bring greater devastation to Southern California, for as long as the church prays, the Lord will not relent until repentance and change occur. Without repentance, a major part of California will be utterly destroyed. Either way, God's heart has been touched concerning the spirit of seduction that emanates from Southern California, and He will not let up until it is removed. Let us pray that the easier way—repentance—will be taken.

This is not the time for the church to abandon California, but to labor with even more boldness, which is the message of Acts *4:31*. The move of the Holy Spirit in the new millennium will be greater than any other witnessed in this state, which has seen so much of God's glory. Los Angeles really can become "the city of angels." San Francisco and San Diego can become great beacons that shine all the way to Asia. Where sin abounds there is even more grace for those who carry the light.

Spiritual Earthquakes Throughout the World

Along with what is taking place in the natural realm, major spiritual earthquakes are about to take place in the church throughout the world. Pressure has been building up at certain points in the foundations that have been laid, and they are about to shift, creating major shock waves. These shifts are going to upset the status quo and result in some serious "structural damage" to the visible church. But only that which can be shaken will be shaken; the ministries and individuals properly lined up with the true foundations of the faith will not be damaged. When these great spiritual earthquakes are over, most of the church will be in much closer harmony with the Lord, and the church as a whole will be much more stable.

A great shift is imminent, however, in the practical application of our ministry as ambassadors of the kingdom.

WE ARE AMBASSADORS

When Paul said, "We are ambassadors for Christ" (2 Cor. 5:20), this was such a stunning statement that it must have shocked those who read it. In the days of the Roman Empire, the position of ambassador was highly esteemed. Communication between Rome and its ambassadors could take months each way. Therefore, only those people considered most loyal and single-minded would be chosen for such a position, which sometimes required making major decisions in the name of the Roman government.

Even with the most trusted men in these positions, ambassadors would only be assigned to a country for two or three years before being brought back home. Governments knew that after even a short time in the host country, ambassadors would tend to take on some of the traits of that culture, which could make them sympathetic to it. When this occurred the ambassador might be inclined to serve the interests of the host country more than those of his home.

There is a sense in which we must try to accommodate those to whom we have been sent so that we do not become *unnecessarily* offensive. The apostle Paul said, "to the Jews I became as a Jew" (1 Cor. 9:20). However, almost universally, Christians, churches, and even missionaries have compromised their effectiveness for the kingdom of God because they have become too sympathetic to the spirit of the culture in which they live. We have been sent to represent the kingdom and to be effective witnesses. This will often require that we move in a *spirit opposite to* the prevailing spirit of that nation.

THE POWER OF DIFFERENCE

One of the most devastating misconceptions that dilutes the church's witness is the belief that we can best reach those who are from our own backgrounds. If we come out of a business background, we feel called to reach businessmen. This seems reasonable, but it is contrary to the Lord's strategy, which is why He sent Peter to the Jews and Paul to the Gentiles.

According to our prevailing philosophy of missions, He should have sent Paul to the Jews; certainly they could have better identified with the "Pharisee of Pharisees" than with Peter. And Peter, being a common fisherman, would have surely been more compatible with the Gentiles. But the Lord did not want His disciples to fit in—He wanted them to stick out!

Both Peter and Paul were cast into roles that made them offenses to those they wanted to reach. There was only one way that either of them could accomplish his mission—he had to have the anointing! Both men were thrust into utter dependency on the Holy Spirit, and that is when the Holy Spirit is best able to do His work.

When Peter left the place of his anointing and tried to go to the Gentiles by visiting Antioch, he got into such serious trouble that Paul had to publicly rebuke him because "he stood condemned" (Gal. 2:11–14). Likewise, when Paul tried to go to the Jews by visiting Jerusalem, he was met with trouble. I submit to you that there was an easier way for Paul to get to Rome. Many of our ministries stay in trouble because we do not stay in the place of our anointing, which is the only place where we will ever have true spiritual authority. Just as a policeman in Charlotte, North Carolina, does not have authority in Toronto, Canada, so we must learn to stay within the realms to which we have been appointed if we are to be effective.

This principle is valid spiritually as well as geographically. Many prophets have fallen from grace because they tried to become teachers, just as many teachers have fallen from grace because they tried to become prophets. Many evangelists have fallen because they tried to become pastors, and vice versa. This does not negate the fact that some have dual, or even multiple, callings, but we must never presume to go beyond the sphere to which we have clearly been called.

When we try too hard to be like those to whom we are sent, we compromise our position of spiritual authority. This does not mean we should purpose to be different in everything. Our authority is not in being different but in abiding in the Holy Spirit. We will be different if we abide in Him and are true to the work He is doing in us. As the Lord Jesus stated: "You are those who justify yourselves in the sight of men, but God knows your hearts; for that which is highly esteemed among men is *detestable in the sight of God*" (Luke 16:15, emphasis added).

If we are compelled to act in a way that will make us acceptable to men, we will be doing what is detestable to God. The reverse is also true; the things that are highly esteemed with God are detestable in the sight of men. Somebody is going to detest what we are doing. Who do we want it to be?

THE FEAR OF GOD

To properly represent God's kingdom, we must fear God more than we fear men. The prophet Elijah made one of the great biblical statements that sums up what is required of a true ambassador. In what appears to be his first public prophecy, made before the king of his nation, he declared: "As the LORD God of Israel lives, *before whom I stand*, there shall not be dew nor rain these years, except at my word" (1 Kings 17:1 NKJV, emphasis added). Elijah told Ahab, the king of

Israel, that Elijah was not standing before Ahab—he was just a king, merely a man. Elijah did not live his life before men, even the most prestigious of men, but before God.

For the church to accomplish her mandate for the twenty-first century, she will need the kind of authority that Elijah walked in and more. To lead people into a true conversion, we do not want them to feel comfortable with our message or us. We want them to feel very uncomfortable! For true conversion, people must be convicted of their ways, which contrast with God's ways. The apostle Paul knew this. He said, "If I were still trying to please men, *I would not be a bond-servant of Christ*" (Gal. 1:10, emphasis added). Paul acknowledged that his bodily condition had been a trial to the Galatians (Gal. 4:13–14). This required them either to be repelled by him or to receive him as "an angel of God," which they did. When people are attracted to the gospel because they are attracted to us, we should seriously wonder about both the state of our lives and the truth of the gospel we are preaching.

As the Lord establishes His foundation in the church, it will often be moving in a direction opposite the movements in society, resulting in the greatest confrontation between the church and the social order since the beginning of time. The power behind the church is God's irresistible power, and the church will prevail. The resulting "earthquakes" will devastate only those building on the wrong foundation.

RISE UP

The retreat of the church has reached its limit. Now the advance will begin, and it will gain momentum until the whole world takes notice. She will march resolutely to the field of battle. Even nature will quake and shudder as a witness that the foundations of heaven and earth are moving in *opposite* directions. But our God will prevail, and our victory is assured. This is the time to be bolder than we have ever been before. There is no turning back. In fact, the time has come to concentrate our forces on the important issues of our time.

A CONCENTRATION OF FORCES

The Scriptures frequently use military metaphors to describe our spiritual conflict because the principles are similar. One of the oldest and most effective military strategies is called *concentration of forces*. This strategy was employed in the most decisive military victories in history, including the Persian Gulf War.

Most battles unfold along individual lines of confrontation. From these lines each side will try to maintain defensible positions while probing the enemy lines to find a point where a breakthrough can be made. If such a breakthrough can be accomplished, the entire enemy line will collapse and retreat to keep from being surrounded by the penetrating forces.

The spiritual battles for people's hearts are likewise formed along spiritual lines of confrontation. Just as most wars include different battles on different fronts, the same is true of our present spiritual conflict. Some of the battle lines now being fought are on the fields of our children, music, the media, and our cities. Even though we are all in the same army of God, it is appropriate for many Christians to become aligned with a specific force fighting a specific battle.

THE BATTLE FOR OUR CHILDREN

One of the most desperate spiritual battles of the twenty-first century will be for the hearts of our children. This battle has been raging throughout the twentieth century and is actually going to intensify in the new millennium. If we do not gird ourselves for this increasing contest for the hearts and minds of our children, we will begin to lose our children to the enemy on an unprecedented level. We cannot be content to just hold our ground—we must aggressively go for a breakthrough. The enemy is seducing our children with a counterfeit for the true desire of their hearts: a genuine relationship with the powerful, wise God who loves them.

Created for Fellowship

With the intensity of the battle increasing, our children will not be kept in the fold by just a good youth program. Nor will good sermons or good Sunday school lessons satisfy them. God who is Spirit created humans to hunger for a relationship with the supernatural, and this hunger is acutely felt during adolescence. If adolescents are denied a relationship with the supernatural power of God, they will be extremely vulnerable to experimentation with evil, supernatural powers. Even though witchcraft grew at a staggering rate during the twentieth century, it will grow even faster in the new millennium if the church does not increase its supernatural influence. True Christianity is a supernatural walk, as the Bible makes abundantly clear.

We must also become more discerning if we want to protect our children.

The Need for Discernment

In the battle for the hearts of our children, the enemy is not going to play fair; he is going to employ the most horrible and cruel means available to him. He is already circulating books, movies, television programs, and music of such demonic power that an unprotected soul will be subject to spiritual oppression or possession. Unfortunately, many Christians do not recognize the enemy until he is well within their camp and has established a powerful stronghold. If the church does not wake up in this area, there is going to be an astonishing increase of violence committed by children against their parents or other children.

One such incident occurred in April 1999 in the small Southern town of Kittrell, North Carolina. The mother, Debbie Bawcum, walked into her twin sons' bedroom at about 9:30 at night and saw a hunting rifle sitting on a bed. She had previously asked her husband, an avid hunter, not to keep weapons in the house. She quickly moved to take the gun from the boys.

That was when the shooting began. One of the boys shot Debbie in the arm and then gunned down her husband when he came bounding up the stairs to help her. The gunfire also hit her daughter, Robin.

The twin boys who killed their dad were eleven years old. "They had this look on their faces," Debbie Bawcum said. "They weren't my boys. They had these blank looks. For a few minutes, they weren't my sons."[1]

This example is not intended to impart fear but wisdom. We cannot give our children's minds over to the world and expect them to grow up as Christians. We really do live in enemy territory, but regardless of our theology or eschatology, our purpose here is not to hide but to raid the enemy at every opportunity.

Parents who fail to discipline their children according to biblical mandates will find themselves being disciplined by their children—or worse. Those who fail to monitor and control the books their children read, the music they listen to, or the movies and television programs their children watch, will soon see forces of evil arising in their children of the most extreme and demonic type.

Now is the time to pray as never before for all Christian parents, Christian youth workers, and children's book authors. (We need also to pray for all teachers, principals, and school boards.) The church must start to recognize that its children's and youth ministries are as important as any other ministry in the church. Children's and youth ministers are not called to be baby-sitters, but equippers of a generation that has been destined from the foundation of the world to stand and confront the enemy in the world's darkest hour. The Lord will greatly bless, prosper, and anoint congregations who devote their resources to their children's and youth ministries.

The reason many of our children and youth have rejected the church is because they have not yet seen the real church. When they do see true Christianity, they will desire it because this walk of faith will reflect the way people were created to live. Church is twenty-four hours a day, seven days a week. We must be delivered from our bondage to buildings and programs if we are going to be a part of the mighty force the Lord is now assembling.

Finally, the most important thing we can do for our children is to get closer to the Lord ourselves. As appealing as the culture of the church can be, nothing in the universe is as appealing as the Son of God. When He is lifted up, all men are drawn to Him.

THE BATTLE FOR MUSIC

Music will be another great battleground during the twenty-first century. In many ways the new millennium will be like a recycled

1960s, only the intensity will be increased. Just as the music of the Beatles and other groups gave direction to the great social upheavals of that period, music is going to play a major role in setting the spiritual climate of this millennium.

The Universal Language

Music is called "the universal language" because of its ability to cross almost every social and political barrier. Music is also a spiritual language that can reach beyond the intellect to touch the heart. Those who create this universal-spiritual language hold a powerful weapon in the war for our hearts. The Lord is calling forth an army of musical warriors who will be used like spiritual artillery to bombard some of the enemy's greatest strongholds, such as racism, drugs, pornography, and spiritualism.

Crossover artists. Some of God's minstrels will become crossover artists who will reach secular audiences. The Lord is going to give the youth alternative role models to the popular, yet morally degenerate, stars of pop music. It is important that these minstrels not look religious or talk "religionese." Neither should they copy the world's style. These singers and musicians are true evangelists who are called to just sow seeds that others will reap.

Country music. Country music's recent popularity is no accident. This music was born in the church, and the Lord wants to reclaim it for His purposes. He is calling many more top country music artists, and if they respond, He will mightily use them. If they do, country music, which has always been considered the music of the lower classes, is about to receive more class and esteem than any other form of music. If they do not, country music will slide back into relative obscurity.

Worship music. New worship music will also arise with a fresh new sound. This music will span the generations and become popular with old and young alike. Many of the Lord's minstrels will experience being caught up into the heavens to hear the music of heaven. Others will receive music and spiritual songs in dreams and visions. The power of this heavenly music will radically impact Christians' everyday lives by imparting a true spirit of worship and adoration for the Lord. This music will also draw multitudes of unbelievers to the faith.

Music evangelism. The church must recognize its minstrels as front-line soldiers in the battle for our generation. A new vision for music evangelism is going to arise so that many music ministries will become recognized as true missionaries instead of mere entertainers. These ministers and missionaries need to be spiritually equipped and supported, just as any other ministry. Music will be one of the main spiritual battlegrounds of the new millennium since it has the potential for providing one of the greatest spiritual breakthroughs in the war against darkness.

THE BATTLE FOR THE MEDIA

The media should not be considered our enemy. There are enemies of the faith in media, and some are in powerful positions, but we must esteem the freedom of speech and the press as one of our greatest blessings. It is counterproductive for us to spend our time complaining about the liberal news media, governments, or other problems when that same time and energy could be spent praying for them. One of the most revolutionizing truths that many of us need to comprehend is that *the Lord really does hear our prayers. He has delegated the awesome authority to us that what we bind in heaven will be bound on earth and what we loose in heaven will be loosed on earth.* Christians should pray for every radio station, television station, newspaper, or other source of information in their geographical region until they become standards of news coverage that are committed to truth, integrity, and fairness.

For the last forty years, English has been the second language taught in schools of almost every nation, including the former Soviet Union. Now the news that is broadcast around the world on CNN and other international stations is understood in this common language. Individual newscasts on secular stations spoken by heathen reporters will accomplish more for the spreading of the gospel than the Christian networks have accomplished during their entire existence. This is not to imply that the Christian networks are not accomplishing anything. But when secular, spiritually neutral newscasters promulgate the news of revival and the great acts of God, it will have an unprecedented impact on viewers.

THE BATTLE FOR OUR CITIES

Each battle for a specific truth is also being fought over a different spiritual landscape with different strategies. The key to victory in each battle is to accomplish a *breakthrough*. In the last few years there have been some changes in the spiritual atmosphere over certain cities, such as Los Angeles, but at best we have only pushed back the enemy lines a little bit in some areas. We still have not had a real breakthrough on this front. When we see one city truly taken for the Lord, Christians all over the earth will rise up with unprecedented zeal to take their cities, and many more will be secured as spiritual fortresses of truth and righteousness.

The advances that have been made in the battle for our cities have caused many more Christians to become aligned with the strategy of spiritual warfare for our cities. This has created a significant mobilization of forces. The key to the breakthrough will be overwhelming force at a single point along the enemy lines. The enemy lines in this battle include every city and town, but the major points of conflict include just a few where the churches are coming together in unity to see revival come to their city and change the spiritual atmosphere. If just one world-class city is taken, the enemy will be in retreat in other major cities of the world. These lines need to be strengthened and advanced as far as possible.

BUILDING THE SAME WALL

As in Nehemiah's time, each family will be given a specific part of the wall to complete. However, all of us will be working on the same wall to stand together as one people. Those who devote themselves to knowing God's healing power will not only be tolerant of those who devote themselves to search the Scriptures, but will also rely on them for teaching, edification, and correction. When those who have devoted themselves to searching the Scriptures and teaching have need of healing, they will also know where to go. As we are all able to specialize in specific callings, the light we are given will become more focused. And when light is focused enough, it becomes a laser.

As we mature in understanding the entire scope of the battle and our place in it, as we are able to recognize those who are on our side even though they may have a different function, the Lord will be able to give us spiritual laser weapons powerful enough to penetrate even the greatest of the enemy's strongholds.

10 THE RELIGIOUS SPIRIT

In the dream I was given on February 16, 1995, which was published as *The Final Quest*, I saw the Lord Jesus standing in the Garden of God under the Tree of Life. It seemed that the entire army of God was there, kneeling before the Lord Jesus. He had just given us the charge to return to the battle for the sake of our brothers who were still bound.

The Lord was not what we might consider to be strikingly handsome in appearance but was rather ordinary. Even so, the grace with which He moved and spoke made Him the most attractive person I had ever seen. He was beyond human definition in dignity and nobility. No painting that has sought to capture what He looked like could ever do it, but somehow most of those I had seen resembled Him. As I looked, I understood how He was everything that the Father loves and esteems.

The Lord continued His exhortation, "I have given you spiritual gifts and power, and an increasing understanding of My Word and My kingdom, but the greatest weapon you have been given is the Father's love. As long as you walk in My Father's love, you will never fail. The fruit of this tree is the Father's love, which is manifested in Me. This love, which is in Me, must be your daily bread."

After I had been in the Garden of God for a while, the angel began to lead me back to the gate. I protested that I did not want to leave. Looking surprised, the angel took me by the shoulders and looked me in the eyes. That is when I recognized him as the angel Wisdom. "You never have to leave this garden," he said. "This garden is in your heart because the Creator Himself is within you. You have desired the best part, to worship and sit in His presence forever, and it will never be taken from you."

Loving God is the greatest commandment and the greatest gift that a person can possess. Jack Deere, a former professor at Dallas Theological Institute and author of *Surprised By the Power of God*, once said, "Passion for the Son of God will conquer a thousand evils in our hearts and is the most powerful weapon against evil in our lives." That is why one of the enemy's most deceptive and deadly attacks on the church is meant to divert us from this ultimate quest of love. His strategy is to keep us focused on the evil in our lives, knowing that we will become what we are beholding (2 Cor. 3:18). This tactic comes in the form of a *religious spirit*, which is the counterfeit of true love for God and true worship.

Let me give a simple definition of this deadly enemy of true religion: *A religious spirit is an evil spirit that seeks to substitute religious activity for the power of the Holy Spirit in the believer's life.* Its primary objective is to have Christians holding to a form of godliness, although they have denied its power (2 Tim. 3:5). This religious spirit is the "leaven of the Pharisees and Sadducees" (Matt. 16:6) about which the Lord warned His disciples.

Jesus called these contrary teachings "leaven" because the religious spirit operates like leaven in bread. Rather than adding substance or nutritional value, leaven only inflates bread. The religious spirit also does not add to the life and power of the church; instead, it feeds the human pride that caused the first Fall and the fall of almost everyone since then. Satan knows that God will not inhabit any work inflated with pride. God will even oppose that work. So one of the evil one's primary strategies against us is to cause us to fall to pride, and religious pride is the ultimate of this deadly evil.

Satan also knows that once leaven gets into the bread, it is most difficult to remove. Pride, by its very nature, is the most difficult stronghold to correct or remove. A religious spirit keeps us from hearing God's voice by having us assume that we already know what God is saying and what pleases Him. This delusion is the result of believing that God is just like us, that our opinions are in fact His opinions. We are deluded to believe that rebukes, exhortations, and words of correction in the Scripture are for other people, not us.

The primary characteristic of the Pharisees was their tendency to see what was wrong with others while not being able to see their own faults. If this is a problem in your life, you have already begun to think about how much someone you know needs to read this. It may not even have occurred to you that God put this into your hands because *you* need it. In fact, we all need this warning. It is imperative that we get free of this devastating deception and stay free. We will not be able to fully worship the Lord in Spirit and truth until we do.

The church's confrontation with the religious spirit will be one of the epic battles of the last days. Everyone will be fighting in this battle. The only issue to be determined is: Which side will you be on?

THE GREAT DECEPTION

One of the most deceptive characteristics of the religious spirit is that it is founded on zeal for God. We tend to think that zeal for God cannot be evil, but that depends on *why* we are zealous for Him. No one on earth prayed more, fasted more, read the Bible more, or had a greater hope in the coming of the Messiah than the Pharisees. Yet, they were the greatest opponents of God and His Messiah. The young Saul of Tarsus was motivated by zeal for God while he was killing and imprisoning Christians before his own conversion. That is probably why he came to have such a profound understanding of this evil stronghold. As Paul wrote of his Jewish brethren: "I bear them witness that they have a *zeal* for God, but not in accordance with knowledge" (Rom. 10:2, emphasis added).

The Lord had little trouble with demons while He walked the earth. They would quickly bow to Him and beg for mercy. Instead, the conservative, zealous, religious community crucified the Word when He came to walk among them. The same is still true. All the cults and false religions combined have not done as much damage to the true moves of God as the infiltration of the religious spirit, since genuine Christians easily discern cults and false religions. However, the religious spirit has thwarted or diverted possibly every revival or movement to date, and it still retains a seat of honor throughout much of the visible church. In the end times, a manifestation of this religious spirit will take his seat in the very temple of God (which is the church), declaring himself to be God and getting almost the whole world to follow him.

THE TWO FOUNDATIONS

Like most of the enemy's powerful strongholds, the religious spirit builds its work on two basic foundations—fear and pride. *The religious spirit seeks to have us serve the Lord to gain His approval, rather than knowing that our approval comes through the cross of Jesus.* Therefore, the religious spirit bases its relationship to God on personal discipline rather than on the propitious sacrifice of Christ.

Fear and pride are the two basic results of the Fall, and our deliverance from them is usually a long process. That is why the Lord even gave Jezebel "time to repent" (Rev. 2:20–21). However, even though the Lord gave Jezebel this time, He rebuked the church of Thyatira for tolerating her (v. 20). We can be patient with people who have religious spirits, giving them time to repent, but we must not tolerate their ministry in our midst while we're waiting! If this spirit is not confronted quickly, it will do more damage to the church, our ministries, our families, and our lives than possibly any other assault we can suffer.

Now let's look at how the fear that motivates a religious spirit is often based on guilt.

FEAR AND ITS FOUNDATION OF GUILT

Eli, the priest who raised Samuel, is a good biblical example of someone who ministered in a religious spirit founded on guilt. Eli had so much zeal for the Lord that when he heard that the Philistines had captured the ark, he fell over and died. He had spent his life trying to serve the Lord as the High Priest, but the first word given to Samuel was one of the most frightening rebukes in the Scriptures—for Eli!

For I have told him that I am about to judge his house forever for the iniquity which he knew, because his sons brought a curse on

themselves and he did not rebuke them. And therefore I have
sworn to the house of Eli that the iniquity of Eli's house shall not
be atoned for by sacrifice or offering forever. (1 Sam. 3:13–14)

Eli's zeal for the Lord was based on sacrifices and offerings that were
supposed to compensate for his irresponsibility as a father. Guilt can
also stir us on to great zeal for the Lord, which usually results in our
attempt to use sacrifices and offerings as an atonement for our failings.
This is an affront to the cross, which alone atones for our guilt. Such
zeal will never be acceptable to the Lord, even if we can make sacrifices
forever. We should note here that the Lord did not say that Eli's sin
could not be forgiven. He just said that Eli's attempts to atone for his
own sin by sacrifice and offering would never work.

This does not mean that we should avoid doing things to please the
Lord but that our motive should always be pleasing the Lord for *His* joy,
not for our acceptance. One is God-centered, and the other is self-centered, and that self-centeredness is an attempt to circumvent the cross.

It is also noteworthy that one of the sins of Eli's sons was that they
"despised the offering of the LORD" (1 Sam. 2:17). They appropriated
the sacrifices and offerings brought to the Lord for their own selfish use.
Those gripped by this form of a religious spirit will often be the most
zealous to preach the cross, but this is a perversion because it emphasizes *their* cross more than the cross of Jesus. They delight in their self-abasement, rather than in the cross of Christ, which alone makes us
righteous and acceptable to God.

The foundation of fear is guilt. And the foundation of pride is
idealism.

PRIDE AND ITS FOUNDATION OF IDEALISM

Idealism, a form of humanism, is one of the most deceptive and
destructive disguises of the religious spirit. Idealism tries to impose
standards on others that are beyond what God has required or has
given grace for. For example, those controlled by this kind of religious
spirit may condemn anyone who is not praying two hours a day as
unspiritual. God may want us to pray two hours a day, but He will first

call us to pray ten minutes a day. Then, as we become so blessed by His presence, we will want to spend more and more time with Him until we will not want to quit after ten minutes, then an hour, then two. This way our grace has grown through love for Him and His presence, not because of pressure or guilt.

Because of their idealism, persons with a religious spirit will usually seek the perfect church and refuse to be a part of anything less. They constantly criticize their church. Those who are led by the Holy Spirit, who is called "the Helper," may also have high hopes for their church, but they can still give themselves in service to some of the most lowly works to help these churches grow in vision and maturity.

When a religious spirit is founded on pride, it is evidenced by *perfectionism*, where everything is black or white. This develops into extremes as it requires that everyone and every teaching be judged as either 100 percent right or 100 percent wrong. Only Jesus could comply with such a standard. When we impose such standards on others or ourselves, the result is serious delusion. True grace imparts a truth that sets us free, showing us the way out of our sin or to higher levels of spiritual maturity.

People with a religious spirit can point to problems with great accuracy, but they usually offer no solutions, except to tear down what has already been built. This is the enemy's strategy—to nullify progress and to bring about a discouragement that will limit future growth.

God's grace leads us up the mountain step-by-step. The Lord does not condemn us because we trip a few times while trying to climb. He graciously picks us up and encourages us so we can make it to the top. We should never condemn ourselves for not being there yet, *as long as we are still climbing*.

If we had to wait until we were perfect before we could minister, no one would ever qualify. Just look at the condition of the apostles who were left with the charge to build the church. At the cross, in Jesus' time of greatest need, all but John scattered from Him, denied Him, and betrayed Him. How many pastors would leave their church for a weekend with such a crew to run things? Yet, Jesus could leave His church with such men, not because He was trusting them but because He trusted the Holy Spirit. Perfect obedience and understanding should always be our goals, but they will never be found within ourselves. We will find them only as we come to abide perfectly in the Perfect One.

One of the greatest delusions of all is that we are already complete in our understanding, or 100 percent accurate in our perception or actions. This closes us to further understanding and correction. Yet Paul said we "see through a glass darkly" (1 Cor 13:12 KJV), so we are compelled to always be open to greater accuracy in our beliefs and teachings.

Jesus blessed Peter and turned the keys of the kingdom over to him just before He had to rebuke him and call him "Satan" (Matt. 16:23). Right after this great blessing of receiving the keys of the kingdom, the enemy deceived Peter, yet the Lord did not take the keys away from him. When Jesus gave the keys to Peter, Jesus knew that Peter would soon deny Him. Those two incidents are not the only times Peter stumbled. Many years after Peter used the keys to open the door of faith for both the Jews and Gentiles, the last-called apostle, Paul, had to rebuke Peter publicly because of his hypocrisy. Even so, Peter was promised to sit on one of the twelve thrones that will judge the twelve tribes of Israel.

The Lord's leadership style was to provide a place where His followers could make mistakes and learn from them. If we required our children to be perfectly mature in everything, it would be counterproductive, actually stifling their growth and maturity. The same is true in the church. We must bring correction for mistakes, because that is how we learn. However, this correction must encourage and edify, not condemn and crush initiative.

Finally, one of the most powerful forms of the religious spirit is built upon *both* fear and pride.

THE FOUNDATION OF BOTH FEAR AND PRIDE

Those who are bound by both fear and pride will go through periods of deep anguish and remorse at their failures, resulting in a repentance that is simply more self-abasement and produces yet more sacrifices in an attempt to appease the Lord. Then they will flip to the other extreme, where they become so convinced they are superior to other Christians or other groups or movements, they are not teachable and are unable to receive reproof.

This religious spirit is so slippery that it will wiggle out of almost any attempt to confront it. If you address the pride, the fears and insecurities will rise up to attract sympathy. If you confront the fear, it will change into religious pride masquerading as faith. This type of spirit will drive individuals or congregations to such extremes that they will inevitably disintegrate.

Now let us examine our own hearts by looking at some of the warning signs of a religious spirit.

SOME WARNING SIGNS OF A RELIGIOUS SPIRIT

Most of us are subject to the religious spirit at least to some degree. Paul exhorted us to "test yourselves to see if you are in the faith" (2 Cor. 13:5). Go through the warning signs below and check the ways you might have a religious spirit.

_____ 1. *The tendency to see your primary mission as tearing down what you believe is wrong.*

This person's ministry will produce more division than lasting works.

_____ 2. *The inability to take a rebuke, especially from those you judge to be less spiritual than yourself.*

Think back on how you responded the last few times someone tried to correct you.

_____ 3. *A philosophy that will not listen to other people—"only to God."*

Since God usually speaks through people, this is an obvious delusion and reveals serious spiritual pride.

_____ 4. *The inclination to see more of what is wrong with other people and other churches than what is right with them.*

John saw Babylon from the valley, but when he was carried to a "high mountain" he saw the New Jerusalem (Rev. 21:10). If we only see Babylon, our perspective is wrong. Those who are in a place of true vision will focus on what God is doing—not on any human achievement.

_____ 5. *Overwhelming guilt that you can never measure up to the Lord's standards.*

This is a root of the religious spirit because it causes you to base your relationship with Him on your performance rather than on the cross.

_____ 6. *The belief that you have been appointed to fix everyone else!*

The self-appointed watchmen or sheriffs in God's kingdom are seldom involved in building anything; they keep the church in a state of annoyance and agitation and may cause serious divisions.

_____ 7. *A leadership style that is bossy, overbearing, and intolerant of the failure of others.*

As James said: "But the wisdom from above is first pure, then peaceable, gentle, reasonable, full of mercy and good fruits, unwavering, without hypocrisy. And the seed whose fruit is righteousness is sown in peace by those who make peace" (James 3:17–18).

_____ 8. *A sense that you are closer to God than other people or that your life or ministry is more pleasing to Him.*

This is a symptom of the profound delusion that we draw closer to God by who we are rather than through Jesus.

_____ 9. *Pride in your spiritual maturity or discipline, especially as you compare yourself to others.*

True spiritual maturity involves growing up into Christ. When we begin to compare ourselves with others, it is obvious that we have lost sight of the true goal—Jesus.

_____ 10. *The belief that you are on the cutting edge of what God is doing.*

This includes thinking that you are involved in the most important thing that God is doing. Again, this is spiritual pride and self-centeredness, even if it were true. Those who are entrusted with the truly important missions have the grace to fulfill them because God "gives grace to the humble" (James 4:6).

_____ 11. *A mechanical prayer life.*

When you start feeling relieved that your prayer time is over, or when you have prayed through your prayer list, you should check your condition. You will never feel relief when your conversation is over with the One you love.

_____ 12. *Doing things so people will notice.*

This is a symptom of the idolatry of fearing people more than we fear God, and it results in a religion that serves people instead of God.

_____ 13. *Being overly repulsed by emotionalism.*

When people who are subject to a religious spirit encounter the true life of God, it will usually appear excessive, emotional, and carnal to them. True passion for God is emotional and demonstrative. Remember how David danced when he brought the ark of God into Jerusalem? And remember how this repulsed his wife, Michal, and she was barren from that day on (2 Sam. 7:23)? Such a critical spirit will lead to spiritual barrenness.

_____ 14. *Using emotionalism as a substitute for the work of the Holy Spirit.*

Do you think that weeping and wailing must accompany repentance? Or that one must "fall under the power" to be truly touched by God? Even though both of these can be evidences of the true work of the Holy Spirit, you are beginning to move in another spirit if you require these manifestations.

During Jonathan Edwards's meetings in the First Great Awakening, some of the toughest, most rebellious men fell on the ground and stayed there for up to twenty-four hours. Such seemingly strange manifestations fueled the Great Awakening, since these men were truly changed. Even so, Edwards stated men who faked these manifestations brought an end to the Great Awakening more than the enemies of the revival.

_____ 15. *Keeping score in your spiritual life.*

Do you feel better about yourself because you go to more meetings, read your Bible more, or do more things for the Lord than other people do? These are all noble endeavors, but the true measure of spiritual maturity is getting closer to the Lord.

_____ 16. *Being encouraged when your ministry looks better than others' ministries.*

This includes getting discouraged when it seems that other ministries are looking better or growing faster.

_____ 17. *Glorying more in what God has done in the past than what He is doing in the present.*

God has not changed; He is the same yesterday, today, and forever. The veil has been removed; we can be as close to God today as anyone in the past. A religious spirit always seeks to focus our attention on making comparisons rather than simply drawing closer to the Lord.

_____ 18. *The tendency to be suspicious of or oppose new movements or churches.*

This is an obvious symptom of jealousy, a primary fruit of the religious spirit—or of pride—which asserts that God would not do anything new without going through us. Of course, the Lord rarely uses people with such a mentality.

_____ 19. *The tendency to reject spiritual manifestations that we do not understand.*

This is a symptom of pride and arrogance that presumes our opinions are the same as God's. True humility keeps us teachable and open, patiently waiting for fruit before making judgments. That is why we are exhorted to "prove all things; hold fast that which is good [not what is bad]" (1 Thess. 5:21 KJV).

_____ 20. *An overreaction to carnality in the church.*

Far more carnality likely exists in the church and a lot less of the Holy Spirit than even the most critical person would think. We must learn to be delivered from our carnality and to grow in our submission to the Holy Spirit. But the critical person will want to annihilate those who may still be doing things in the flesh 60 percent of the time (but are making progress because they were 95 percent last year) instead of helping them along the way.

_____ 21. *An overreaction to immaturity in the church.*
The Lord tolerates a certain amount of immaturity. My four-year-old is immature compared to my fourteen-year-old, but that is okay. In fact, he may be very mature for a four-year-old. The idealistic religious spirit only sees the immaturity without considering the other important factors.

_____ 22. *The inability to join anything that you do not deem as being perfect or near perfect.*
The Lord joined humans here on earth and even gave His life for the fallen human race. The apostles that He called and released to build His church would probably have made most people's list of "The Least Likely to Succeed." Such will be our nature, too, if we abide in Him. We will not just see people as they are but also for whom they can become.

_____ 23. *If while reading these signs you were thinking about how they applied to someone else, you may have a serious problem with a religious spirit.*

SCORING ON THE TEST

I will let you determine how you scored on this test. Just remember, Paul did not tell us to test our neighbor or our pastor, but ourselves. I confess that every one of these issues has applied to me, and I am sure that much of it still does. These are all the fruit of having eaten from the spiritual Tree of the Knowledge of Good and Evil, and it takes a process of having our minds renewed to get free of its influences.

Now that we know how affected each of us is by the religious spirit, let's look at the forms of a religious spirit, not only to keep from being infected by this spirit ourselves, but also to protect ourselves from someone who has a religious spirit.

THE FORMS OF A RELIGIOUS SPIRIT

I have seen five forms of a religious spirit: a counterfeit gift of discernment, a spirit of Jezebel, self-righteousness, the martyr syndrome, and some self-help psychology. Let's begin with the counterfeit gift of discernment.

1. THE COUNTERFEIT GIFT OF DISCERNMENT

A religious spirit gives birth to a counterfeit gift of discernment of spirits. This counterfeit gift thrives on seeing what is wrong with others rather than seeing what God is doing to help them along. (If you checked number 4 or 6 on the self-test, you tend to have a counterfeit gift of discernment.) Its wisdom is rooted in the Tree of the Knowledge of Good and Evil, and though the truth may be accurate, it is ministered in a spirit that kills.

Suspicion, which is motivated by rejection, territorial preservation, or general insecurity, causes this counterfeit gift. However, the true gift of discernment can only function with love. Whenever someone submits a judgment or criticism about another person or group, I disregard it unless I know that person truly loves the other person or group and has an "investment" of service to them.

When Paul warned the Corinthians about those who ministered in a religious spirit that sought to place a yoke of legalism on the young church, he declared that "such men are false apostles, deceitful workers, disguising themselves as apostles of Christ. And no wonder, for even Satan disguises himself as an angel of light. Therefore it is not surprising if his servants also disguise themselves as servants of righteousness" (2 Cor. 11:13–15).

That is why Saul of Tarsus, the "Pharisee of Pharisees," was so enraged against the church. Religions that are based on works will tend to become violent easily, especially when confronted with those who live by faith. This includes "Christian" religions where a doctrine of works has supplanted the cross of Christ.

Those who are driven by religious spirits may try to destroy those they oppose by means other than physically taking their life. Many of the onslaughts of slander instigated against some churches and ministries are the ragings of this religious spirit.

The spirit of Jezebel is another form of the religious spirit.

2. THE SPIRIT OF JEZEBEL

Jezebel was the ambitious, manipulative wife of King Ahab, Israel's weak leader who allowed her to dictate policy in his kingdom. Basically, the spirit of Jezebel is a combination of the religious spirit and the spirit of witchcraft that is the spirit of manipulation and control. This spirit is often, but not always, found in deeply wounded women. The way women were treated in biblical times, and the way Jezebel was treated by being given to a foreign king as a political gesture, makes it somewhat understandable that she turned out the way that she did, but it is not excusable. Every trial in our lives will either make us bitter or better, and the cross will heal every spiritual wound if we will turn to it. Those who are deeply wounded who do not go to the cross can open themselves up to this evil spirit.

Jezebel was the greatest enemy of one of the old covenant's most powerful prophets, Elijah, whose ministry represented preparing the way for the Lord. The Jezebel spirit is also one of the enemy's most potent forms of the religious spirit that seeks to keep the church and the world from being prepared for the Lord. This spirit attacks the prophetic ministry because that has always been a primary way in which the Lord gives timely, strategic direction to His people. Jezebel knows that by removing the true prophets, the people will be vulnerable to her false prophets, which always leads to idolatry and spiritual adultery.

When a void of hearing the true voice of the Lord exists, the people will be much more prone to the deception of the enemy. This is why the enemy always tries to sow pride in people. A religious spirit produces religious pride so that God will not communicate with those who are proud. That is why Jesus called the religious leaders of His own day "blind guides" (Matt. 15:14). Those men knew the messianic prophecies better than anyone else in the world. Yet, they could look right into the face of the One who was the fulfillment of those prophecies and think that He was sent from Beelzebub!

Jezebel's prophets of Baal were also given to sacrifice, even being willing to flail and cut themselves so their god would appear. A primary strategy of the religious spirit is to get the church devoted to sacrifice in a way that perverts the command for us to take up our crosses daily. This perversion will have us putting more faith in our sacrifices than in the Lord's sacrifice. It will also use sacrifices and offerings to try to get God to manifest Himself. This is a form of the terrible delusion that we can somehow purchase the grace and presence of God with our good works.

The third form of a religious spirit is self-righteousness.

3. SELF-RIGHTEOUSNESS

We do not crucify ourselves for the sake of righteousness, purification, spiritual maturity, or to get the Lord to manifest Himself; this is nothing less than conjuring. We are "crucified with Christ" (Gal. 2:20). If we crucify ourselves, it will only result in *self-righteousness*. This is pride in its most base form because it gives the appearance of wisdom and righteousness. The apostle Paul warned:

Let no one keep defrauding you of your prize by delighting in self-abasement and the worship of the angels, taking his stand on visions he has seen, inflated without cause by his fleshly mind, and not holding fast to the head, from whom the entire body, being supplied and held together by the joints and ligaments, grows with a growth which is from God. If you have died with Christ to the elementary principles of the world, why, as if you were living in the world, do you submit yourself to decrees, such as, "Do not handle, do not taste, do not touch!" (which all refer to things destined to perish with the using)—in accordance with the commandments and teachings of men? These are matters which have, to be sure, the appearance of wisdom in self-made religion and self-abasement and severe treatment of the body, but are of no value against fleshly indulgence. (Col. 2:18–23)

The religious spirit will make us feel good about our spiritual condition as long as it is self-centered and self-seeking. Pride feels good; it can even be exhilarating. But all of our attention is on how well we are doing or how we compare to others—not on God's glory. (If you checked numbers 8, 9, 10, 15, or 16 on the self-test, you have at least some degree of self-righteousness.) This results in our putting confidence in discipline and personal sacrifice rather than in the Lord and His sacrifice.

Of course, discipline and the commitment to self-sacrifice are essential qualities for every believer to have, but the motivation behind them determines if we are being driven by a religious spirit or by the Holy Spirit. A religious spirit motivates through fear, guilt, or pride and ambition. The motivation of the Holy Spirit is love for the Son of God.

Delighting in self-abasement is a sure symptom of the religious spirit. This does not mean that we do not discipline ourselves, fast, or buffet our bodies as Paul did. It is the perverted delighting in this, rather than in the Son of God, that reveals a problem.

Deceptive Revelation

In Colossians 2:18–19 Paul explained that people who delight in self-abasement will often be given to worshiping angels and taking improper stands on visions they have seen. A religious spirit wants us to worship anything or anyone but Jesus. The same spirit given to worshiping angels will also be prone to exalting humans excessively. We must beware of anyone who unduly exalts angels, men, or women of God or uses visions he has received to gain improper influence in the church. God does not give us revelations to prove our ministry or so people will respect us more. The fruit of true revelation will be humility, not pride. The Scriptures teach that Christians do have these experiences and that they are useful and needed when used properly. The key word in this text is that we should beware of those who are having such revelations *and* are being "inflated" by them.

A religious spirit will always feed our pride, whereas true spiritual maturity will always lead to increasing humility. This progression of humility is wonderfully demonstrated in Paul's life. In his letter to the

Galatians, estimated to have been written around A.D. 56, he declared that when he visited the original apostles in Jerusalem, they "added nothing to me" (2:6 KJV). In a sense, he declared that he had as much as they did. When he wrote to the Corinthians, he called himself the "least of the apostles" (1 Cor. 15:9). And in about A.D. 61, he declared himself to be "the very least of all saints" (Eph. 3:8). Finally, when he wrote to Timothy in approximately A.D. 65, he declared himself to be the "chief" of sinners (1 Tim. 1:15 KJV), adding that God had mercy on him. *A true revelation of God's mercy is the greatest antidote for the religious spirit.* The religious spirit will not remain long when we grow in true humility.

Remember that the manifestations of a religious spirit are a counterfeit gift of discernment; a spirit of Jezebel, which is manipulation; self-righteousness; and the martyr syndrome, which we will examine now.

4. THE MARTYR SYNDROME

To be a true martyr for the faith is one of the greatest honors that we can receive in this life. When this is perverted, it is a tragic form of deception. When a religious spirit is combined with the martyr syndrome, it is almost impossible for that person to be delivered from his deception. At that point, any rejection or correction is perceived as the price he must bear to "stand for the truth," which drives him even farther from the truth and any possibility of correction.

The martyr syndrome can also be a form of the spirit of suicide. It is sometimes much easier to "die for the Lord" than it is to live for Him. Those who have a perverted understanding of the cross often glory more in death than they do in life. The goal of the cross is the resurrection, not the grave.

Finally, we need to look at how some forms of self-help psychology can lead to a religious spirit.

5. SELF-HELP PSYCHOLOGY

The self-help psychology movement is a subtle attempt to replace the power of the cross in the church. This humanistic psychology is "another gospel" and another form of the religious spirit. Indeed, Paul warned us:

> As you therefore have received Christ Jesus the Lord, so walk in Him, having been firmly rooted and now being built up in Him and established in your faith, just as you were instructed, and overflowing with gratitude. See to it that no one takes you captive through philosophy and empty deception, according to the tradition of men, according to the elementary principles of the world, rather than according to Christ. (Col. 2:6–8)

We all need "inner healing" to some degree, but much of what is being called inner healing is nothing less than digging up the old man and trying to get him healed. We need to kill the old man and leave him. The way to heal our spiritual wounds is not a procedure or formula, but simple forgiveness. When we go to the cross and find true acceptance, based on the blood of Jesus, we will find a perfect love that will wash away all bitterness and resentment.

This seems too simple, but that is why Paul said: "But I am afraid, lest as the serpent deceived Eve by his craftiness, your minds should be led astray from the simplicity and purity of devotion to Christ" (2 Cor. 11:3). Salvation is simple. Deliverance is simple. The enemy's major strategy is to dilute the power of the gospel by having us add to it. That is how he deceived Eve.

The Lord had commanded the man and woman not to eat from the Tree of the Knowledge of Good and Evil because they would die. When asked about this command, Eve replied that they could not eat from the tree "*or touch it*" (Gen. 3:3). The Lord had not said anything about touching the tree. Adding to His commandments is just as destructive as taking away from them. People who think they can flippantly add to the Word of God do not respect it enough to keep it when testing comes. If Satan can get us to add or subtract from Scripture, he knows he has caught us just as he did Eve.

Many "Christian" philosophies and therapies seem wise, but they attempt to substitute for the Holy Spirit in our lives. Some people do need counseling, and many Christian counselors do lead people to the cross. Yet, others are simply leading people into a black hole of self-centeredness that will consume them and try to suck in everyone else around them. In spite of the Christian terminology, this philosophy is an enemy of the cross of Christ.

Finally, how do you know if you are free from the infection of a religious spirit? Here is the test of a true messenger.

THE TEST OF A TRUE MESSENGER

In Ezekiel 37, the prophet was taken to a valley full of dry bones and asked if they could live. The Lord then commanded him to prophesy to these bones. As he prophesied they came together, came to life, and became a great army. This is a test every true ministry must pass. The true prophet can see a great army in even the driest of bones. He will prophesy life to those bones until they come to life, and then become an army. A false prophet with a religious spirit will do little more than just tell the bones how dry they are, heaping discouragement and condemnation on them, but giving no life or power to overcome their circumstances.

Apostles and prophets are given authority to build up and tear down, but we have no right to tear down if we have not first built up. I will give no one the authority to bring correction to the people under my care unless that person has a history of encouraging people. You may say that eliminates the ministry of the prophets, but I say that those "prophets" need to be eliminated from ministry. As Jude said of them, "These are grumblers" and faultfinders who are "hidden reefs in your love feasts" (Jude 11–16). As an old proverb declares, "Any jack-ass can kick a barn down, but it requires a skillful carpenter to build one."

The Lord's leadership style was to provide a place where His followers could make mistakes and learn from them. If we required our children to be perfect, it would be counterproductive, actually stifling their growth and maturity. The same is true in the church. We must bring correction for mistakes, because that is how we learn, but it must be a correction that encourages and frees, not one that condemns and crushes initiative.

Even so, as Eli gave us an example, woe to shepherds who feed and care for the sheep but fail to correct them. The true grace of God is found between the extremes of the spirits of faultfinding and unsanctified mercy (showing mercy to the things that God disapproves of). Either extreme can be the result of a religious spirit. True religion is not a heavy yoke, but the greatest freedom and the greatest joy that the human soul can ever experience. That can only come from knowing the Lord and having fellowship with Him. When we see His glory, we will no longer be so captivated by our own positive or negative qualities; His beauty will capture our souls. Even the twenty-four elders cast their crowns at His feet (Rev. 4:10). That is the goal of the true faith— to see Him, to abide in Him, and to reveal Him. This may sound too easy, but it is the only answer to our great dilemma.

The world is becoming increasingly repulsed by religion. However, when Jesus is lifted up, everyone will be drawn to Him. Because the whole creation was created through Him and for Him, we all have a huge, Jesus-size hole in our soul. Nothing else will ever satisfy us or bring us peace but a genuine relationship with Him.[1]

PART 3

THE CHURCH AND
THE 21ST CENTURY

---

11 THE NEW AGE AND THE KINGDOM OF GOD

The New Age movement has become a powerful force in the devil's strategy to blind the world to the gospel of Jesus Christ. One reason why this movement has been so effective is because many New Age teachings closely mirror the great truths of the gospel, but then carry them to conclusions that are in conflict with the most central of all Christian truths—the cross.

Because of the seriousness of this deception, it is understandable that the church has developed a knee-jerk reaction to the very words *new age*. Even so, the way we combat darkness is not to run from it, but to take our stand on the truth, and push it back. Light is more powerful than darkness. When we open our shades at night, darkness does not come into our rooms, but rather the light shines out into the darkness. We need not fear darkness if we know the Light, Jesus.

WHAT IS THE NEW AGE MOVEMENT?

The New Age movement is basically a combination of witchcraft and Hinduism disguised to make it acceptable to white-collar professionals. This form of spiritualism is targeting this group for an important reason. For almost 5,800 years of the earth's 6,000 years of recorded history, nearly 95 percent of all workers were agricultural. In just a little over a century, that statistic has been reversed so that now less than 5 percent of the workers in the West are farmers. This change is the result of technological advances, which make it possible for this 5 percent to produce more than the 95 percent could in the last century.

When the Lord predicted that "knowledge will increase," few understood the degree to which this would happen. In the mid 1950s, white-collar workers exceeded the number of blue-collar workers in the West. Since that time this majority has grown until it is now estimated that, in the near future, blue-collar workers will go the way of agricultural workers, composing only a small fraction of society. Information is the most valuable commodity in the world, and the job of accumulating, interpreting, packaging, and transferring knowledge is the largest industry on earth.

Those involved in this industry are not only the most numerous, but also the most wealthy and most powerful. They are also the group that the church has become increasingly unsuccessful in reaching, which has helped to feed the proliferation of the New Age movement and other cults. God created us to have fellowship with Him. He is Spirit, and there is a spiritual void within us until this fellowship with Him is restored. True fellowship with Him is a supernatural experience because God is supernatural. The void created when we do not have this fellowship is a hunger for the supernatural. If we do not satisfy it with a relationship with God, the devil will be quick to fill it with his substitutes.

THE POWER OF GOD

The day of supernatural neutrality is over. Those who do not know God's true power through the Holy Spirit will become increasingly subject to the evil and counterfeit supernatural powers of the enemy. People whose fears or doctrines have led them to avoid God's supernatural power will find themselves, and especially their children, easy prey to evil.

Paul explained that "the kingdom of God does not consist in words, but in power" (1 Cor. 4:20). Satan knows this and is quite content to fight his battle on the level of words (doctrines, and so forth). Regardless of how well we argue our true doctrines, Satan has little problem conquering those who do not know the power of God. Righteousness is the result of believing in our hearts, not our minds;

those who do not know God's power believe in Him only in their minds.

In light of the foolishness of the Pentecostal, Charismatic, Full Gospel, and Third Wave movements, it is easy to understand why many shy away from the gifts of the Spirit. But this, too, is one of the tests that separate true believers from those who just know creeds or doctrines. God has called the foolish things of the world to confound the wise. Only the humble will come to what He is doing, and He will give His grace only to them.

The more secularized the society, the more people will hunger for the supernatural. That is why atheists tend to be drawn to the basest forms of witchcraft and the black arts, which they think are natural human powers within man. Churches that have rejected God's supernatural power have already succumbed to influences from the New Age movement. Others succumb to the spirit of the age in other forms. Not only do they tolerate perverted people and unbelievers as members, but they even ordain them as pastors and leaders.

Many of these churches and denominations have become increasingly irrelevant, with little or no power to attract converts. And these denominations and movements are almost all shrinking because they have become irrelevant and boring, even to their own people. Contrary to this, the denominations and movements that preach and walk in the supernatural power of God are not only growing, but they are by far the fastest-growing religious movements in the world when measured as a single group.

The apostle Paul declared, "My message and my preaching were not in persuasive words of wisdom, but in demonstration of the Spirit and of power, *that your faith should not rest on the wisdom of men, but on the power of God*" (1 Cor. 2:4–5, emphasis added). The conflict between the kingdom of God and the kingdom of evil is not just a conflict between truth and error (though it is that), but it is also a confrontation of supernatural power. Both sides are seeking to fill the spiritual void created by the Fall.

To claim to be a biblical people if we do not walk in God's supernatural power is a contradiction. The entire history of God's dealings with the human race has been demonstrated by supernatural power. Jesus did not just talk about God's power to heal, save, and deliver; He healed the sick and cast out demons. Jesus stated that as the Father sent Him into the world, so He sends us (John 17:18). He expected His disciples to heal the sick and cast out demons as they preached the kingdom. Jesus does not change. If we are going to preach the gospel, we are to preach it as He did, demonstrating God's love and power.

Churches that do not walk in power will become more and more inadequate to deal with the increasing power of evil during the end times that are prophesied in Revelation. The first defense against this deceptive supernatural power is to know the true power of God, so we must "desire earnestly spiritual gifts, . . . especially that you may prophesy" (1 Cor. 14:1). "God is spirit, and those who worship Him must worship in spirit and truth" (John 4:24).

Most believers now desire spiritual gifts, but they must *earnestly* desire them if they are going to receive them. Jesus has decreed that each of us must ask, seek, and knock in order to receive. When someone says, "I am open to receive the gifts of the Spirit," it is usually a cop-out. This person is often too fearful or too prideful to risk failure. Those who are just "open" for the Lord to use them are almost never used.

Other people often resist the Spirit by saying, "We are to seek the Giver, not the gifts." That sounds pious, but it is not biblical. Certainly we are to seek the Giver more than the gifts, but we are commanded to seek the gifts also; they are not mutually exclusive. Seeking to walk in the gifts of the Spirit is one form of seeking God, and even more important, it is being obedient.

Love is the greatest gift, and we are told that it is the more excellent way. However, the two Scriptures that surround this chapter both encourage us to seek spiritual gifts. In 1 Corinthians 12:31, we are told to "earnestly desire the greater gifts." In 1 Corinthians 14:1, we are told to "pursue love, yet desire earnestly spiritual gifts, but especially that you may prophesy." The gifts do not cancel out love; instead, they are to be used in love.

Still other people's hearts have been hardened by false doctrines that say God no longer moves supernaturally. However, in recent years some of the world's most brilliant theologians and apologists, who used to believe that God no longer moves supernaturally, have been won over after witnessing just one genuine miracle. *Genuine* is the key here; those who love and seek to walk in God's true power are turned off by the fakery and hype often associated with some ministries that do not have real power. However, many who believe that the Lord no longer moves supernaturally are seekers of truth, and when they witness the authentic, they will change their theology.

True Christianity is *the true word of God verified by the true power of God.* Jesus went about both to "do and teach" (Acts 1:1). Often, He performed miracles before He taught, because He knew that people who had an undeniable encounter with God would be far more open to what He would say to them. The same is true today; demonstrations of God's power transform intellectual concepts into a true faith in the Lord's teachings. It takes both the word and the power of God to change the inner man. The spiritual void in the heart must be filled by a true fellowship with God if we are going to be free of the spiritual influence and power of the enemy.

Because New Age philosophy is basically a counterfeit spiritual authority, we will only be completely free from its power when we are completely submitted to the power and authority of God. If we are not, we will become increasingly subject to witchcraft in some form as we draw closer to the end of the age. The Battle of Armageddon is fought in the "valley of decision." That day, everyone on earth must make a decision: We must choose between the power and authority of God and the power and authority of the evil one.

To overcome the New Age movement, we must also keep these people from stealing our words and perverting our teachings.

WE CANNOT ALLOW THE ENEMY TO STEAL OUR WORDS OR TEACHINGS

We also cannot allow the enemy to steal our words, our practices, or our teachings. The words *new age* do not belong to the devil, but to the Lord, and we must take them back. Much of the success of the New

Age movement has come from stealing the high ground of hope for the future from the gospel. This is the church's special domain, and we must refuse to surrender a single acre of it to the enemies of the cross.

A fundamental truth of the gospel is that a new age is coming. An age of peace, righteousness, and justice will prevail over the whole earth. That is the age in which Jesus Christ will rule as the Prince of Peace, the King of kings, and the Righteous Judge. This is the true message of the new age to come, which the church is called to preach and the enemy is trying to subvert through the New Age movement.

Almost every aspect of New Age teachings is a counterfeit of the true hope of the gospel. However, just as we do not quit using real currency because someone has made counterfeit currency, we must not abandon a single truth of God's coming kingdom. If counterfeit money is circulating, we must become more familiar with what is real so we can recognize the false. We must do the same with the essential truths of the kingdom. The enemy would not be after these truths if they were not important.

OUR MISGUIDED FOCUS ON THE END OF THE AGE

One way the New Age movement has been able to steal the crucial high ground of hope for the future is through the church's tendency to overfocus on the end of the age. *This is not just the end; it is the beginning of a new age in which Christ will rule over the earth!* For the church to reclaim the high ground of hope for the future, we must proclaim the *beginning*, the coming of the kingdom. Hope for the future is central to the power of the gospel. The age that is coming belongs to the Lord, and the message of the new age belongs to *Him*.

When the Lord came to earth the first time, He came to purchase our redemption with His own blood. As Psalm 24:1 declares, "The earth is the LORD's, and all it contains, the world, and those who dwell in it." The price for the entire earth, and all of its inhabitants, was fully paid at the cross.

After His resurrection, Jesus could have destroyed the devil and taken His rightful domain over the earth right then. Instead, it was the Father's plan that a people would first be redeemed from the earth to become joint heirs with the Son of God. They would then rule with Him in the age to come. The Scriptures testify that the Lord will return to redeem the earth from all consequences of the Fall. Peter referred to this as the "restoration of all things" (Acts 3:21), and this is why all of creation is groaning and travailing (Rom. 8:19–22).

The Scriptures are clear that the end of this age will be accompanied by a time of trouble such as the world has never experienced. These biblical prophecies cannot be changed, and we must teach them if we are going to present the whole truth. Even so, the Scriptures are also clear that even the time of greatest darkness will be one of glory for the Lord's people (Isa. 60:1–5). This glory is not just coming on us so we can look good! His glory will appear on us because we will be living in the reality of the age to come and experiencing His glory right now.

THE NEW AGE RIGHT NOW

The greatest hope the Lord gave us about His kingdom was that it is "*at hand*" (Mark 1:15, emphasis added). Those who hear and believe Him can live in His kingdom now! Even though we walk on the earth, we are also seated with Him in the heavenly places (Eph. 2:6). The miracles He performed were evidence that the kingdom was available to any who could see it by faith. When He cast out demons, He said, "If I cast out demons by the Spirit of God, then the kingdom of God has come upon you" (Matt. 12:28).

The message of the last trumpet in the book of Revelation is: "The kingdom of the world has become the kingdom of our Lord, and of His Christ; and He will reign forever and ever" (Rev. 11:15). Those who live in the reality and power of His kingdom *now* will preach the message of the kingdom. We do not wait for the millennium for Jesus to reign over us. His kingdom is already "*at hand.*"

Those who have the Holy Spirit of God have more power abiding in them than all the demons have combined. We are not to be ignorant of the devil or his schemes, but we do not need to fear the devil or anything he will try to do. When we walk in the light, the demons fear *us*. John wrote:

Beloved, do not believe every spirit, but test the spirits to see whether they are from God; because many false prophets have gone out into the world. By this you know the Spirit of God: every spirit that confesses that Jesus Christ has come in the flesh is from God; and every spirit that does not confess Jesus is not from God; and this is the spirit of the antichrist, of which you have heard that it is coming, and now it is already in the world. You are from God, little children, and have overcome them; because greater is He who is in you than he who is in the world. (1 John 4:1–4)

We have already overcome the antichrist if we know Jesus. Our gospel will cease to be true to the degree that Jesus is not central to our lives. Even heaven would not be heaven unless He was there. Our hope is in the King, not just the kingdom. Satan will try to offer all the elements of the kingdom of God without Jesus; that is the essence of the New Age movement. Our message of the kingdom is that Jesus is King!

At the very time that darkness is covering the earth, the glory of the Lord will arise. This will cause the nations to turn to the Lord's people. In the end, the church will become all she has been called to be—the pure, spotless bride of Christ. Then her light will be even more brilliant against this backdrop of darkness.

The Gospel of Hope

In a recent prophetic experience, I found myself in the radar room of a warship, and the Lord was standing right next to me. As I looked at the radar screen, a single, small blip appeared—straight ahead and getting closer.

Instinctively, I ordered the ship to turn to the right, but the blip stayed in front of us, continually getting closer. I then ordered the ship to turn to the left. The blip still appeared directly in front of us, drawing ever closer. Finally, I braced for the impact. Nothing happened—not even a jolt. And then the blip was gone. I asked the Lord, "What was that little blip?" "It was the great time of trouble," He answered. "It is coming, and there is nothing we can do to avoid it. However, it is only a little blip on the screen of all that God is about to do, and as long as we stand with Him, we will not even feel it."

I was astonished, but I know this is true. Against eternity, the entire Great Tribulation is but a tiny blip on the screen. Weighed against the awesome power of our God, the great time of trouble is not enough to even register on the scale.

Why do thoughts of the end times consume so much of our attention? We do need to understand coming troubles and be prepared for them, but by no means should the coming troubles dominate our attention or our message. Our preparation for the coming troubles is simple—we are to stand with Jesus. To abide in Him, we must prepare for any future troubles in *faith*, not in fear. No other religion or philosophy in the world has a hope that can compare to the hope we have been given for the age to come.

As I prayed for the wisdom to build our Moravian Falls community, the Lord gave me three basic instructions. He said that He had designed the land for us, so we needed to build structures that would fit into the landscape, and "not offend the land." He also said we needed to consider our neighbors, because love does no harm to a neighbor. The Lord then said, "What you build will need to last for a thousand years! Build with future generations in mind, because I will return to reign over the earth. You need to build for the age to come, not the one that is coming to an end."

We know that the Lord is about to judge the earth. As Paul wrote, "Behold then the kindness and the severity of God" (Rom. 11:22). God is both severe and merciful, and His judgment will be both severe and merciful: severe to those who resist Him, and merciful to those who seek Him. All His ways are perfect, and even His judgments are for redemptive purposes:

> Let the heavens be glad, and let the earth rejoice;
> Let the sea roar, and all it contains;
> Let the field exult, and all that is in it.
> Then all the trees of the forest will sing for joy
> Before the LORD, for He is coming;

For He is coming to judge the earth.
He will judge the world in righteousness,
And the peoples in His faithfulness. (Ps. 96:11–13)

God's judgments are to be sought, not resisted. If we are living in obedience, we do not need to fear even the greatest times of trouble.

THE GLORIOUS HOPE

The message Jesus has entrusted to the church is a far more glorious hope than any utopia or age of Aquarius that the humanists or spiritualists predict. Our message is the *kingdom of God*. The message Jesus preached was not the gospel of salvation, although that was contained in His message. Neither was His message about the church. In all of His messages, He only made a few brief references to the church.

His message was *the kingdom*, and this is the message we have been given to preach. This does not belittle the importance of our salvation, nor negate the high place of the church in His plan. However, the message of the kingdom is bigger than these. Great truths are included in the message of the kingdom, but they are never intended to eclipse it.

The message of the kingdom is essentially one basic but all-encompassing truth—Jesus is the King! He reigns, and His kingdom will be an everlasting kingdom. When He returns to set up His kingdom on the earth, He will not just do away with war, He will bring the whole creation into harmony. The lion will lie down with the lamb. Children will be able to safely play with cobras. Not only will sickness and disease be removed from the earth, but even death will have been abolished. The nations will drink from the River of Life, and eat the fruit of the Tree of Life:

And he showed me a river of the water of life, clear as crystal, coming from the throne of God and of the Lamb, in the middle of its street. And on either side of the river was the tree of life, bearing twelve kinds of fruit, yielding its fruit every month; and the leaves of the tree were for the healing of the nations. And there shall no longer be any curse; and the throne of God and of the Lamb shall be in it, and His bond-servants shall serve Him; and they shall see His face, and His name shall be on their foreheads. And there shall no longer be any night; and they shall not have need of the light of a lamp nor the light of the sun, because the Lord God shall illumine them; and they shall reign forever and ever. (Rev. 22:1–5)

The true message of the kingdom must contain both God's kindness and severity. He is coming to bring peace, but He is also coming with a rod of iron to strike the nations. Both the Lion and the Lamb must be included in the kingdom's message.

The darkest and coldest time of night is just before the dawn. For a little while, it may get colder and darker, but then the day of the Lord will come: no more mourning, no more pain, no more hunger, no more disease. No parent on earth will ever again abuse an innocent child, and no one will try to injure or defraud a neighbor. Truth will prevail over every lie, and love will prevail over the whole earth. There is a new age coming, and it will be more glorious than any utopia, philosophy, or religion that has ever been conceived by human hearts.

A Vision

War and Glory

In August 1993, I had a vision of the church that was represented as an island in the middle of a sea. Many different types of buildings were all over this island, each of which I understood to represent a different denomination or movement. These buildings seemed to clash with each other architecturally as very old ones were next to very modern ones. A war was going on between many of the buildings, and most of them looked like bombed-out shells. People were still living in the buildings, but most were starving and wounded.

Two dark spirits over the island were directing this war. One was named Jealousy, the other Fear. Every time one of the buildings suffered damage or people were wounded, these spirits congratulated each other.

I then saw two powerful and frightening spirits rise over the sea. These became storms. One was named Rage, the other Lawlessness. They were stirring up the sea and causing great waves to crash onto the island. Soon these storms became so large that they seemed even more threatening to the island than the war.

I felt that the people in the city had to be warned about these storms, and several apparent watchmen were trying to do this, but no one would listen. The people only debated and argued about whether the watchmen could be trusted. This was remarkable because anyone who just looked up could see the storms for themselves, but no one would look up.

These wars had left so many people wounded that the hospitals—movements or denominations that were giving healing—were fast becoming the largest buildings on the island. As these hospitals grew, the other warring factions had no respect for them as a place where even their own wounded were being cared for; instead they were soon more resolved to destroy them than the other buildings.

As the war continued, even those who were not badly wounded had the appearance of phantoms, or they became grotesquely deformed from starvation and disease. People were attracted to any building receiving a supply of food. The others then targeted the building. I could not comprehend how even a war could be so cruel—and yet this was the church!

In the midst of the battle, men were still trying to add to their buildings, or start new ones, but it was futile. Whenever one building would start to rise a little higher than the others, or any time a new building was started, it would become the main target of all the other buildings, and it would quickly be reduced to rubble.

I was then shown many powerful leaders who were conducting this war. All of them had the same word on their foreheads: Treachery. I was surprised that anyone would follow someone with that written on them, but people did. I was reminded of 2 Corinthians 11:20, "For you bear with anyone if he enslaves you, if he devours you, if he takes advantage of you, if he exalts himself, if he hits you in the face."

A REMNANT

However, there were people who appeared as lights in almost every building. These lights refused to take part in the fighting, but spent their time trying to repair the buildings or nurse the wounded. Even though it was impossible to keep up, they did not stop trying.

Each of these lights had the power to heal wounds, and this power increased as they worked. Those who were healed became lights just like those who healed them. These individuals were now able to do more than the hospitals because of the ruthlessness of the attacks on the hospitals. Understanding this, the hospitals dispersed their people as healing teams that spread out across the island and moved into many of the other buildings.

Many small camps were around the perimeter of the island. Some of these were involved in the war between the buildings, and seemed intent on trying to destroy all of the buildings so they could bring the people to their camps. The leaders of these camps had the same word, Treachery, written on their foreheads.

A few of these camps were not involved in the war, and they, too, appeared as lights. These were growing in authority, but it was a different authority. They had authority over events. They were praying to stop small battles and to keep small storms away, and it was happening as they prayed.

The two spirits over the city that were stirring up the two great storms became very intimidated by these small camps. I felt that these intercessory groups were actually close to having the authority to stop the major battles and big storms that were obviously the source of agitation of these large spirits.

THE TRAGEDY

Multitudes of boats and ships were all around the island, waiting to enter the city as soon as the fighting stopped. Many of these boats were full of refugees from other wars, and many were wounded. There were also ships bearing kings, presidents, and people who appeared wealthy and prosperous. They were all afraid of the storms, but they could not enter the city because of the fighting. They were groaning and screaming so loud, in obvious despair, that I was surprised that no one in the city could hear them; no one even seemed aware that they were out there.

Then I saw the Lord standing and watching. His glory was so great that I wondered why I had not seen Him before, or why everyone in the city did not stop to worship Him. To my amazement, no one was able to see Him. I looked into the eyes of some of the people, and they were all so bloodshot that I was surprised that they could see anything.

I wondered why the Lord did not stop the fighting; instead, He seemed content to just watch. As if He had understood my thoughts, He turned and said to me, "This is My church. These were the houses people tried to build for Me. I knocked on the door of each one, but they would not open to Me. I would have brought peace because I will only dwell in the city of peace."

Then He turned and indicated the people in the ships: "If I allowed all of these people to come to the city now, they would just be used in the war. When their cries become louder than the war, I will build a place for them."

Then He looked at me with great earnestness and said, "I allowed this to happen so that it will never happen again!" It is hard to convey the power of this statement, but it imparted to me a deep understanding that He allowed this conflict to continue out of profound wisdom. He then said, "Until you understand this, you cannot understand what I am about to do."

When the cries of those in the boats became louder than the conflict in the city, the Lord gave a command, and the sea was released. Great tidal waves arose and began to sweep across the island until they covered the buildings. The spirits that were storms joined the spirits over the island, and they all almost doubled their previous size. Then the island completely disappeared under the darkness of the spirits and the raging sea.

The Lord did not move as this was happening. I knew that my only protection was to stand as close to Him as possible. I could not see anything but Him during this great storm. As I looked at His face, I could see both hurt and resolve.

Slowly, the storms died down and the tides receded. The individuals who were the lights in the buildings emerged and remained standing where the buildings had once been. Then the Lord, who had been on the edge of the island, moved to the center and said, "Now I will build My house."

All of those who were lights started turning toward the Lord. As they turned, they became even brighter, and each group was changed into a living pillar right where they stood. Soon it became obvious that these pillars were the framework of a building, which would almost cover the entire island.

The pillars were different colors, shapes, and sizes. It was hard to understand how all of these, being so different, would work as a single framework. However, the Lord seemed very pleased with each one, and they did eventually fit together.

Then the ships and boats started landing on the island. Each ship or boat was from a different country or race of people. Soon I began to think that, even as large as the building was, there were too many people. The Lord looked at me and said very sternly, "We will build as many rooms as we need—no one will be turned away."

This was said so sternly that I resolved never again to consider turning people away as an option. I also pondered how the biggest problem before was how to get people to come to the buildings. Now the biggest problem was what to do with all the people.

When each ship arrived, the people on it were led straight to the Lord. He looked into the eyes of each one and said, "If you trust Me, you will die for Me." When one said, "I will die for You," He immediately thrust His sword right through their heart. This caused very real pain. To those who tried to avoid the sword, it was obviously even more painful. To those who relaxed, it did not seem to hurt as much.

These people were then taken to a cemetery with the word Obscurity over the gate. I felt compelled to follow them. Those who had been stabbed were checked to see if they were really dead before they were buried. Some clung to life for a long time, and were laid off to one side. Those who were buried began to arise quickly as great lights, just like those who had survived the storm. I noticed that they were not staying in their tombs the same length of time. Some of them arose before those who were clinging to life were even buried.

When I first looked at this cemetery, it looked like a dreadful place, and I did not think that it fit on this now-glorious island. As I left the cemetery, I turned to look back at it, and it looked beautiful. I could not figure out what was different. Then one of the workers said to me knowingly, "The cemetery has not changed—you have."

I looked at the building, and it was even more glorious than I had remembered. I looked at the island, and it had become much more beautiful. I remembered the Scripture, "Precious in the sight of the LORD is the death of His godly ones" (Ps. 116:15). The worker, who was still looking at me, said, "You have not died yet, but were changed just by being close to those who have. When you die, you will see even more glory."

Those who were emerging as lights from the cemetery were each being led to their own place in the building that had their name on it. Some joined the walls; others joined the pillars. Some became windows or doors. They remained people even after they became a part of the building.

THE TEST

I returned to the Lord's side. Standing in His presence was so wonderful I could not imagine why anyone would not be willing to die for Him, but many of the people coming from the ships refused. They backed away from Him at the request. Many of these went back to the ships, some of which left and some of which remained in the harbor.

A few of the people who refused to die stayed on the island and were allowed to walk about freely, and even enter the house of the Lord. They seemed to love to bask in the glory of it all. Many of these began to shine with a glory, too, but they never had the glory within themselves—they only reflected what was coming from the others.

As I was thinking that it was not right for these people to be allowed to stay, the Lord said to me, "My patience will win many of these, but even those who never give Me their lives, I love and am pleased to let them enjoy

My glory. Never turn away those who love My glory." These people really did enjoy the presence of the Lord that radiated from the house, but they seemed timid and retreated when the Lord Himself came close to them.

I watched as those who had refused to die for the Lord began to act as if His house were their own, and had been built for them. I wanted to be angry at their great presumption, but I could not feel anger. I understood that I could not be angry because I was standing so close to the Lord. This forced me to make the decision to stay close to Him or to move away so I could be angry.

I was surprised that this was a difficult decision, but it honestly was. Out of fear at what was arising within me, I stepped closer to the Lord. He immediately reached out and grabbed me as if I were about to fall off a cliff. I looked behind me and was astonished to see that I had been on the very edge of one. Had I taken that step away from the Lord to feel the anger, I would have stepped off the cliff.

The Lord then said to me, "In this house I can tolerate presumption more than anger. That anger would start the war again." I was overwhelmed with the knowledge that I had not yet made the decision to die for Him, and that I, too, had been presumptuously feeling possessive of both the house and the Lord. When I saw this great evil in my own heart, I was appalled and immediately begged the Lord to destroy my evil heart with His sword.

RESURRECTION LIFE

When the Lord pierced my heart, I was surprised to feel so little pain; it seemed to have been so hard on others. He then said, "Those who request death die easier." I remembered His statement in Matthew 21:44: "And he who falls on this stone will be broken to pieces; but on whomever it falls, it will scatter him like dust."

I did not remember being carried to the cemetery, but just as if no time at all had passed, I emerged from it again. Now the glory of everything I saw was unspeakable. I looked at a rock and loved it. I looked at trees, the sky, and clouds and could not believe how wonderful they were. A sparrow seemed more glorious than any bird I had ever seen. I wondered at the great treasure that this little bird was, and why I had not appreciated it like this before.

I looked at the presumptuous people. Not only did I feel no temptation to be angry, I loved them so much I would have let them all pierce my heart again if it would have helped them. I began to think of how blessed I was to be able to meet them and be with them. Now I actually wanted them to stay and could not comprehend how I was ever tempted to be angry with them— they were much greater treasures than the sparrow!

Then the Lord stood next to me. Though I did not think it was possible, He was much more glorious than before, and I was able to bear it. He said, "This is why the death of My people is so precious to Me. Those who seek to save their life always lose it, but those who lose their life for My sake find true life. Now you know true life because you know love."

Then I looked at the house and all of those who composed it. Everything and everyone seemed to stir up a great feeling of love that was more wonderful than anything I had ever felt before. I wanted to talk to each one, but I did not want to leave the Lord's side, since His presence was even more compelling. Knowing my thoughts, He said, "You need never fear leaving My side, because I have made My abode in you and I will be with you everywhere you go."

As I watched the presumptuous people, who were enjoying all of the blessings and even thought of themselves as the reason for them, I realized they really were not even a part of what was being built. Having just been one of them, I also knew how shallow their enjoyment was, compared to what it could be, and a great compassion came over me. As I continued watching, these people gradually became thinner in substance until they were just like the phantoms I had seen in the former city. Again I thought of the Lord's words, "Those who seek to save their life will lose it, but those who lose their life for My sake will find it."

Then I looked at how the building kept getting higher. The higher it went, the more glory it exuded and the farther it could be seen. This resulted in even more ships and people coming through the storms that were still raging, but seemed unable to affect the island. As I wondered how high the building could get, the Lord turned to me again, and, as if He were answering my thoughts, said, "There is no limit to how high we can build this, because I am the foundation and love is the cement."

This caused me to look at the cement. It was transparent but radiated a great power. I wondered how I had not noticed this before; it was now so obvious and captivating. I started pondering how I seemed blind even to the greatest wonders of this building until the Lord directed my attention to them. This caused me to turn back to the Lord and to watch everything to which He gave His attention.

Then the Lord began looking at the people who now composed the building. As I looked at them again, I was immediately struck by the fact that they were more than people—I knew that they were the "new creation" that had transcended the old creation. They had bridged the gap between the physical and spiritual realms and were clearly a part of both. They were unquestionably supernatural, which did not mean that they were not natural, but were far more natural than anything "natural" I had ever seen. They made everything else seem like a shadow, and this sense increased as they continued to change.

Soon the glory that was coming from them could be both seen and felt. The feeling was not like a touch but like an emotion. As I walked close to this glory, it made me feel so good. It was like a wonderful intoxication—not one that clouded the mind but illuminated it. I felt somehow ennobled, not with pride, but with a powerful sense of destiny. I also felt a profound security, as if I were in complete harmony with the ground, the atmosphere, and especially the Lord and His house. This feeling was so good that I never wanted to move again.

With the addition of each new boatload of people, the transformation of those already a part of the building continued, and the glory of the whole building increased and expanded. Everyone in the building greatly rejoiced when each new group of people came.

SHARING THE GLORY

When those who came from the cemetery took their place in the building, those who were already a part tried to give the new ones their own glory. As they did this, the glory radiating from the Lord would increase, and He would give even more to those who had given their own glory away. Those who were the most devoted to this sharing would be the ones used to start the next level of the house that kept going higher and higher.

I thought of how opposite this was from the jealousy that had prevailed previously in the city. I then tried to ponder the jealousy to understand it more, but it was almost impossible to do—it seemed as unreal as if it had only existed in bad dreams. The joy of sharing was so great that not doing it now seemed incomprehensible. The more the glory was shared, the more each one received to share.

I knew that all of us would be spending eternity just seeking others with whom to share the glory. I had a strong sense of knowing that the Lord would be creating many new worlds just for us to have new places to share His glory. I then knew that this was why He had created the universe with such diversity, and why He created it to continually expand at a rapid pace. He had set in motion a glorious chain reaction that would never stop! There were no limits on time or space, and we would need every bit of it!

THE STORMS RETURN

Suddenly my attention was turned toward the storms that had continued to grow in the sea. To my shock they had grown larger and faster than the house of the Lord, and were now coming toward the island.

Great waves covered the island, and the building disappeared from my view, even though I was still very close to it. The fury of this storm was beyond comprehension, but I felt no fear at all. I had already died to this world and had a life that could never be taken from me. As wonderful as the island had become, I was just as happy to die physically so that I would be free to carry the glory of the Lord to the rest of the universe. It really would have been hard to choose whether to stay or go, so I just rested and waited.

Gradually the storms abated, and the building reemerged. Both the building and the island were much smaller, but even more glorious. Then I noticed that the storms were just offshore and were returning. This happened several times, and each time the building would emerge smaller, but more glorious. Each time this happened the storms were also much smaller—they were wearing themselves out on the island. Soon the storms could only generate small waves that posed no threat of any real damage. The glory of the house was now beyond any human description.

Then the clouds dissipated altogether into the most beautiful sky I had ever seen. As I gazed into the sky, I realized that it was filled with the glory that was being emitted from the house. There was no damage from the storm, though the house was much smaller. Even so, the glory now coming from the house was much greater than before, and was reflected by everything. I felt that it was so great, it must already be extending far beyond the earth.

Then the vision changed, and I was alone with the Lord. All of the great feelings were gone—even the love. He looked at me earnestly and said, "The war is almost over. It is time to prepare for the storms. Tell My people that no one with His brother's blood on His hands will be used to build My house."

I was trying hard to listen to these words in order to heed them, while still thinking about the great love I had felt. He then said, "This was a dream, but it is real. You have known everything that I have shown you in this dream in your heart. Now believe with your heart, and My love will be real to you again. This is your quest—to know My love."

12 Civil War in the Church

There have probably been few times in history when there were more reasons for expecting a major advance for the cause of Christianity than there are in the twenty-first century. Renewal of the church is taking place around the world. Reconciliation movements are confronting important strongholds such as racism and other roots of division and injustice. Powerful new movements are affecting men, women, and children, awakening them to their place and destiny in the church. Worldwide, almost 200,000 new believers are coming to the Lord each day.

In spite of its problems, Christian television has done much to help break down the barriers between denominations and movements. Catholics now watch Baptists, and Presbyterians watch Pentecostals, with everyone learning that there is merit to others' beliefs. Many Christian events draw believers together from across the spectrum of the body of Christ, and genuine interchange is taking place. There is probably more unity in the church today than at any time in the last one thousand years.

This is a cause for rejoicing and hope. Even so, some of history's greatest watershed events came at a time and in a way that seemed most improbable. That is why we are warned that when people cry "peace and safety," sudden destruction will come. I believe that this may apply to the present church unity. The greatest test of our unity may soon be on us. All that is happening today will be a foundation for a future, greater unity. The enemy intends to use the coming great test for our greatest defeat, but if we are properly prepared, it can become an opportunity for one of our greatest victories.

On February 23, 1996, I was shown for the third time that the church was headed for a spiritual civil war. I was first given an impression of this in 1988. Then at the beginning of 1995, I saw it again in a dream, which I wrote as part of *The Final Quest*. I believe that this was the same conflict I was shone in the vision I titled *War and Glory* in the previous chapter. On February 23, 1996, I was told that it was time to warn the church to prepare for this great war with the resolve to fight until there was complete victory—the complete overthrow of the accuser of the brethren's strongholds in the church.

Such a victory sounds like a good thing to fight for, but for a long time the battle to win this victory will look like one of the church's greatest defeats. The accuser will arise from some of the most unexpected places and people. This will, in fact, be one of the cruelest battles the church has ever faced. Like every civil war, it will cause brother to turn against brother as we have never before witnessed in the church.

When a prophet is shown impending negative events, it can be for the purpose of thwarting the enemy's schemes. However, I do not believe that this one can now be stopped *or that the Lord wants it stopped*. This battle must be fought. It is an opportunity to drive the accuser out of the church and for the church then to come into a unity that would otherwise be impossible. Like the cross, the very event that Satan expected to destroy his enemy is the very occasion that will cause his own defeat.

What is coming will be dark. At times Christians will be loath to even call themselves Christians. Believers and unbelievers alike will think that it is the end of Christianity as we know it, *and it will be*. Through this the very definition of Christianity as known by the world will be changed—*for the better*. The church that emerges will be full of unprecedented grace, truth, and power. Remember, when the great darkness came on the world the day Jesus was crucified, the greatest light of all followed it: the resurrection.

The impending civil war in the church will parallel the American Civil War in many ways, since the great spiritual issues that must be settled in the church are a counterpart to the political problems America faced before the Civil War.

Parallels Between Two Civil Wars

Until the first battle of the American Civil War, no one on either side expected the war to last more than a few months, or to cost more than a few hundred casualties. The ultimate cost in lives, property, and damage to the soul of the nation was a profound shock. Likewise, the conflict the church is headed for will be unimaginable to almost everyone before it happens. That will cause a serious lack of preparation. This will seriously prolong the conflict.

Slavery was not tolerable in America, and its presence in a free country with such a spiritual destiny could not be endured. Neither is the spiritual slavery and oppression now existing in much of the church tolerable; it must be eradicated before the last-day church can come into her full purpose. Pseudo-spiritual leaders who use control, fear, and manipulation to keep believers in bondage impose this spiritual slavery. They do this with a "plantation mentality." They are so possessive with the people in their domains that they act as if they own them, which is the basis of slavery.

CAUSES OF THE SPIRITUAL CIVIL WAR

Just as with the American Civil War, spiritual slavery and oppression will become the primary issue facing the church. This will be the first cause of the spiritual civil war.

1. Spiritual Slavery

You may protest, "What are you talking about? There is no spiritual slavery in the church today, and most of us are free from spiritual oppression." That's probably right. More than half of the United States were also "free states" before the Civil War, but the rest had a deadly cancer that had to be removed, or the whole nation would have died. The same is true of the church. Many believers in the world today are held under a spiritual "plantation mentality": Leaders are only seeking to build and maintain their own spiritual estates and are doing it mostly through spiritual slave labor. Some are benevolent toward their people unless they try to leave, and others are as spiritually ruthless and cruel as most slave owners were.

Here we are speaking of spiritual enslavement and oppression, but its perversion of our spiritual character is no less devastating than slavery was. How could America, otherwise the freest nation on earth, abide such cruelty? She couldn't. No nation can long abide that kind of contradiction and hypocrisy in its midst. Neither can the church continue to abide many of the present contradictions in her teachings and practices. These issues must be addressed.

Great Britain, under the leadership of men like John Wesley and William Wilberforce, showed that the terrible institution of slavery could be removed from a nation by the power of the truth. Britain repented and removed the cancer from her midst without a civil war. She did this by first making the ownership of slaves spiritually and socially unacceptable, then by passing civil laws to enforce these obvious truths.

America took a different path, trying for decades to compromise the obvious and appease the offenders. This only made the ultimate cost of the inevitable changes much greater. Likewise, inevitable changes are coming to the church. We are right now determining how much these changes will cost us. Satan's strand of three cords (the *control spirit*, the *political spirit*, and the *religious spirit*), by which he is yoking multitudes of believers, must be confronted and removed. The longer we compromise with them, the more costly their ultimate removal will be. As America could never have become a great nation while tolerating slavery, neither can the church come into her ultimate glory while tolerating the spiritual strongholds and bondage now forced on so many. As Paul said, "Now the Lord is the Spirit; and where the Spirit of the Lord is, there is liberty" (2 Cor. 3:17).

For true worship to exist, there must be liberty. That is why the Lord placed the Tree of the Knowledge of Good and Evil in the

Garden. There could be no true obedience unless Adam and Eve were free to disobey.

Freedom is essential for true worship and true obedience or for any place that the Spirit of the Lord will come. The use of guilt, pressure, manipulation, and control to compel people to do what we think they should do is not tolerable in the church of Jesus Christ, who came to set those same people free.

Again, the main point in the impending spiritual civil war will be the institution of slavery—or the institutions of spiritual slavery. When I speak of "institutions of slavery," I am not necessarily speaking of denominations, but rather of any organization, including denominations or movements, that holds its people in spiritual bondage. The longer we compromise with institutions that manipulate or control for the sake of unity or for any other reason, the more it will ultimately cost us to remove the cancer from our midst.

A major secondary factor in the American Civil War, and one that many contend was the primary factor, was simple economics. One of the greatest powers of bondage at the end of the age will be that of money over people.

2. Money

Money will be the ultimate false god at the end of the age. That is why the "mark of the beast" is an economic mark, and why "the love of money" is called "a root of all sorts of evil" (1 Tim. 6:10). A god is not just something you bow down to, but something you trust.

Big ministry can be big money. Because many churches and ministries are built with considerable debt, financial pressures can cause leaders to do things they would not otherwise do. Many of the coming conflicts between movements, denominations, and individual churches will be deeply rooted in the power that money now has over the church. Leaders will use doctrinal differences or other issues as justification for their attacks on their brothers, but the real cause will be over a loss—or a potential loss—of money.

Stewardship is one of the most crucial matters for every leader to understand and walk in during these times. If we compromise the biblical standards here, we will fall into one of the most devastating traps of the enemy.

Another cause for the American Civil War was the compulsion for many in the South to simply preserve their way of life or their traditions. The same is true of the church.

3. Traditions

There are many good traditions we should honor, but many traditions are substitutes for a living relationship with the Lord. One of the powers of a religious spirit is to cause people to honor the things that God has done in the past in order for them to justify their opposition to what He is presently doing.

The Pharisees (who loved the Word of God and esteemed both the traditions and a hope in the coming Messiah) rejected and opposed Jesus more than anyone else when He came. They worshiped their traditions more than God, so when He came without having the same regard for those traditions, they could not receive Him. Those who put their security and faith more in their traditions than in the living God will oppose almost everything that He is doing. A huge portion of the church will attack any new movement that arises in the church. The more anointed a new movement is, the more these traditionalists will be threatened by it, and the more vehemently they will attack it.

Another cause of the American Civil War that will parallel the impending spiritual conflict is the demand for states' rights on the part of the secessionists. Territorial rights will also be a cause of the spiritual civil war.

4. Territorial Rights

The Southerners' call for states' rights might have seemed like a call for liberty, but it was actually the demand for an unholy right of self-will and independence. If liberty had truly been in their hearts, why would they also demand to keep their slaves in bondage? (Note: For those who might be wondering, I am a white Southerner, born in North Carolina and raised in Richmond, Virginia. My ancestors were slave owners. However, I am not writing this out of guilt, but simply because this is what I was shown.)

Likewise, many today who are vehemently demanding their own independence from organizations and denominations often yoke their followers with character-crushing doctrines of fear to keep them under their control. Such people will be some of the primary vessels for the accuser in the coming conflict.

Besides these causes, there are other parallels between the Civil War and the coming spiritual war in the church.

OTHER PARALLELS

The coming spiritual civil war will be a war between the forces of the union and the forces of confederacy. There is a true unity movement, and there is a counterfeit one. The first is based on the relationship we have in Christ that makes us all family. The other is based on political expediency—alliances or organizations created to maintain their way of life that they do not want to change.

It should also be noted that the Union itself remained divided throughout the entire American Civil War. There were peace movements, riots and demonstrations, even occasional violent clashes. Yet these people remained a part of the Union. We can also expect problems and divisions within the part of the church that is fighting for true liberty and the preservation of a true union. Even so, the forces of the true union will work out their differences and prevail. (Union and confederacy in this case do not imply north and south portions of our country.)

THE BLUE AND THE GRAY

Like the American Civil War, the coming spiritual civil war will also be between the blue and the gray. In dreams and visions, blue often represents heavenly mindedness (the sky is blue), and gray speaks of those who live by the power of their own minds (the brain is often called "gray matter"). This civil war will be a conflict between those who may be genuine Christians but live mostly according to their natural minds and human wisdom, and those who follow the Holy Spirit.

It seems to be a contradiction, but after a point the only way the Union could be preserved was for a leadership to arise that would be willing to fight a civil war to preserve the Union. Likewise, the church is coming to that point. The only way she can attain a true unity is for her leaders to fight the forces of spiritual slavery and oppression.

The unity of the church is one of the most important issues with the Lord. One of His own most pressing prayers on the night before He laid down His life for the church was "that they will be of one heart and mind" (John 17:21, author's trans.). However, He also prayed for us to be sanctified in truth (John 17:17). He gave His life to set us free from the evil one's yoke. Jesus prayed for unity based on truth, not just political expediency or compromises fashioned to keep peace at any cost. Peace at the cost of truth or the liberty of the Spirit is a yoke of bondage that only leads to greater division. Just as the very leaders who seemed to bring the greatest division to the nation were the only ones with the vision and resolve to save it, the same will be true in what is coming on the church.

Some of the noblest souls in the American Civil War caused multitudes of unnecessary deaths and greatly prolonged the war by fighting for the wrong side. Their allegiance was based more on territory than principle. Robert E. Lee claimed to disagree with what the South was fighting for, but he said he could not take up arms against his native Virginia. How many lives could have been saved and how much devastation avoided, if he (and other people like him) had chosen sides based on principle rather than territory?

Unfortunately, the same will be true of the impending spiritual civil war. Those people who have more allegiance to a position, or an organization, than to genuine spiritual principles will likewise end up fighting on the wrong side, even though they may be able to justify it in a thousand ways. These, too, will cause many unnecessary casualties.

For a long time it looked as if the South were going to win the Civil War, and likewise for a time it will look as if the forces of spiritual slavery and rebellion will prevail, but they will not. As I wrote in *The Final Quest*, this war will cause the Lord's champions to ascend the mountain into higher realms of the Spirit. As they do, faith, hope, and charity will be revealed, and seen from even greater distances than would have otherwise been possible.

Another parallel between the Civil War and the coming spiritual civil war will be the forces that compose the winning side.

The Forces of Victory

Few today realize that near the end of the Civil War, almost one-third of the Union troops were black. Some historians have rightly stated that the Union probably could not have won without them because of the widespread antiwar movements in the North. When leaders of the Christian forces of union determine to fight for the essential principles of liberty and truth, the black church will arise to fight. They will be the primary forces to bring about the ultimate victory.

Because of the destiny of the black church in America, she has been subjected to the most severe systematic attacks of the enemy. He has continually tried to sow seeds of control and manipulation within the leadership, and he is using Islam to attack the black church from without. However, a new generation of black leaders will cast off all forms of manipulation and control; they will be the great spiritual liberators who will help lead the entire body of Christ through what is coming.

After this great spiritual civil war, there will no longer be a white church and a black church. Neither will many of the present distinguishing characteristics that categorize Christians into groups continue to exist. There will be an entirely new definition of Christianity, which the Lord Jesus Himself has already written: The world will know us by our love.

The Lord is also going to raise up spiritual leaders like Abraham Lincoln, which is another parallel between the two wars.

A New Breed of Leader

These new leaders will be willing to fight a civil war to preserve the union. Like Lincoln, under the greatest of pressures from forces within the church and through what appear to be constant defeats on spiritual battlefields, they, too, will hold their course and not compromise until there is a complete victory. God gave America Abraham Lincoln, and He will do no less for His church.

Abraham Lincoln is considered one of the most remarkable leaders of all time. After his assassination, Lincoln was almost immediately recognized as one of our greatest presidents. However, before his death he was one of the most despised presidents ever to hold the office. Not just in the South but even in the Northern states, Lincoln was constantly chided and ridiculed. Many of the nation's best leaders refused to be associated with him and would not serve in his government. Even so, he did the best he could with what he was given, believing that if the Lord was with him, he could not fail. We must do the same. The leadership that must lead the church through what is coming will not be here to win popularity contests. They must do their jobs as unto the Lord, because few people in their own time will appreciate them.

From the beginning of history, the first strategy of every leader in a war is to demonize his enemy so he can galvanize support and mobilize his forces. One of Lincoln's greatest accomplishments was to wage such a bloody conflict without once demonizing his enemy. Possibly Lincoln could have won the war much sooner if he had done this, as the North never did fully mobilize. However, Lincoln kept focused on his ultimate goal—the preservation of the union. That goal would have been more difficult, if not impossible, if he had demonized the South. Until the end he treated his enemies with the utmost dignity and respect. He even visited Southern troops in hospitals, because he continued to maintain that they were all Americans, even if they had been led astray.

Lincoln faced defeat after defeat on the battlefield. He faced the possibility of losing his reelection as president to an advocate of peace at any cost. However, Lincoln kept his vision on the ultimate purpose of unity, which was an extraordinary grace. This was also a characteristic of one of the greatest leaders in the Bible, King David, who fought a civil war with the house of Saul (2 Sam. 3). However, David always honored King Saul, even when Saul sought David's life, even when there was war with the house of Saul, and even after that war was over.

As the spiritual civil war starts to unfold, we, too, must always remember that we are not warring with flesh and blood, but we are actually fighting for the liberation of the very ones on the other side of the conflict. Lincoln's vision of unity included the South as a part of the Union, and to consider them anything other than Americans was to contradict his basic vision. Regardless of how deceived people may be, if they have embraced the cross of Jesus Christ, they are our brothers and sisters, and the very ones our Savior gave His life to save. We are not fighting against people but against the forces that deceive and bind them.

In a vision Philip Elston had several years ago, he saw the Lord standing with His arms outstretched. Soldiers in blue and gray uniforms were marching past Him on both sides and were laying their bloody swords on His arms. The Lord resolutely looked into the eyes of each one, saying, "No one who has his brother's blood on his sword will be used to build My house." We must never use our swords against our brothers, but only against the cords of evil that are binding them.

Some people with great influence in the body of Christ are children of their "father the devil" (John 8:44) just as there were in Israel when the Lord walked the earth. These stumbling blocks must be confronted and exposed, and then either converted or removed from their place of influence in the church. Neither the Lord nor the apostles refrained from confronting such people, exposing them, and when necessary, removing them from the church. As in the first century, these people can be distinguished by their attempts to yoke the church with bondage or sow doctrines the Scriptures call leaven.

So what can we do if this spiritual war is going to happen?

PREPARING FOR THE SPIRITUAL CIVIL WAR

I believe we should support all the movements working to bring about the unity of the church because God has sent them. These movements are meant to strengthen our unity for what is coming. We should also do all we can to reconcile with those with whom we have differences. Some we now think of as enemies will be our best friends in what is coming. And some we now think of as our best friends may become our enemies. We must do all we can to strengthen every relationship and reconcile with those we can.

We should also do all we can to strengthen the essential truths of our faith within ourselves and within others whom we are called to serve by leading. The true unity of the faith will never come at the compromise of our beliefs. We are called to follow the Lamb, not just an organization. Those who have built their spiritual lives or positions of leadership on obeying an organization, rather than seeking to follow the Lord, are in the most serious jeopardy of becoming stumbling blocks.

We are called to overcome evil with good. We cast out darkness with the light. Allow the Lord to search your heart for any way you might be using a controlling spirit, manipulation, or means other than the Holy Spirit to try to accomplish your purposes. Let us now judge ourselves, lest we be judged. If we will humble ourselves now, He will lift us up at the proper time.

Some of the greatest revivals in our nation's history took place among the Southern troops during the Civil War. Many Southern generals were leaders of the revival. The Lord came to save the rebels, among which we were all found at one time. Let us never forget that we are here to save people and set them free. The church will soon be singing "The Battle Hymn of the Republic" with much greater fervor and understanding.

Finally, we might take some direction from the vision that preceded this chapter.

WAR AND GLORY

To review the vision I titled "War and Glory," I saw an island with many different types of buildings, which I knew represented denominations or movements. The architectural clash between these buildings was so striking that it was grotesque. It was as if they were all so intent on being different, they didn't care to blend together. I could not imagine anyone desiring to enter this city, even if there had been no conflict.

The church is doing much more damage to herself through infighting than the enemies without are able to do. At the time of this vision, I was consciously surprised that the Lord did not intervene in this destructive fighting. Yet, those who were fighting against the other denominations or movements were all disqualified from being a part of the house the Lord built.

This reminded me of King David, who was not allowed to build the temple of the Lord because he was "a man of war" and had "shed blood" (1 Chron. 28:3), although this did not disqualify him from salvation or from being considered one of God's great men. I felt that many true saints, and even great people of God, were tragically disqualifying themselves from this most wonderful work by becoming embroiled in this spiritual civil war. This even caused them to lose the light that they had; only the peacemakers and those who were trying to repair and build instead of tearing down radiated with light in this vision.

I think that it was significant that almost all, if not all, of these buildings contained those who were true lights. These may appear as small lights now, but they will be the foundation on which the Lord will build His house.

Because the sea sometimes represents mass humanity in Scripture (Rev. 17:15), the multitudes are going to rise up in great waves that will destroy much of the present, visible structure of the church. Those who are true lights will not be swept away by the waves because those who walk in truth have a foundation that cannot be shaken.

The Lord's command to release the sea did not cause the sea to rise up, but just removed that which was restraining it. The sea then came against the island with fury, as if it were being controlled by a great hatred. I believe this represented a great hatred against visible, institutional Christianity that will arise, and the Lord will allow it to destroy these institutions.

When these great tidal waves had stopped, there were no Christian institutions as represented by the previous buildings. However, all of the real Christians remained. I do not think that it is wrong to keep trying to repair these structures (as the Lord honored and preserved those who did), but this vision affirmed deep within me the need to focus on building people.

Even though the earlier buildings were destroyed, they each contained people who were to be pillars in His house. The house of the

Lord was a brand-new building, but those who became its main supports were from almost every denomination and movement. The Lord is "the wise Man who brings forth from His treasures things both new and old." The Lord does have new wine to serve, but Isaiah 25:6 declares that the Lord will also serve "refined, aged wine." The Lord will not use *either* the old or the new but *both* the old and the new.

The Lord's house was built in the midst of the increasing storms of rage and lawlessness. It radiated as an even greater light because of those storms. I was encouraged that the Lord will build a church on this earth that will reflect His glory. This age will not end until He builds it.

It could not be any other way. When the Lord threatened to destroy Israel, Moses warned God that people would say that the Lord could bring people out of Egypt, but He could not lead them into the promised land. The Lord will have a testimony through the church that will last for all eternity. That testimony will be that not only can He forgive the sins of His church, but He also has the power and wisdom to deliver her from her sins and make her into a glorious bride without spot or wrinkle.

A Vision

The Next Wave Is upon Us

On May 11, 1992, I had a vision of a surfer floating on a short surfboard, gazing at the beach, lazily drifting and dreaming of the big wave. I knew that this surfer somehow represented the church in America. While this surfer was drifting, the very wave he was dreaming about was getting closer and closer, but he did not know it. I knew that unless he woke up and looked around very quickly, the wave was going to come crashing down on top of him. The result was not going to be a smooth ride! I also knew that his board was too short for the huge wave that was coming.

By the time this surfer did hear the sound of the wave and turned to look, it was too late. What had been the desire of his heart became a terror because he was not ready for it. The wave turned the surfer over and over, smashing him onto the bottom several times and breaking his board. I feared for his life, but he survived with many cuts, bruises, and a few broken bones.

I watched the surfer lying on the beach in great pain. Soon the terror of possibly dying passed and a deep wisdom replaced it. He gazed back out over the sea. Even though he was so broken and hurt he could hardly move, an awesome resolve and dignity came over him. I knew he would come back to ride the waves again.

Next I saw this surfer in a hospital with a room that looked out over the ocean. He was still gazing out over the sea, but instead of dreaming, he was now planning. Then I saw him standing on the beach, not only healed but also far more muscular than he had been before. Beside him stood the largest surfboard I have ever seen. Even though the sea was calm, he knew that the biggest wave of all was already in motion beyond the horizon. He was ready to ride the wave, but fears were rising up in him. If he did not quickly dismiss them and get moving, he would not be able to paddle out far enough and would again be in great jeopardy from the wave.

Many other surfers who looked like professional bodybuilders were standing on the beach. They all had the same short board the first surfer had at the beginning. *These bodybuilders really did not seem interested in the waves at all, but just in showing off their bodies, which to me looked grotesque. I knew their large, bulging muscles were not really as strong as the first surfer's, whose muscles seemed more natural. They had built their bodies for show, but he had built himself up for strength.*

13 CATCHING THE NEXT WAVE

America has experienced many great moves of God, but two of them were so powerful and far-reaching that *revival* was not an adequate word for them. These were so extraordinary in their social and spiritual impact, historians have called them Great Awakenings. During these great outpourings of God's grace, it seemed as if the entire nation awakened from its spiritual slumber to the bright realities of the kingdom of God. Some cities and towns experienced almost universal conversion, and whole regions were swept into the truth of the gospel. Great social changes were made and morality increased—not with the passage of laws, but with the changing of hearts.

One of these awakenings preceded the Revolutionary War, and the next preceded the Civil War. Both Great Awakenings, and both of these wars, radically changed the spiritual and social fabric of America. Another "great awakening" is coming. It, too, will have the potential to profoundly change our country. The cross and righteousness are going to be popular again. The truth of creation will not only be taught in the schools, but it will also be believed as the only logical answer to our existence. Prayer will not only be allowed in schools, it will be encouraged. The fear of God will sweep across the land like a tidal wave, crushing the frail humanistic ideologies that have so long exalted themselves as reason.

In the previous great awakenings or revivals in church history, very few individuals were anticipating the move of the Holy Spirit. In almost every one of the awakenings, the existing churches and ministries were damaged by the new move, simply because the groups were not ready for it. Some of these had to actually resist the revival just to survive. In contrast, today there seems to be almost a universal expectation of impending revival, but very little has actually been done to prepare for it. The next wave of the Holy Spirit is in reality bigger than we have dreamed, but because we are dreaming, instead of preparing, we are now in serious jeopardy from the very wave we have been hoping to see.

Moves of the Holy Spirit are often compared to waves because their characteristics are common. If the Holy Spirit moves in waves, how do we catch them so as to be carried in the direction that He is going? Six basic steps that a surfer uses can give us significant insight into what we, too, must do to catch the waves of the Holy Spirit.

STEPS TO CATCH THE NEXT WAVE

To catch the wave we must:

1. Be adequately trained and in shape.
2. Have the proper board (vehicle or ministry).
3. Discern where the wave is going to break.
4. Be properly positioned.
5. Be watching so that we can start paddling with the wave at the proper time.
6. Be ready to act without hesitation when the wave breaks.

Let's look at each of these steps individually.

1. BE ADEQUATELY TRAINED AND IN SHAPE

Every time the Lord has shown me the coming harvest, He has shown it to me in two great waves. There may be more than two waves, but I know there will be at least two. The first one will be so great that almost everyone will believe that it is the great harvest that is the end of the age. Yet, another wave coming after it will be much greater. The millions of new believers who become Christians on the first wave will be called to be laborers in the second. These people must be properly equipped and prepared for the greater wave.

The first wave of revival will only be a blessing to churches that have been using their time wisely and have been truly equipping the saints to do the work of the service. This wave will actually be judgment to every ministry that has not properly equipped its people.

In the vision that preceded this chapter, the first surfboard was so short that it was obviously inadequate for even a good-size wave, much less the awesome one that came. This picture speaks of the inadequacy of the current vehicles, outreaches, and ministries of the church. Even if the surfer had seen the wave in time, he could not have ridden it— he would have either had to quickly paddle into the beach, or out beyond where the wave was going to break to watch it go by.

Like this surfer, the present church is in danger of getting nothing more than a good beating and a good lesson out of the impending move of the Holy Spirit. Even though the church has been hearing from the Lord about the impending ingathering, we have not been acting on His words and actually taking practical steps to be ready for what is coming. But this beating will immediately bring wisdom and resolve to be ready for the next one and to have the proper vehicle for riding it. The time we spend recovering from the injuries of the impending wave must be spent in planning for the next one; then our plans must be turned into action.

To ride the wave that is coming, we will also need to be *much* stronger than we are now. Strength comes from *exercising*. When the surfer returned to the beach, he had the physique of a bodybuilder, one who had built himself up for strength, not just for show.

The body of Christ must likewise be built up. Every muscle and every limb, or every individual part of the body, must be properly exercised and brought to full strength. For decades, we have been preaching on Ephesians 4 about equipping the saints for the work of service. Now is the time to start doing it.

Many will become involved in this "spiritual bodybuilding" just for show. These people will be more devoted to impressing each other than to preparing for the next move of the Spirit. They will not really have the proper equipment for, or even be aware of, what is going on in the sea of humanity. Those who build their congregations for show will actually look grotesque and will not have the proper skills for riding the wave of the Spirit—or even be in the water when it comes.

Still another factor is required if we want to catch the biggest wave—we must resist catching the smaller ones, which means we must have the proper board.

2. HAVE THE PROPER BOARD

There are patterns to incoming waves that experienced surfers learn to recognize. Patience is required if they are going to ride the biggest and best wave. Likewise, in the Spirit we can give ourselves to many movements and become involved in many projects, but are they what we have been called to? How many of these are only working to displace us from our position when the big one comes?

I don't say this to discourage anyone from devotion to service and ministry. Indeed, the only way that we will be in shape and skilled enough to catch the big wave is by practicing on smaller ones. However, when we have been adequately prepared, and we know that the big one is coming, we must let the smaller ones go by. Many who miss the great moves of God do so because they are already too busy.

Obedience, not sacrifice, will keep us in the will of God. I do not think that I have ever met a true Christian who did not long to be in the center of God's activity. However, we must know that not all good activity is His activity. We must also understand that it is not possible for all of us to be a part of everything God is doing. The most important issue is not just catching the "big wave" but catching the one He wants us to catch. At the same time, we must cheer on those who may be catching the bigger waves, and the smaller ones, if they are in God's will.

First, the church must be adequately trained and in shape; second, we must have the proper board; and third, we must discern where the wave is going to break and get there.

3. DISCERN WHERE THE WAVE IS GOING TO BREAK AND GET THERE

Every move of God is built on the foundation of the previous moves. If we are going to discern where the next move of God is going to break, we need to discern the nature and pattern of previous ones. We must understand the spiritual "continuation principle." Even the Lord had to properly honor those who had gone before Him and prepared His way; He submitted Himself to John's baptism to "fulfill all righteousness." The chief priests and elders asked Him, "By what authority are You doing these things, and who gave You this authority?" Jesus answered them, "I will ask you one thing too, which if you tell Me, I will also tell you by what authority I do these things. The baptism of John was from what source, from heaven or from men?" (Matt. 21:23–25).

The Lord's response to their question was not an attempt to deflect the question, because the answer to His question was the answer to their question. Jesus had credentials. John was there as the representative of the old order, sent to declare that Jesus is the One of whom all the prophets and wise men from the beginning spoke.

If we arrogantly point to previous movements as the old order and declare ourselves to be of the new order, we have almost certainly disqualified ourselves from being a part of the new order. Only those who view the previous movements with honor and immerse themselves in their message and teachings will be qualified to receive the next level of authority. For any new movement to abide long on the earth, it must honor its spiritual fathers and mothers.

James gave an interesting exhortation concerning the treatment of the law, the "movement" that preceded Christianity: "Do not complain, brethren, against one another, that you yourselves may not be judged; behold, the Judge is standing right at the door" (James 5:9).

However, we are foolish if we do not learn from the mistakes of previous movements. The potential for the same faults exists within us. We must seek the grace to stand in those areas. The same forces of darkness that were able to sidetrack those moves of God will seek to steer the coming awakening away from its purpose. Just as the truth of the gospel has never changed, the deception that opposes it hasn't either.

It could be argued that if the first two Great Awakenings had not been diverted from their courses, the wars that followed them would not have been necessary. I believe the Lord intended to use the awakenings to make the needed social changes, like the end of slavery. But once political forces diverted the awakenings, the wars became inevitable. If these moves of God had been allowed to run their courses, we would have avoided the destruction and the deep, enduring scars that always result from war.

The next great awakening in America is also intended to cause sweeping spiritual and social changes that will make a future conflict unnecessary. When it comes, we must continually humble ourselves and pray for it to stay on its intended course. We must be vigilant to guard against the political forces that will seek to divert it for their own agendas. Although we may agree with the morality of these agendas, the strategies proposed for accomplishing them will be devastating to the awakening, and ultimately to the nation. It would be helpful to start reading about past revivals to prepare ourselves for the next wave.

To catch the next wave, the church must be adequately trained and in shape; we must have the proper board; we must discern where the wave is going to break and get there; and we must be properly positioned to meet this wave.

4. BE PROPERLY POSITIONED

As we keep our vision on the goal of seeing the water move as far up the beach as possible, and holding all of the ground that we can take, we will be in a better position to move forward with the next wave rather than retreating and undercutting it. It does not matter who leads a wave as long as the Leader gets the glory. To have any other attitude is to be as deluded as the donkey's colt that Jesus rode into Jerusalem. Could this animal have thought that all of the commotion and adoration was for him instead of the One riding on his back?

Unfortunately, relatively immature leaders lead most new movements. This is because the mature leaders often become "old wineskins," too inflexible to receive the new wine. The Spirit, who requires flexibility and openness, must lead spiritual movements. Sometimes the only ones He can find who are flexible enough are the immature, because they do not have preconceived ideas. Immature leaders are, therefore, more prone to be dependent on the Holy Spirit than on their experience, allowing Him to direct as He chooses. This is probably why the Lord chose such unlikely and "unqualified" men as the foundational leaders of His church. They were so unqualified that they desperately depended on His grace and guidance.

Rarely does a spiritual leader arise with great experience and wisdom, combined with a sensitive dependency on the Holy Spirit. However, such leadership is certainly preferable to that of the immature person who allows the Holy Spirit to lead, but whose lack of experience allows other influences to gain entry. For this reason, the Lord always seems to give leaders of previous movements the opportunity to lead the next one. The greatest leaders will know how to let the Holy Spirit lead and have the experience and discernment to keep the movement out of the hands of those who are lawless or legalistic.

Joshua and Caleb are two biblical examples of those who combine maturity and experience with flexibility and dependence on the Holy Spirit. Certainly they showed their dependence upon the Holy Spirit when they alone said, "We can take the land, despite the giants." Then, even though they had believed God, they had to wander in circles with the Israelites until all members of the unbelieving generation perished. This must have been a much greater test of their faith than seeing the giants or fortresses in the land. Such faith will be required for the movement that leads the church across her Jordan River into the battle for her promised land.

This faith can only be the result of two great spiritual factors. First, true faith is not encouraged or discouraged by the condition of the people, because it is not faith in people but in God. Second, true faith always views present conditions from the perspective of eternity. That is why the great men of faith in Scripture were content to know the prophetic promises without having to receive these blessings in their own time.

True faith does not look at people, and it does not look at the temporary. Some of the Lord's most anointed messages caused the crowds to shrink. Truly wise people will not be overly encouraged when others gather around them or discouraged when they depart. If we receive our encouragement from humans, it only proves that we have received our authority from them. If we receive our authority from above, no one can take it away. That is why Jesus fled to the mountains when the multitude came to make Him king. If people make you king, then people will also rule you, regardless of your title.

One of the greatest stumbling blocks to walking in true ministry is the tendency to take the people's yokes instead of the Lord's. The people's yokes will have us busy doing many things that appear good and fruitful, but they will not have us doing the Lord's will.

How many of us could begin a revival that stirs an entire city, then give that work into the hands of others so that we could witness to just one man? Philip did this (Acts 8). Philip could be entrusted with such authority and power to stir a city because of his obedience. If he had just been focused on people, or the temporary, he would never have left Samaria. However, it is probable that the fruit of that one Ethiopian eunuch's conversion was much greater than the revival in Samaria. Centuries later missionaries were astonished to find so many Christians already in Ethiopia. This fruit had been hidden to the human eye, and probably even to Philip, but it was certainly credited to his account.

One of the great leadership lessons in nature is found in migrating waterfowl such as geese and ducks. They fly in V formations because the lead bird creates a draft that makes flying easier for those who follow closely behind. However, since the lead bird is working so hard cutting through the air, it will only stay on the point for a while; then it will drop back to the end of the formation to rest. This rotation allows the birds to share the burden of leadership, and they all benefit from the draft when others are leading.

If a bird refused to give up this leadership position at the proper time, it would slow down the whole flock. Those who give up their position at the proper time will have a chance to rest while following in the wake of others, enabling them again to assume the point at another time. Seldom in church history has any leader been on the cutting edge for more than a few years. For a leader to give up leadership is difficult. We can see a clear demarcation point in the lives of those who refuse to do this; at that point they stop going forward and start attacking those who are still moving ahead.

Getting to the destination is the goal of the flying geese, not being honored as the point bird. Whenever our own position becomes a goal in itself, we will become a hindrance to the advancement of the church. A leader can have great influence and control other people long after he has lost the true anointing for spiritual leadership. King Saul certainly did.

However, Saul's counterpart, King David, was not just an extraordinary leader in his own time. David had the wisdom to realize the limits of his authority. When he understood that it was not his destiny to build the temple, he began gathering materials to pass on to his heir to make his job easier. The greatest leaders not only know how far to go themselves—they know how to prepare for the next generation, and when to pass on the scepter.

To catch the next wave, we must be properly positioned to meet the wave, and we must be watching so we can paddle with this wave at the proper time.

5. BE WATCHING SO WE CAN PADDLE WITH THE WAVE AT THE PROPER TIME

Some people position themselves properly but hesitate to move until the wave is on them. These people are in as much danger of missing the wave as those who have not positioned themselves at all. A major source of this hesitancy is a religious spirit rooted in human idealism that will not move until something is "totally God."

A minister once congratulated a farmer on the precision and lushness of his cornfield, remarking, "You could not have done that without God." "I agree," said the farmer, "but He could not do it without me either. You should see the field I let Him grow by Himself. It's all weeds!"

This story makes an important point. The Lord does not do anything without His people. God commissioned Adam to "cultivate the garden." As Psalm 115:16 states, "The heavens are the heavens of the LORD; but the earth He has given to the sons of men." That is why He will not do anything unless we pray. He has delegated to the church the awesome responsibility to bind and loose on the earth. However, when we pray for things, such as revival, we should start preparing for them.

Even the greatest man of God is an earthen vessel, imperfect and frail. As James explained, "We all stumble in many ways" (James 3:2). Every true move of God has begun with a considerable amount of humanity mixed in. There will always be tares among the wheat. If you are going to wait until all of the tares are removed, you will miss the entire harvest.

The Opposition

Each wave will try to make it as far up the beach as it can. Then the wave recedes, undercutting the next wave, making it break sooner than it would otherwise. Seldom have those who were a part of one move of God gone on to be a part of the next move. Usually those of a previous move are retreating as the next wave advances, creating a clash that hinders the incoming wave.

Throughout church history, those who were a part of one move of God have tried to resist and undercut those of the next move. However, even though this has continually been our history, it does not have to be our future. Before the end, a movement will so capture the hearts of those in the previous movements that they will join the advance rather than continue the retreat. When this happens, the church will begin a spiritual advance that will not be stopped until the end of the age.

Looking at some of the historic factors that have caused others to retreat can help us discern these stumbling blocks. The first dangerous delusion is for us to think that we would never oppose a true move of God. Yet, it has happened to some of the greatest men in church history.

Andrew Murray is a good example of a great man of God with a passion for seeing revival come to the church, yet he failed to recognize the revival he had spent his entire life praying for. The cause for this tragic failure was simple. The revival that he hoped for, and even prophesied, did not come in the form he was expecting. Though he earnestly desired again to see the release of spiritual gifts within the church, he was offended by the package they arrived in.

Finally, we need to be ready to act without hesitation when the next wave comes.

6. BE READY TO ACT WITHOUT HESITATION

Even though the surfer in my vision was properly prepared and had a suitable board for riding the next wave, the enemy used the negative experience of the previous wave to hit him with a fear that could have hindered him from accomplishing all that he had prepared for. All of our preparation and work will come to nothing if we are not utterly committed to getting back in the water and walking by faith, not by fear.

Yet this surfer was now fully equipped. He was not only healed but far more muscular than before. Beside him stood the largest surfboard I had ever seen. He was ready. For the big one, we need to be ready.

A Vision

A Bridge to Revival

In a vision in 1997, I saw the transition period between renewal (which works to heal and awaken the church) and revival (which results in the salvation of the lost and the empowering of believers to challenge the spiritual darkness of the times). In the vision, this period was portrayed as a bridge between two fields. The first field progressed from what looked like fallow ground, overgrown with weeds and littered with debris, to land that was plowed and sown. I knew that this field represented the work of renewal.

At the end of this field, a bridge was under construction, which was being built with different-size stones, from very large ones to those that were very small. The names on each stone represented a different movement or ministry—and in some cases individual people. This bridge was built without sides, making it a little precarious to cross, but this also enabled it to be easily widened to accommodate more traffic, which was constantly being done.

The stones on this bridge were all different, but they fit together like interlocking pieces of a puzzle. This made the entire bridge very strong. The undergirding pillars were made out of what appeared to be pure light. However, this light also had substance. The pillars along one side had the fruit of the Spirit written on them. Those on the other side had the gifts of the Spirit. The interlocking girders had biblical truths written on them. I felt that these pillars were strong enough to hold any weight that could possibly be put on the bridge. In a strange way it seemed as if this bridge were holding up the earth—not the other way around.

The workmen on the bridge were a diverse group of people, from very young children to the very elderly, men and women, and seemingly from all races. Businessmen and -women were working right next to those who looked as if they were homeless. I recognized artists, musicians, athletes, news correspondents, soldiers, and policemen. These had been transformed into apostles, prophets, evangelists, pastors, teachers, administrators, those with gifts of helps and other ministries. They seemed to fit perfectly with the diversity of the stones they were setting into their place on the bridge.

As these people constructed the bridge, they were under constant attack from flies and from stones that were being thrown at them from seemingly every direction. Over them there were dark clouds that I recognized as spirits of depression. Regardless of the attacks, these workmen never stopped their work. In fact, they hardly paid any attention to the attacks. When one of the workers was severely wounded, he or she would be carried over the bridge into the other field. Then one of the workers from that field would take his or her place on the bridge.

The field on the other side of the bridge was composed of plants that were just beginning to sprout as well as those with an abundance of fruit that was ripe for harvest—all mixed together. Some of this field seemed to be tended very well, with the plants in straight rows and with almost no weeds. Other parts were so overgrown with weeds and other plants that they looked almost impenetrable. Yet, the abundance and quality of the fruit even there were extraordinary. One thing that stood out to me as I looked at this field was that I only recognized a few of the many different types of fruit.

Those who had been wounded while working on the bridge were quickly healed as they ate some of the ripened fruit from this field. However, they did not return to the bridge; instead they began tending that field. Where the faces of those working on the bridge were filled with determination and a certain urgency, the faces of those working in the field seemed more relaxed, even though the fruit was ripening faster than they could gather it. This was not the relaxed attitude that comes from the peace of the Lord, but rather one that seemed to stem from an unholy casualness.

Also, very poor coordination existed between those who were picking the fruit and those who were carrying it to the place where it was cleaned and packaged. Coordination also seemed to be lacking among the pickers. They wandered about, working where they wanted to. Then I noticed the faces of those who were cleaning and packaging the fruit. They seemed overly harried and were therefore dropping and losing more of the fruit than they were getting into the packages.

I could see bottlenecks everywhere that were devastating to the efficiency of the entire harvest. All the people just seemed to be doing their own thing with no supervision. More laborers were badly needed for the abundance of the harvest, but I knew that more laborers would only make the situation worse if there were no supervisors. One of the workers on the bridge then said to me, "You must start praying for the apostles to come. We must have apostles." It seemed as if every worker on the bridge turned to acknowledge the importance of this.

Then the same kinds of attacks that came on the workers on the bridge came on the workers in the field. Here the flies did not just harass them, they also started to devour the fruit. Then stones would come in waves, knocking some of the fruit from the plants and wounding some of the workers. I knew that the flies were lies, and the stones were false witnesses and accusations. Some of the workers kept working during these attacks, but most would stop, and some would even leave the field.

Finally, some of those who had crossed the bridge formed teams to protect parts of the field. Workers then returned to those parts of the field. Some would try to gather the fruit that had been knocked from the plants by the stones, but it would rot very fast, and most of it was lost.

Those who crossed the bridge immediately started harvesting the fruit. The ripe fruit was put into a great assortment of different types and sizes of baskets. Some of the workers harvested fruit that was not yet ripe simply because they did not recognize the fruit and could not tell if it was ripe. This created arguments between the harvesters. Finally, a supervisor appeared. His first directive was for the laborers to harvest only the fruit they recognized and knew was ripe. This brought striking peace on all the workers in that area. The resolve and confidence of the harvesters grew dramatically just because someone supervised.

Even though multitudes began crossing the bridge, it did not seem that there were nearly enough workers to keep up with the fruit that was becoming ripe. I saw the work of widening the bridge so that more people could cross to be one of the most urgent tasks. At the end of this vision, my whole attention was on the bridge. I was given time to study many of the stones. As I looked at each individual stone, I would start to know its strengths and weaknesses and the movement or ministry that it represented. My attention was especially drawn to the individuals whose job it was to see that the different stones fit together, as I was impressed again by how the interlocking of these different stones was the strength of the bridge. Some of these I will explain in a general sense in the next chapter.

14 | WHY REVIVAL TARRIES FOR AMERICA

Over the last century and a half, the American church has been accustomed to being on the cutting edge of spiritual advances. However, in the last few years, she has fallen behind in the spiritual activity found in many other regions of the world. One question people frequently ask me is: "Why does the Lord seem to be doing so much in other countries and so little in America?"

Let me define exactly what I mean by *revival*. In this context, I am defining *revival* as "a restoration after a decline of true religious faith among those who have become indifferent." Obviously, I am also including the awakening and salvation of those who are not believers so that the social fabric of society is changed by righteousness.

Revival is coming to America. It is imminent. I believe that the American church has a prominent place on the bridge that I saw in the vision I shared in the last chapter. However, in America powerful stumbling blocks have arisen whose primary purpose is obviously to oppose and, if possible, even thwart the coming revival. We must address these stumbling blocks if we are going to receive the full benefit of this awakening. Even though I do not believe that these stumbling blocks will be able to stop the revival altogether, they can limit its scope, depth, duration, and fruit.

The Scriptures teach that the harvest will begin with the tares being taken out first (Matt. 13:30, 41–43, 49), and this has been going on for some time. This may be painful for a season, but this pain will be appreciated when the full harvest begins, and we are able to avoid making some of the same mistakes that they have been causing. Just as there has been a period of the Lord cleansing His church by exposing sin, we are now entering a period when He will remove the stumbling blocks. Though sin is, of course, a stumbling block to God's purposes, the primary stumbling blocks to God's moves that have now set themselves up as strongholds in the church are rooted much more in pride than in moral transgressions.

In one of the remarkable statements made in the New Testament, Peter said that we should be "looking for *and hastening* the coming of the day of God" (2 Peter 3:12, emphasis added). Is it possible that we can have something to do with "hastening the coming of the day of God"? Yes! Obviously, Peter would not have said this if it were not possible. If we can hasten the coming of His day, we can also delay it. Therefore, it behooves us to honestly address the stumbling blocks causing revival to tarry for America.

STUMBLING BLOCKS TO REVIVAL

Two stumbling blocks prevent revival from occurring in America: pride and unholy skepticism.

1. PRIDE

Some American Christians seem to think that what is happening in the United States is all God is doing. This mentality has often caused us to miss what He is doing in other places, losing the cross-pollination from other great moves of God. Just as any flock that only interbreeds will get weaker with each succeeding generation, every church, denomination, or movement that does not interrelate with other movements will get weaker with each succeeding generation. This has been the case with many in America over the last few decades.

If we will look closely at the true condition of the church in America, we will discover that we have been very shallow in our faith and in our fruit. Our lack of historical perspective and comprehensive worldview has caused us to develop theologies and eschatologies incomprehensible to the rest of the international body of Christ, inhibiting further interrelations.

The great scandals involving television evangelists during the 1980s did much to discourage the American church, but the end result has been healthy. These scandals caused us to take a hard look at some erroneous theology, spiritual pride, and other issues that laid the foundation for these mistakes. Proverbs warns us: "Pride goes before destruction, and a haughty spirit before stumbling" (Prov. 16:18). We must understand how this pride entered if we are going to get rid of it and advance again. Then, we must keep it out so that we do not stumble when we *do* advance. The Scriptures warn that "God resists the proud, but gives grace to the humble" (James 4:6 NKJV).

The Grace by Which We Stand

The apostle Paul referred to "this grace in which we stand" (Rom. 5:2). No one can stand except by God's grace. This may sound like a mere cliché, but some clichés are crammed with reality. This one is a profound biblical truth! Peter's experience is one of the great examples of this in Scripture. When Jesus told him that he would deny the Lord, Peter responded by protesting, "No way. I would never do such a thing." Instead of clinging to the Son of God and praying for help, Peter thought he knew more than Jesus did!

Pride is thinking that we can stand on our own—that we do not need God. This attitude caused the Fall in the beginning and has been involved in every fall since. Peter was no coward. That same night, he had charged a detachment of Roman soldiers and temple police by himself (John 18:3). However, by morning he could not even stand before a servant girl! The Lord did not cause Peter to fall; He just removed the grace by which Peter was standing.

Galatians 6:7 states, "Do not be deceived, God is not mocked; for whatever a man sows, this he will also reap." If we want to reap grace, we must sow grace. If we sow judgment, we will reap the same. We have been clearly warned:

> Do not judge and you will not be judged; and do not condemn, and you will not be condemned; pardon, and you will be pardoned. (Luke 6:37)

Therefore you are without excuse, every man of you who passes judgment, for in that you judge another you condemn yourself; for you who judge practice the same things. (Rom. 2:1)

During the 1970s and 1980s, the American church fostered many doctrines and attitudes that seemed especially designed to feed our pride. This set us up for a great fall. Even if individually we did not hold to some of these doctrines, we were only preserved from doing so by the grace of God. Every public fall was meant to bring conviction on all of us.

Someone once said, "If you do not change your direction, you will end up where you are headed." I submit that the church in America does not want to end up where she is now headed. Our bitterness and lack of forgiveness of those who, in a sense, took the fall for all of us restrain the grace that releases genuine revival. We must learn the lessons that led to such tragic falls; but we must not do it in a spirit of bitterness, or we ourselves will fall.

David as an Example

None of the men who were publicly defrocked in the twentieth century have yet transgressed to the degree that King David did in his affair with Bathsheba. Not only did he commit adultery, but he also murdered one of his most faithful men in order to cover it up. It was probably for this reason that all of Israel joined Absalom in a conspiracy against David (2 Sam. 15:13).

It may have been hard to understand how David could still be God's man after such behavior, but the Lord never removed the anointing from David. In spite of all the appearances, Zadok the priest recognized that the anointing was still on David and remained faithful to him. Because of this, God blessed Zadok with the promise that his sons would always minister in the presence of the Lord. Today we are in desperate need of the discernment of Zadok.

David's sin did not catch the Lord by surprise. When He called David, He knew that this evil was in his heart, and that in the right circumstances it would be exposed. He used David before the fall and afterward. It could be argued that David's greatest prophetic psalms were written after his fall. His sin caused him to know the depths of his Redeemer's grace. Knowing that grace enabled God to raise David to even greater spiritual heights.

In one of the most unfathomable demonstrations of God's grace in Scripture, the Lord actually anointed David and Bathsheba's son, Solomon, as the heir to the throne and made him a direct ancestor of Jesus. How could He possibly do this? Does this not actually condone adultery and even murder? Of course not! It is simply another revela‑ tion of God's great grace and heart for redemption. He can and will take even our worst mistakes and use them for good. It is no less of a marvel that the Lord would choose Solomon than that He would choose the sons of Adam to become His own sons and daughters, and that He would even determine to make His abode among us.

Some of the leaders who have stumbled in our time will be raised up again. In fact, some of them will go on to reach even greater spiritual heights. This will be a testimony to the world that our God really is a God of redemption, and He has the power to redeem even our most tragic mistakes.

Does this imply that we should sin so that an even greater grace can come? Paul replied to those who asserted such foolishness:

What shall we say then? Are we to continue in sin that grace might increase? May it never be! How shall we who died to sin still live in it? Or do you not know that all of us who have been baptized into Christ Jesus have been baptized into His death? Therefore we have been buried with Him through baptism into death, in order that as Christ was raised from the dead through the glory of the Father, so we too might walk in newness of life. (Rom. 6:1–4)

Because of David's repentance he was restored, and the Holy Spirit was not taken from him. Even so, the law of reaping and sowing still applied, and David paid a high price for this sin. His household was never to know peace again; the sins of the fathers were passed on to his children. To sin so grace might increase is to "trample under foot the

Son of God" (Heb. 10:29) and to set in motion repercussions that are never worth the fleeting, shallow pleasure inherent in the sin.

Even though David's sin released the seeds of tragedy in his own family, the Lord preserved David's throne so completely that it will last forever. Jesus Himself is seated on the throne of David. The Lord extended His grace to David so freely because David had shown so much grace toward his predecessor, Saul. Even after the Lord had removed the Holy Spirit from King Saul, David would not lift his hand against the king during his most terrible atrocities because he was "the LORD's anointed" (1 Sam. 24:6). The Lord would have to remove him because the Lord had put him in authority, regardless of how tragic Saul's error.

Many fallen men of God will use "Don't touch the Lord's anointed" as a shield to protect themselves against correction. Does this mean that we must allow known sin to continue and those who commit it to continue in leadership in the church? No. But we must carefully follow the biblical mandate for bringing correction, lest we put ourselves in jeopardy. (See Chapter 3 and Matt. 18:15–17.)

This is not to imply that we should just be blind to mistakes. The Scriptures are brutally honest about how they portray even the greatest spiritual heroes. However, their mistakes were not written to punish or humiliate them; they were written for the sake of instructing others who would come after them. They were not written to expose scandalous activities or, worse, to attack those who threaten us or are difficult for us to understand.

God's intent is to restore sinners, not just to expose them: "Brethren, even if a man is caught in *any trespass*, you who are spiritual, restore such a one in a spirit of gentleness; each one looking to yourself, lest you too be tempted" (Gal. 6:1, emphasis added). If we do not bring correction in the right spirit, we can open ourselves to the same temptations and sin. Regardless of how anointed we are, or how repulsed we are by certain sins, if God removes the grace from our lives because of pride, we can fall to what we may abhor the most.

Pride is the first issue that inhibits revival in America; unholy skepticism is the second.

2. UNHOLY SKEPTICISM

American journalism has crossed a line that has made it one of the primary platforms of the "accuser of the brethren" and a major stumbling block to spiritual advancement in this country. This extends beyond secular journalism to include much of the Christian media, which, at times, has proved to be even less honorable and truthful in its reporting than the secular press. Many of the basic policies of the Christian media are founded more upon a humanistic philosophy of journalism than on biblical principles. Today, the Christian media is one of the greatest sources of a deadly poison that is sowing destruction in the Western church—the spirit of unrighteous judgment.

There is a pure form of skepticism (the kind displayed by the Bereans who searched the Scriptures to verify Paul's and Barnabas's message—Acts 17:11) that wants to see the best until it is proved wrong. Another form of skepticism, however, wants to see the worst in others because that somehow makes this person look bigger or at least feel better about his own flaws. That kind of doubt is the most tragic. When the chronicles of this earth are read on the great Judgment Day, I believe we will learn that this evil doubt was far more deadly than cancer or AIDS. Great souls rise to even greater heights by lifting others higher.

Evidenced by the News Media

Since the 1960s, the news media of the West, including the Christian media, seem to have been almost completely overtaken by this dark side of skepticism. It is now almost unthinkable for a Christian journalist to write an article about a church, a movement, or an event without making some derogatory observations. This is often done through hearsay or even gossip in its lowest form. The targets of the slander are not even contacted for their side of the story. Make no mistake about it; those who pass on gossip are just as guilty as the originators. All of this is usually done under the guise of information or in an effort to protect the people from error. However, are we really protecting them when we commit one of the most serious errors of all? Those who set themselves up as judges in the church are in jeopardy of being stumbling blocks. This does not imply that we should overlook sin or poor leadership, but the Scriptures are clear about how we should deal with such things. When we depart from these Scriptures, we put ourselves in far worse jeopardy of ultimate judgment than those we judge.

Does such journalism justify departure from the biblical exhortation: "Let no unwholesome word proceed from your mouth, but only such a word as is good for edification according to the need of the moment, that it may give grace to those who hear" (Eph. 4:29)? *Edification* means "to build up." Is our criticism intended to build up or just tear down? Answering this simple question can help protect us from making a terrible transgression.

In Matthew 18:15–17 Jesus gave the procedure to keep us from becoming stumbling blocks. Not following this procedure, especially in journalism, has inflicted more damage on the church than the heresies we try to expose. We are exhorted in James 3:13–18:

Who among you is wise and understanding? Let him show by his good behavior his deeds in the gentleness of wisdom. But if you have bitter jealousy and selfish ambition in your heart, do not be arrogant and so lie against the truth. This wisdom is not that which comes down from above, but is earthly, natural, demonic. For where jealousy and selfish ambition exist, there is disorder and every evil thing. But the wisdom from above is first pure, then peaceable, gentle, reasonable, full of mercy and good fruits, unwavering, without hypocrisy. And the seed whose fruit is righteousness is sown in peace by those who make peace.

Alexander Solzhenitsyn once said, "The press has become the greatest power within the Western countries, exceeding that of the legislature, the executive, and the judiciary. Yet one would like to ask: According to what law has it been elected, and to whom is it responsible?" Solzhenitsyn's question is valid for Western society and especially for the church. The Lord appointed elders to give the church both protection and direction, not journalists. We should be very thankful for the freedom of the press that we enjoy, but all freedoms come with responsibility.

Where Are the Elders?

The office of elder was the highest and most respected appointed office in the local church. The very meaning of the word *elder* implies a certain degree of longevity in faithful service to the church before a man was given this influence.

Writing can be an aspect of a biblical ministry, and some journalists have obvious spiritual ministries as teachers and pastors. Some of these people have complied with the biblical standards for leaders in the church, and their faithfulness and wisdom over a period of time should enable us to recognize them as true elders. However, complying with the biblical procedures for bringing correction in the church is critical for elders, or they, too, can become stumbling blocks. Paul warned the elders he had appointed for the church at Ephesus that "from among yourselves men will rise up, speaking perverse things" (Acts 20:30 NKJV). Just because we have been recognized or appointed to an office does not mean that we cannot fall.

Many who are sources of the prevailing critical spirit now permeating the church are standing on a carnal platform of influence rather than a true anointing. Some received their position from professional training in schools founded on a humanistic philosophy of journalism. This philosophy has the appearance of wisdom and a genuine search for truth, but is in conflict with the Truth Himself. Others have been given a true commission from God, but have succumbed to the spirit of the world. Secular schools may be able to teach us the mechanics of writing, but the philosophy they impart to their students has been devastating to Christian media.

John said, "The whole world lies in the power of the evil one" (1 John 5:19). The ways of the world are not God's ways. The apostle Paul exhorted: "In reference to your former manner of life, you lay aside the old self, which is being corrupted in accordance with the lusts of deceit, and that you be renewed in the spirit of your mind, and put on the new self, which in the likeness of God has been created in righteousness and holiness of the truth" (Eph. 4:22–24).

If we're going to be created in righteousness, holiness, and truth, we must put on a new self and live by a philosophy different from that of the world.

Good Intentions

Many Christian journalists enter the field intending to provide an alternative source of information to the secular media. This is a noble vision and is truly needed. The church is called to be the pillar and support of the truth. However, the accuracy of reporting in Christian journalism seems to be no higher than in secular journalism—it merely has a more spiritual slant. The investigative reporting done by Christian journalists on the events I have personally witnessed, or about people whom I know personally, has been shockingly dishonest. Some were so prone to the use of gossip, hearsay, and conjecture that they could rival some supermarket tabloids. Truth is our most precious commodity, and we cannot continue to allow it to be compromised.

To whom are Christian journalists accountable? To what standards are they held accountable? Who gave them authority to bring correction to the church?

These are important questions. Just as the secular media can now manipulate public opinion and often dictate public policy sometimes even more effectively than our elected officials, Christian journalists can do the same. Who gave them this power? Did it come from an ability to be articulate, or because of God's anointing and commission? Do any of us have the right to massive influence in the church just because we have the marketing ability to distribute our magazines, newsletters, or programs?

I am honestly not trying to point the finger at others without including myself. When I received the commission from the Lord to begin a publishing ministry, I received a stern warning. I was told that much of what was done in the name of Christian journalism, God called gossip, and that He was going to judge the industry because of it. I did not receive this warning from a man, but directly from the Lord, and my ears are still ringing with it.

James warned, "Let not many of you become teachers, my brethren, knowing that as such we shall incur a stricter judgment" (James 3:1). It is a most sober matter to have influence in the Lord's own household! Let us be very careful how we attain it and how we use it. Paul explained that he did not presume to go beyond the sphere of authority that was appointed to him (2 Cor. 10:14–18). We all have realms of authority, but if we go beyond them, we will be in jeopardy of going beyond the grace that has been given to us to stay in the Way.

Judgment on Journalism

During recent years, Christian television ministries have come under intense judgment. At one time the trust and esteem of televangelists probably sank lower than that of any other professional group. It is not over yet, but this judgment is now beginning to come on journalism. The unholy foundations of journalism are about to be shaken, but judgment begins "with the household of God" (1 Peter 4:17). Christian journalism is soon going to come under the same kind of judgment as television ministries.

In the next millennium, we will enter a period when the unholy skeptics of Christian magazines, journals, newsletters, and newspapers will receive the same judgment they measured out to others. Even those who have tried to be honest and fair, but have been operating on a humanistic foundation, will see their foundations collapse.

Can this judgment be avoided? I believe the Scriptures clearly teach that all impending judgment can be diverted by genuine repentance. We can judge ourselves lest we be judged. Yet repentance is more than asking for forgiveness for our wrongs—repentance is going back to where we missed the turn and getting on the right road, which often includes restitution when we have injured others.

In writing this, I do not point the finger of judgment at any particular group or ministry. When Paul Cain and I wrote a prophetic bulletin addressing the "spirit of intolerance" in the religious right, we were often asked why we did not name particular groups or people. I can honestly say we didn't because we were not thinking of any particular groups or individuals. When Paul received this word, he hardly even knew what the religious right was, and I considered myself a part of the "religious right" that needed to be convicted.

I know some who are specifically guilty of what I have addressed here. I have gone to some in private about these matters and try always to be open to go to others. I am trying to keep them from the terrible fate of being stumbling blocks through their reporting or writing. If there is no repentance, I will continue through the rest of the process outlined in Matthew 18. I know others who follow the same process.

The Grace of True Authority

Possibly the main reason the church is so full of unrighteous judgment is because no format exists for righteous judgment. Until the elders take their proper place in the city gates, we will continue to be subject to the judgment of the secular media and heresy hunters. Regardless of how well intentioned they are, they sow division and unrighteous judgment that are as damaging as the heresies themselves.

Church leaders on every level must address this issue if we are going to accomplish our purpose for this hour. Unrighteous judgment can be seen as a source of most of the conflicts in the world, and the church is called to be the light of this world. That is, we are called to have the answers to the world's pressing problems. But how can we bring righteous judgment to the world if we cannot even judge ourselves?

America is the only nation on earth made up of people from every other country. Our unique spiritual and physical constitution has positioned us to be in the best place to address some of the ultimate issues at the end of this age. Many of the issues that are now our weaknesses and even our stumbling blocks will be turned into strengths and stepping-stones to a much higher place than we have been. Let us address them and overcome them with a devotion to live by the highest standards of God's grace and righteous tolerance that will glorify our Lord's name. When He saw our condition, He did not condemn us, for we were already condemned. Instead, He gave His life to save us. Let us do the same for one another.

Finally, what stepping-stones are hastening the coming revival? In my vision in 1997, I saw a few of them and their strengths and weaknesses.

THE STEPPING-STONES TO REVIVAL

In the vision I related previously about the bridge, I saw stepping-stones to revival. These were the stones being placed in the bridge, some of which I will relate here.

PRAYER MOVEMENTS

In my vision interlocking prayer movements spanned the bridge, from side to side and from one end to the other, all the way across. These stones touched the earth on both sides. Whenever a worker could not find a piece to fit, he or she would look among the prayer movements and always find one. Not only were these the most numerous and prominent stones, they also tied the entire bridge together. Their strength was their flexibility; they were able to fit almost anywhere. Their weakness was the same as their strength. They were so flexible and easily shaped that the footprints of those crossing the bridge could be impressed in them, causing them to bend out of shape. They could be bent back; however, this cost the workers a lot of time.

I was told that the soul of these movements was Seoul. From there a mushroom cloud arose and spread over the entire earth. This spiritual radiation was an energy that pierced the flesh of man, and there was nowhere to hide from it. These prayer movements somehow softened and prepared all flesh for the gospel.

British Revival

So many of the workers on this bridge were from London that it became known as "London Bridge." London once ruled an empire that spanned every continent to the point that a popular saying was "The sun never sets on the British Empire." In a way, the bridge between renewal and revival will ultimately span the earth, connecting people, cultures, and nations. What the British did in the natural realm foreshadowed building this bridge that the Lord's messengers will cross to carry the gospel of the kingdom. This is also why one of the main recipients of the renewal movements was the British, including the British Commonwealth nations. They are called to be the primary builders of this bridge to revival. This was also one reason for the great Welsh Revival, and the blueprints for this bridge can be found in Wales.

That the British were so involved in the construction of this bridge caused many to trust it. However, for others this was a reason for distrust. British involvement was a serious bottleneck until German and Jewish builders joined the British movements in this work. Then everyone seemed to trust the bridge, and the bottleneck was opened.

The Brownsville Revival

The Brownsville Revival in Pensacola, Florida, was a stone that many seemed to want to step on as they crossed from the renewal side to revival. This brown and red stone was not attractive, but these colors represented devotion to service and to the cross. Brownsville's great strength was its willingness to sacrifice for the Lord's purposes. Its main weakness came from this same willingness. Its people could be lured into making sacrifices that God had not called them to make. Because the enemy cannot stop them, he will try to push them too far.

This stone was being stretched to the point where it could be easily broken. Even so, many laborers for the coming harvest will get their marching orders at Brownsville. Those who chose to step on that stone became some of the most confident, effective harvesters when they reached the revival field.

As people came out of the first field, their shoes were covered with mud. As they progressed across the bridge, the mud rubbed off on the stones, and their shoes became clean. I felt that the shoes represented the message of the gospel. Since Pensacola was one of the first stones in the bridge, it was caked with mud from the shoes of those who were just starting to cross. Because of this, that stone needed constant cleaning to keep from becoming a stumbling block to those starting to cross the bridge. I was reminded of the proverb: "Watch over your heart with all diligence, for from it flow the springs of life" (Prov. 4:23).

Specific Cities

A long span of stones in the middle of the bridge seemed to represent specific cities across America. Following Pensacola were Jacksonville,

Florida; Mobile, Alabama; then Baton Rouge, Louisiana; Dallas and Fort Worth, Texas; Phoenix, Arizona; and Los Angeles, California. I felt that works were going to rise up in each of these cities that were crucial to this bridge, and they would ultimately be linked closely together. These stones did not go all the way across the bridge, but together they reached more than halfway.

Then stones representing cities in the islands of the Pacific and on the continent of Asia became prominent. Singapore; Hong Kong; Sydney, Australia; and a number of cities in India all stood out to me because they were colored like British flags. This seemed to represent the British influence that in some way had prepared them for their destiny. (I later prayed about this and was reminded that the British spread the English language and culture in preparation for what is coming, just as Alexander the Great helped spread the use of the Greek language in preparation for the spreading of the gospel in the first century.)

The Baptists

The Baptists have a high purpose in preparing for the coming harvest, and they will provide many of the laborers for the harvest at the end of the age. The strength of the stone that represented the Baptists was that it was made out of very strong elements. Its weakness was that it was so strong, it had a hard time bonding with the concrete and other stones on the bridge. Even though it was hard for the workers to use, it was worth it because it added greatly to the strength and size of the entire bridge.

The Dream Center

The name on this stone is the nickname for the Los Angeles International Church, and I believe this is its name in heaven. This stone was shaped like a triangle; its small point faced the beginning of the bridge, and the stone continually got broader as it proceeded toward the other side. This stone reproduced other stones that were shaped like little anchors that represented hope. These were placed next to stones that were pale and weak, which gave them strength. Together I felt that these stones enabled the bridge to carry more weight. However, these stones were also very fragile. They were easily scratched and could even be crushed. These represented the beginning of hope—which can be a very fragile thing.

Promise Keepers

The stone that represented the national men's movement Promise Keepers was very broad but not long. I felt that this represented its inclusiveness and possibly its endurance. What enabled it to be broad also caused it to be dangerously thin in places. Even so, it was a prominent part of the bridge. Because of this the enemy hurled two large rocks—Jealousy and Division—at it, trying to hit the places where it was thin in order to shatter it.

Women's Movements

Numerous stones represented different women's movements. Many of these were very large. Some were prayer movements, which were shaped like arrowheads. Arrows shot from these stones would strike down the attacks thrown at the other movements, such as those coming at Promise Keepers. One common characteristic of these stones was that they all had the ability to absorb heat from the sun. This kept the entire bridge warm so that ice could not form on it. The heat from these stones also kept the people moving across the bridge. This was essential because many wanted to stop on a certain stone, but they couldn't because their feet would begin to burn.

Other Movements

Many other large stones made up this bridge. Some of these were movements I could recognize, but most I could not. This was because I do not think that they yet exist, indicating that many new movements will come forth to be a part of this bridge between renewal and revival. Also many church associations, or fellowships of churches, started banding together. When they did, their size grew and quickly began to widen the bridge.

Almost every spiritual advance in history has come from a movement originally created by spiritual pioneers who eventually settled somewhere, like a denomination. Denominations may now have a place in the purposes of God, occupying spiritual territory while pioneers continue to take more land.

I also saw a large pile of discarded stones of all sizes. These could not be used in the bridge. Some were too brittle and would break too easily. Others were not "living stones." Some had an exterior that looked strong and alive, but just below their thin, fragile surface they were nothing but sand. Others had edges that were too sharp to touch. Many denominations were in this pile, along with a surprising number of movements and ministries.

TROUBLED WATERS

Even though the bridge was still under construction, it was beautiful, emanating life, peace, and great joy. However, the large river underneath it was repulsive, composed of raw sewage, mixed occasionally with large streams of blood. It was such a torrent. It seemed as if the entire earth were discarding its waste into this river. I felt this represented the times in which this bridge was being built. The greatest danger for the workers was to fall into the river or to drop one of the stones into it.

Occasionally, great waves would come down the river that engulfed the bridge. Yet, the waves never really damaged the bridge because of the strength of its pillars. However, both the workers and the bridge had to be washed from the spray of this foul torrent. Some who were crossing the bridge stayed too close to the edge and were swept away by these surges. Each time a wave poured over the bridge it would carry away stones from the pile that could not be used. Eventually the only stones that were left were those that were a part of the bridge.

The church has been in a period of renewal in the twentieth century. Multitudes have been healed and restored. Vision and faith have been rising steadily over the last few years. This has been a wonderful time, but it is merely a preparation for what is coming. In the twenty-first century, we will cross this bridge from renewal to revival. Now is the time for us to ask ourselves if we are ready.

15 PROPHECY FOR THE 21ST CENTURY

The night the *Titanic* sank, one of the ship's officers was sifting through a large pile of requests and recommendations from the passengers on her maiden voyage. The majority were frivolous requests, but the requests were treated as if they were the mandates of royalty. Buried in the pile was a request from a watchman for a pair of binoculars. It was disregarded.

That same watchman was the very one who first spotted the iceberg just before they struck it. Had he been given the binoculars, he might have seen the iceberg in time for the ship to avoid it. For the lack of a fifty-dollar pair of binoculars, the greatest, most expensive ship that had ever been built was doomed, along with the majority of her passengers and crew.

The binocular incident was just one in a whole series of bad decisions made by the captain and officers of the *Titanic*. However, I think this one is especially relevant to the church.

In prophetic dreams and visions, ships often speak of leadership. The *Titanic* was not the only ship sailing the oceans then, and we cannot imply that its message applies to all leaders. However, it was the one almost everyone considered to be so well built that it could not be sunk. That delusion, more than anything else, led to her tragedy. In spite of the incredible series of bad judgments, a simple pair of binoculars would have almost certainly saved the ship that night. This chapter is a call to the leaders of the church to be sure they have a pair of binoculars for the twenty-first century.

The sea is now calm, and many of us are surrounded by unprecedented luxury. The bands are playing; the party is at a high point. Even so, we are approaching some dangerous waters. We may be warm and comfortable now, but we will be introduced to some very cold water if we do not wake up from our stupor.

In the last few years, the need for the prophetic ministry has gone from important to critical. Entire television channels are now devoted to psychics because people are so desperate to hear a supernatural word about their future. Even though prophets have been gifted to do this, the church is not fulfilling this need to let people hear a message from God. Therefore, the devil is quickly filling the void. The most shocking statistic is the number of Christians who are now calling psychics, in clear violation of the Scriptures and contrary to basic discernment. The adage has become true, "If you deny a man food, he will gobble poison."

BURYING OUR TALENTS

The church has been entrusted with the gift of prophecy, words of knowledge, and words of wisdom far superior to anything the devil is producing through psychics. Yet, much of the church remains either oblivious to these gifts or afraid of them. Both of these responses are easy to understand, but neither is justifiable.

We have now come to a time when we can no longer choose to ignore the important gifts the Lord gave to His church through the Holy Spirit. Mature prophets are usually used for strategic prophecies, but individual and personal prophecy should flow throughout the church. Prophecy is not just for prophets. The prophet's calling is to equip the church to know the Lord's voice and to be used in the prophetic gifts.

To release prophecy throughout the church is understandably a terrifying thought to many leaders. However, prophecy is not that difficult for a pastor with the proper biblical foundation to judge. The consequences of not releasing this ministry are quickly becoming far more expensive and destructive than any of the problems that can come with the prophetic. Every birth, spiritual or natural, is painful and messy, but the child is worth it.

In almost every congregation I visit, I meet at least two or three people who have been wounded by the misuse of prophecy. However, I have also met many Christians who have been wounded by a pastor at some time. Do we throw the pastoral ministry out of the church because of this? Of course not, and neither can we throw out the prophetic. The prophetic ministry is not a panacea for everything that ails the church, but it is necessary, or the Lord would not have given these gifts to us.

The Scriptures exhort us especially to seek prophecy for a good reason. This gift helps to release all of the other gifts, and helps the church to maintain a sense of intimacy with the Lord. The quality of any relationship can be judged by the quality of the communication in it. The Lord is not a God who wrote a book and then retired. He desires a close relationship with us, and that requires communication from us. Prophecy is a primary way that He communicates with us. Prophecy is not meant to supplant Scripture, which God gave to establish sound doctrine. Neither was Scripture given to replace the Holy Spirit and the gift of prophecy in our lives.

Because this ministry is so important, it is under constant attack. The most deadly attacks against the prophetic have almost always come from Christian leaders who have either been wounded by a misuse of the prophetic or pseudo-prophetic. These leaders usually claim to love the prophetic and love prophecy, but then go on to use the most extreme examples of problems caused by this ministry—or those who claim to have this ministry. This effectively sows such doubt about the prophetic ministry or gift of prophecy that those who listen to them or read their books will be essentially cut off from the genuine prophetic ministry as well. Certainly those who are called to the prophetic ministry must not cut themselves off from needed correction from other members of the body, but this is a wrong way to bring correction to any part of the body. I have heard and witnessed far worse mistakes made by pastors than I have ever seen come from anyone with an authentic prophetic ministry. I could probably accumulate many volumes of these examples to "bring correction" to pastors, but the real result of this would be to have just about everyone doubt their pastors. I could certainly do the same with the evangelists, using all of the most extreme examples of mistakes made by evangelists, and likewise have everyone doubting them. Is this kind of thing going to get us where we are supposed to be?

It is true that all of God's people are supposed to know His voice, but this does not deny the need for the prophetic ministry. The eye cannot say to the hand, "I have no need of you" (1 Cor. 12:21). We need everything God has given us through His Holy Spirit. King David, one of the greatest prophets in Scripture, had the wisdom and humility to inquire of other prophets at times. He remained open to the prophets for his entire life. He never considered himself so mature that he did not need them.

Even the most prophetically gifted people have a difficult time hearing from God for themselves; they often ask other prophets for personal direction. The Lord obviously could speak to them about their own personal matters. He does speak occasionally, but He usually does not. He has so ordered life that we all need each other. This keeps us humble so He can trust us with more spiritual authority.

Martin Luther was one of the most powerful prophetic voices of the New Testament age. He was just a monk, but he shook the influential leaders and institutions of his time to their very foundations. Not since Paul and Silas compelled the leaders of the mighty Roman Empire to declare that those "who have turned the world upside down have come here too" (Acts 17:6 NKJV) had the world witnessed Luther's revolutionary power. He stood against the greatest darkness of his times, refused to retreat, and drove the darkness back.

The tiny church of Wittenberg, Germany, was hardly as big as many garages are today. But God does not care about size when He determines to do something. When Luther nailed his Ninety-five Theses to its door, the whole earth read them and trembled. No conqueror or political leader in all of history changed the world as much as that one monk. His is one of the greatest testimonies of the power of one humble man. He took his stand on the truth without compromise, and he made the whole world bow its knee to the truth. That is the nature of true prophetic power.

If pastors allow staff and parishioners to exercise the prophetic ministry, they can use the following two discernment principles and the twelve common prophetic deceptions to test these people; they can also educate their congregation to use these guidelines. If you are a layperson or staff member who is interested in a prophetic ministry, you should be willing to work within these boundaries.

DISCERNMENT PRINCIPLES TO TEST PROPHETS

When the disciples asked the Lord about the signs of the end of the age, He began His answer with, "See to it that no one misleads you" (Matt. 24:4). While listing a number of events in these perilous times, He included, "False Christs and false prophets will arise and will show great signs and wonders, so as to mislead, if possible, even the elect" (Matt. 24:24). As we get closer to the end times, we must recognize these false Christs and false prophets.

PRINCIPLE ONE: KNOW THE TRUE

The most important principle for discerning the false is to know the true. The better we know someone, the less likely we are to be fooled when others try to disguise themselves as that person. And the better we know the Lord, the less likely we are to be fooled by any spirit that claims to be Him. Likewise, the better we know true prophecy, the less likely we are to be deceived by the false.

Of course, in Matthew 24:24, the Lord was warning people about those who would claim to be *the Christ*. Many non-Christians and pseudo-Christians have been, and will continue to be, carried away with false Christs. However, false Christs will not fool believers who know the true Christ.

The warning about "false Christs" is not just a warning about those who claim to be Christ. The Greek word for *Christ* can also be translated "anointed." The warning is also meant to be more general: Many will come claiming to be "anointed" of God and be impostors. False prophets will obviously be a much greater danger to the true church than false Christs will.

I have watched a number of churches and ministries devastated by false prophets or false prophecies. Why? For basically the same reason people may be fooled by the false Christ: Those who do not know true prophecy will be easily fooled by false prophecy.

Some of the more glaring examples of this have come through the false prophecies that set a date for the Lord's return. It is most sobering to watch so much of the church get caught up with these prophecies that are in clear contradiction to the Scripture that states, "No man knows the time." Those churches and movements so easily captured by these false prophecies are often those that reject the gift of prophecy as being for the church today.

An example of this was when so much of the church was swept up with the "88 Reasons Why the Lord Will Return in 1988." Every one of the prophetic people I knew at that time, and the movements that were seeking to grow in prophetic ministry, easily discerned this as spurious. It was alarming that so many who were so distracted by this did not seem to confess their mistake after it had become so obvious or even examine how this happened to them. Remarkably, many of these people simply expressed an increased disdain for the gift of prophecy.

If the apostle Paul admitted to having been "foiled by Satan" (1 Thess. 2:18, author's trans.), it can happen to any of us. Our response to this should not be to reject prophecy. Prophecy is such a central theme of Scripture and has been a primary way the Lord has related to His people from the beginning. Our response must be to increase our resolve to know the true so we can quickly discern the false.

It is also biblical wisdom not to be "ignorant" of Satan's schemes (2 Cor. 2:11). Therefore, it is right to examine ways that Satan has fooled either others or us. So, to sum up principle number one, we need to know the true, but we also need to admit our need for God's grace and wisdom, being willing to honestly admit our mistakes.

PRINCIPLE TWO: THE BETTER WE KNOW
THE HOLY SPIRIT, THE SAFER WE WILL BE

One can be a true believer but still be a false prophet or give false prophecies. The Lord Jesus Himself confirmed this in Matthew 24:4–5: "And Jesus answered and said to them, 'See to it that no one misleads you. For many will come in My name, saying, 'I am the Christ,' and will mislead many.'" The Lord did not say that many would say that they were the Christ, but that *they* would come saying that He, Jesus, was the Christ, and yet they would still mislead many. History has testified to the truth of this, as some of the most destructive false prophets stated that Jesus was the Christ, and yet deceived many. How could this happen?

False prophets and false prophecies are founded on deception. The most effective guise of the enemy is to come as "an angel of light" or "a messenger of truth." Just because a prophecy has some truth in it does not make it genuine. Unfortunately, Satan knows the Bible better than most Christians. He is so clever at perverting its message, he even tried it on Jesus, who is the Word Himself. Just knowing Scripture, and being able to bludgeon others into submission with it, does not make one a true messenger. We must ask if someone is "rightly dividing the word of truth" (2 Tim. 2:15 NKJV).

Who will know if the Word is being rightly divided? The One who wrote the Book. Doesn't that leave a lot of room for subjectivity? Yes, it does, and that is dangerous, but it is far more dangerous not to allow for subjectivity in the discernment of truth. Subjectivity is essential. People will not be saved because they know someone else who is saved. The Lord must become our personal Savior, our personal Lord, and truth must be personal if we are really going to know it. For this reason the Bible was meant to be relatively subjective in its interpretation. This was not to promote private interpretations, but to require each of us to be seekers of the Lord and His truth ourselves. We will not keep from being deceived just because we know someone who knows the Bible. Every one of us must know the Spirit of Truth.

Scholars have devised many systems of hermeneutics to remove subjectivity from biblical interpretation. Many of these are excellent guidelines, but regardless of how good our hermeneutics, we will be subject increasingly to deception in the coming times if we do not know and follow the Spirit of Truth. We must recognize that some hermeneutic principles are an attempt to remove our need for the Holy Spirit, regardless of how much the developers give lip service to needing Him. Many of those who react the most to what they perceive to be people's tendency toward "private interpretations" are really reacting to the ability of people to see things differently from the way they do.

To sum up discernment principle two, we will not keep from being deceived without the Holy Spirit. The better we know Him, and the closer we remain to Him, the safer we will be. This is true with doctrine and with prophecy. Once we understand these foundational principles, we must be watchful for twelve characteristic deceptions of false prophets or false prophecies.

TWELVE DECEPTIONS OF FALSE PROPHETS

Following are twelve primary ways we can be deceived and fall into the traps that open us up to false prophecy or false prophets.

DECEPTION ONE: ALLOWING ANY TRUTH, EVEN A BIBLICAL TRUTH, TO ECLIPSE THE CENTRALITY OF CHRIST

Christ is the ultimate purpose of God. As Mike Bickle, pastor of Metro Christian Fellowship in Kansas City, Missouri, once said, "If we do not keep our attention focused on the ultimate purpose of God, we will be distracted by the lesser purposes of God." Those who go to extremes, or become eccentric (which means to be "off center"), do so because they lose their focus on Christ. As Ephesians 1:9–10 states: "He made known to us the mystery of His will, according to His kind intention which He purposed in Him with a view to an administration suitable to the fulness of the times, that is, the summing up of all things in Christ, things in the heavens and things upon the earth."

The central purpose of the church is to reveal Jesus. The apostolic commission was not just to teach truths, but to labor until Christ was formed in His church. Only when He is formed in us can we do the works He did. We must never let any doctrine or emphasis eclipse our simple devotion of being close to Him and becoming like Him. As the apostle prayed: "I am afraid, lest as the serpent deceived Eve by his craftiness, your minds should be led astray from the simplicity and purity of devotion to Christ" (2 Cor. 11:3).

The ultimate goal of the Father is to have all things summed up in His Son. Truths, the church, the ministry, even worship, can become idols if we allow them to take Jesus' rightful place as the central focus of our devotion.

DECEPTION TWO: BECOMING TOO SYMPATHETIC TO INTERESTS OF MEN

We are commanded to love people, but we must not let our hearts be captured by human interests. This happens when we get the two great commandments out of order, which causes us to love people more than we love the Lord. As James warned: "You adulteresses, do you not know that friendship with the world is hostility toward God? Therefore whoever wishes to be a friend of the world makes himself an enemy of God" (James 4:4).

To the degree that we are subject to the influences of fallen humanity, we will be found doing that which is contrary to God. The Lord Jesus said to the Pharisees, "You are those who justify yourselves in the sight of men, but God knows your hearts; for that which is highly esteemed among men is detestable in the sight of God" (Luke 16:15). The reverse is also true; the things that are highly esteemed by God are usually detestable in the sight of men. *Someone* is going to detest what we are doing. Who do we want it to be, God or men?

The Lord Jesus also said, "Woe to you when all men speak well of you, for in the same way their fathers used to treat the false prophets" (Luke 6:26). When the gospel has been preached in its purity and power, it has brought the most vehement persecution from men.

Jeremiah made a most sobering observation: "The prophets prophesy falsely, and the priests rule on their own authority; and My people love it so! But what will you do at the end of it?" (Jer. 5:31). The people will actually love false prophecy, and if prophets are afraid of people, they will end up prophesying falsely to please others.

DECEPTION THREE: HAVING AN UNHOLY FAMILIARITY WITH GOD

True prophetic ministry must have a proper balance between friendship with the Lord and fear of the Lord. John was intimate with the Lord, but Judas was familiar. There is a difference between these two. Even though John was close enough to the Lord to lay his head on His breast, when John saw the resurrected Christ during His revelation,

John fell to the ground like a dead man. That is what Paul meant when he exhorted the church to know both "the kindness and severity of God" (Rom. 11:22).

Amos 3:7 states: "Surely the LORD God does nothing unless He reveals His secret counsel to His servants the prophets." The Lord does this because the prophets are His friends, and He does not want to do anything without sharing it with them. The essence of true prophetic ministry is being that close to God. Even so, Psalm 25:14 adds: "The secret of the LORD is for those who fear Him." Wisdom is to seek to be as close to the Lord as we possibly can be, while at the same time remembering who He is and who we are. Anyone who does not fear the Lord has not seen Him as He is.

One characteristic that is evident in the lives of all true prophets is the pure and holy fear of the Lord. It is a fearful thing to presume to speak in His name when He has not spoken. What could be more of a delusion than to presume to put words into the mouth of Almighty God? Beware of any messenger who does not display this holy fear of the Lord.

DECEPTION FOUR: THINKING THAT YOU ALONE SEE THE TRUTH

Even prophets only see in part. If we are to have the whole picture, we must put our part together with the other parts. In the Scripture quoted above from Amos, the Lord declared that He does not do anything unless He reveals His secret counsel to His servants the *prophets* (plural). Those who only listen to one prophet or teacher are usually a cult. The Lord has composed His body so that we all need each other. And prophets don't just need other prophets; they need the other ministries given to the body just as much as anyone does.

When Elijah complained to the Lord that all of the prophets had been killed and that he alone was left, the Lord rebuked him. The Lord informed him that He had seven thousand other prophets in Israel (1 Kings 19:18). The Lord instructed Elijah to anoint his successor because it was time for Elijah to come home to heaven. The deception that leads to isolation, whether real or perceived, is a deadly one; it can bring an end to the fruitfulness of even the most powerful ministry.

DECEPTION FIVE: BEWARE OF THOSE WHO DO NOT WALK IN WHAT THEY PREACH

A key element for anyone who would walk in a true prophetic ministry is faithfulness to his or her own message: "Who has stood in the council of the LORD? . . . Who has given heed to His word and listened?" (Jer. 23:18). Beware of those who do not walk in what they preach. This is not to say that a prophet cannot make mistakes. However, we need to discern between those who are sincerely seeking to obey and live uprightly before the Lord and those who preach His words but do not obey them.

DECEPTION SIX: PROPHESYING PREJUDICES

Prophets who allow prejudices to influence the words they attach to "thus saith the Lord" will become false. Prejudices can be cultural, religious, racial—the result of unhealed wounds or character flaws. Anyone who feels called to the prophetic ministry or who is sometimes used in prophetic gifts, must heed the exhortation: "Watch over your heart with all diligence, for from it flow the springs of life" (Prov. 4:23). The following are a few of the more common prejudices that can wrongly influence prophecy:

Pet doctrines can wrongly influence prophecies. The Lord does not give prophecies to verify doctrines—He gave the Bible for that. Prophecy was used to write Scripture, but now the canon is complete. Prophecy is not used to verify or establish doctrine. Prophecy may be used to illuminate specific applications of Scripture, such as the revelation that led Peter to preach the gospel to the Gentiles. Beware of using prophecy to verify doctrines, especially those that are ambiguous or obscure.

Bitterness or resentment can also influence the message. The priests in the Old Testament could not have scabs. Unhealed wounds can be a destructive element in any ministry. If we have spiritual scabs, it is because we have not taken them to the cross and applied the balm of forgiveness. Anyone who is walking in unforgiveness can be easily subjected to deception.

Rejection is another problem that can turn a true prophet into a false one. The Lord often allows His prophets to be rejected to deliver them from the fear of man. If they are going to be prophetic, they must learn to live with rejection without becoming reactionary or bitter. If they continue to be overly sensitive, this unhealed wound can affect their perception.

Rebellion is another stronghold that can lead to false prophecy. Rebellion is rooted either in rejection, self-will, or both. This can be deadly to the prophetic ministry. As Samuel warned King Saul, "rebellion is as the sin of witchcraft" (1 Sam. 15:23 NKJV). There can be a fine line between divination and revelation, and rebellious prophets can easily be led into crossing that line. Witchcraft, which is counterfeit spiritual authority, is exactly contrary to prophetic ministry.

The *"party spirit"* or sectarianism can also lead to false prophecy. When prophets derive their recognition from a single organization, there will be pressure to prophesy the "party line." This can make it very difficult to preserve prophetic integrity.

Of course, all of these strongholds can pervert any ministry, not just the prophetic. All of us must esteem the word of the Lord so that we will never let our own opinions or flaws influence what we say in His great name. The more respect we have for this, the more He will trust us with spiritual authority and revelation.

DECEPTION SEVEN: BEWARE OF SOMEONE WHO TAKES MORE AUTHORITY THAN THE LORD HAS GIVEN

Even if the Lord gives a prophet a revelation, that does not necessarily give the prophet authority to dictate policy or to compel others to take action on it.

In the Old Testament, prophets were often called "watchmen" because they were spiritually stationed on "the walls of Jerusalem." From that position, watchmen would be the first to see someone coming. It was the watchman's job to distinguish between friend and foe and to convey what he discerned to the elders who sat in the gates. However, it was not the watchman's job to determine what action should be taken. It was the elders' responsibility to determine if someone was to be let in or kept out of the city or to sound the alarm to mobilize troops.

Unfortunately, many prophetic people fall into the trap of believing that they have the responsibility to see their prophecy brought to pass. From that they will assume the authority to carry it out. This brings many unnecessary conflicts to congregations and ministries, since the Lord has established pastors and elders in the church for that purpose.

Paul talked about how careful he was to stay within the realm of authority that had been appointed to him (2 Cor. 10:12–14). Here he was speaking geographically, but it is just as true spiritually. Paul also said to the Corinthians, "If to others I am not an apostle, at least I am to you" (1 Cor. 9:2). By this Paul acknowledged that he was not an apostle to the whole church. When Paul went to Jerusalem, he was not given apostolic authority in the church there, although he was honored as an apostle to the Gentiles. He could not dictate policy as he could have in the churches he raised up. In Jerusalem, he was just a visiting missionary, esteemed, but not followed.

Some prophetic people fall into the trap of feeling the responsibility to tear down anything that they do not believe is from the Lord. However, prophets only have authority to tear down that which they have been used to raise up. Paul warned the church in Corinth that he had authority to tear down as well as build up because he was the father of the church there.

Would any responsible father let just anyone come in and start bringing correction or dictating policy to his family? I certainly would not let anyone bring correction to a work I had responsibility for unless he had also been involved in building it. If you are a responsible leader of a church or work, and someone who has not been a part of the building claims to be sent to bring correction or set things in order, you have the right to throw him out.

True spiritual authority is built on love and trust. Love and service earn trust. If a person comes to me with a corrective word about what to do in the nursery but has never been willing to work there, I will not even bother to listen. Like most pastors, I get piles of prophecies from people who try to dictate policy in our ministry, and many of them I do not even know! Such misuses of "prophecy" make it obvious why so many pastors come to despise prophecy. These actions may have caused so many problems that any pastor who is still open to prophecy demonstrates extraordinary grace.

Some prophets who claim to be watchmen do not have the proper trust relationship with the elders of the church, and they, therefore, try to usurp the authority of the elders. If church members or staff are called as watchmen, they must allow the Lord to establish their authority with those who have authority and not strive to gain influence themselves.

DECEPTION EIGHT: A WORD THAT DOES NOT COME IN THE DEMONSTRATION OF THE FRUIT OF THE SPIRIT

God denied Moses the blessing of leading the people into their promised land because the Lord told him to speak to the rock to bring forth water, but he struck the rock in anger. As a prophet he represented the Lord as being angry when He was not, and it cost him dearly. It is easy to understand how Moses was frustrated, but prophets must never convey their feelings as the Lord's. Many prophetic people have disqualified themselves from higher realms of authority by representing the Lord improperly.

To think that, because God occasionally uses prophets, He thinks just as they do, or that their feelings are His feelings, is a serious delusion. Prophets must carefully distinguish their own feelings from that which is from the anointing. This is not easy to do even for mature prophets.

Elijah prayed for the judgments of the Lord to come on the people, but it was not out of his own wrath. God's wrath is not like our wrath. Neither is His jealousy like self-centered jealousy. Prophets must always be careful not to represent their anger as being the Lord's, or they might end up like Moses. Whenever a prophet has a word of correction for another ministry or person, the would-be prophet should ask three important questions: Do I love them? Has God given me authority with them? Has the bridge of trust been built so they could be expected to receive what I think I should share?

DECEPTION NINE: SIN

Because prophets are called to *see* for the body, the enemy usually concentrates his attack on them through their eyes. Therefore, pornography or other forms of lust are serious traps. If prophets are going to function as the eye of the body, they must be careful in how they use their eyes. Job showed great wisdom when he said, "I have made a covenant with my eyes; how then could I gaze at a virgin?" (Job 31:1). Job vowed that he wouldn't look on something that would cause him to stumble. If a prophet's eye is on the Lord, his or her whole body will be full of light. If a prophet looks upon lust or other sin, darkness will enter his or her soul. Deception will come from that darkness.

All prophets should remember the Scripture: "But encourage one another day after day, as long as it is still called 'Today,' lest any one of you be hardened by *the deceitfulness of sin*" (Heb. 3:13, emphasis added).

DECEPTION TEN: NEW COVENANT PROPHETS WHO TYPE THEMSELVES AFTER OLD COVENANT PROPHETS

The spiritual gifts of New Testament prophets are basically the same as in the Old Testament, but the function of the New Testament prophet is very different. Many think of prophets as harsh and always looking for what is wrong with people. That was often the nature of the old covenant prophet, because he was under the law and therefore had to represent its severity.

However, the New Testament prophet is under the covenant of grace and truth, and likewise must represent that covenant. The Lord did not come to condemn us, but to save us by laying down His own life. That should be the nature of anyone who is called to speak for Him in this age of grace and truth. Truth without grace will at best be only half the message.

Another major difference between the prophets under these two different covenants is that the old covenant prophets often stood alone; the new covenant prophets, however, are one of a team of ministries that equips the church. Therefore, the new covenant prophet must be properly related to the rest of the team; to do so the prophet must understand the other equipping ministries listed in Ephesians 4: apostles, evangelists, pastors, and teachers.

A serious deception can enter into a ministry when a young, immature prophet tries to live under the old covenant mandate for prophets given in Deuteronomy 18:18–22:

> I will raise up a prophet from among their countrymen like you, and I will put My words in his mouth, and he shall speak to them all that I command him. And it shall come about that whoever will not listen to My words which he shall speak in My name, I Myself will require it of him. But the prophet who shall speak a word presumptuously in My name which I have not commanded him to speak, or which he shall speak in the name of other gods, that prophet shall die. And you may say in your heart, "How shall we know the word which the LORD has not spoken?" When a prophet speaks in the name of the LORD, if the thing does not come about or come true, that is the thing which the LORD has not spoken. The prophet has spoken it presumptuously; you shall not be afraid of him.

This was the standard under the law. Under that covenant anyone who failed in any point of the law was under condemnation to the whole law. However, we cannot put the New Testament prophet under the law without putting the rest of the body under the law as well.

What pastor or teacher could live under a yoke that removed him from his ministry if he made just one mistake? When young, struggling prophetic ministries try to comply with this old covenant mandate, it will seriously distort their development and their character. This yoke makes it impossible for them to acknowledge and learn from their mistakes.

This does not mean that we can compromise the high standards required of one who would speak for the Lord. Mistakes must be addressed and the reasons for them found. No prophet is infallible, which is why new covenant prophecy must be judged. There are even cases where old covenant prophets missed a prediction or prophecy, but were still acknowledged as prophets by the Lord (Jonah, Isaiah, and Elijah all made statements that were not true or did not come to pass). Because anyone can make a mistake, the church is responsible for knowing the Lord's voice.

DECEPTION ELEVEN: PROPHETS WHO SAY THEY ARE NOT REQUIRED TO USE PROPER BIBLICAL PROTOCOL OR PROCEDURE

The prophets under the old covenant were used mostly to bring correction to the Lord's people, but this is not the case in the New Testament. In the New Testament the apostles and elders assumed this duty. This does not mean that a prophet cannot be used to bring correction, but it is no longer a primary responsibility. And when prophets are used this way, they must comply with the new covenant procedure for correction given in Matthew 18 and Galatians 6:1. Anyone who tries to bring correction to someone else publicly and has not first been to him or her privately, and then with another witness, is at best out of order. At worst, they are a stumbling block.

DECEPTION TWELVE: THE PRESUMPTION THAT PROPHECY MUST BE SPECIFIC OR SPECTACULAR

Normally, prophetic words are general. For example, the Lord could have been much more specific with His prophecies in the Scriptures. He could have told of the emergence of America, the dates and places that the world wars would start, or other great events in history in much more detail than He chose to. Prophecy is seldom given to convince someone that the Lord exists, or to testify that we are His messengers. It is given for revealing His strategic will and for awakening the church to her need to prepare for coming events or conditions. The Lord wants prophecy to be general enough to require those who receive it to both know His voice and still have to walk in faith and wisdom. Many have turned a good prophecy into a false one by trying to go beyond what they were given to make it more spectacular.

Paul Cain once said, "Almost every heresy was the result of men trying to carry to logical conclusions that which God has only revealed in part." I think history corroborates that statement.

Finally, both pastors and prophets must beware of the wizard spirit.

UNDERSTANDING THE WIZARD SPIRIT

The "wizard" will be one of the primary forms of false prophets who try to infiltrate the body of Christ. They will usually have a clean, professional appearance, and will often establish their credibility by "prophesying" information that they know in the natural. One of their chief weapons will be flattery. They will divert us from the purposes the Lord has for us by prophesying to us things that are either greater, or seem more glamorous, than what the Lord has given us to do. Scripture warns us about this: "They speak falsehood to one another; *with flattering lips* and with a double heart they speak. May the LORD cut off all *flattering lips*, the tongue that *speaks great things*" (Ps. 12:2–3, emphasis added).

Anyone who is involved in prophetic ministry should also be aware of the following passage from Ezekiel:

> Then the word of the LORD came to me saying, "Son of man, prophesy against the prophets of Israel who prophesy, and say to those who prophesy from their own inspiration, 'Listen to the word of the LORD!' Thus says the Lord GOD, "Woe to the foolish prophets who are following their own spirit and have seen nothing. O Israel, your prophets have been like foxes among ruins. You have not gone up into the breaches, nor did you build the wall around the house of Israel to stand in the battle on the day of the LORD. They see falsehood and lying divination who are saying, 'The LORD declares,' when the LORD has not sent them; yet they hope for the fulfillment of their word. Did you not see a false vision and speak a lying divination when you said, 'The LORD declares,' but it is not I who have spoken?"
>
> Therefore, thus says the Lord GOD, "Because you have spoken falsehood and seen a lie, therefore behold, I am against you," declares the Lord GOD. "So My hand will be against the prophets who see false visions and utter lying divinations. They will have no place in the council of My people, nor will they be written down in the register of the house of Israel, nor will they enter the land of Israel, that you may know that I am the Lord GOD." (Ezek. 13:1–9)

One of the responsibilities of biblical prophets was to confront and expose false prophets. True new covenant prophets must face up to this responsibility. Admittedly, this is one of the most uncomfortable tasks because it will probably make a prophet appear to be self-serving or even self-righteous. Even so, prophets must esteem the interests of the Lord and the welfare of His people above all else.

Just as the Lord promised, at the end of the age, prophecies, visions, and dreams are being poured out (Acts 2:17). These are being given because we will need them for accomplishing our last-day mandate. I look forward to the day when all of us will fulfill God's call on our lives.

THE CALL

In Chapter 1, I mentioned the different armies I saw in a vision published in *The Call*. At the end of that vision I saw a new city, the glory of which was beyond anything I had seen or imagined before. One feature that stood out was the large amount of glass windows in each structure or dwelling. This glass was so clear and clean, and the windows and doors were so situated, that I sensed I was not only welcome in each dwelling but also invited. It was also as if nothing was hidden, and there was no danger of anything being stolen.

Then I looked at the people in the city. They seemed familiar, but at the same time I knew that I had never met anyone like them. They were as I imagined Adam to have been before the Fall. Each one's eyes shone with what seemed to be almost total comprehension, an intellectual depth far beyond even the most brilliant person I had ever known. I knew this to be the result of an order and peace that were completely free of confusion or doubt—or maybe the confusion *of* doubt. They had no self-seeking ambition because all were so confident and had so much joy in who they were and what they were doing. Because all the people were free, they were also completely open. Poverty or sickness seemed incomprehensible.

I then noticed that there were no restaurants, hotels, or hospitals in the city. I understood that none of these were needed because every home was a center of hospitality and healing. Almost every home was open to travelers. Those that were not open were used for special purposes, such as study or long-term healing. I could tell that every home had been built for this great ministry of hospitality, helps, or healing, even those being built on the Highway of Judgment. Because of this, even the Highway of Judgment was appealing. It was apparent that every street was not only safe, but was more desirable than any other road or highway I had ever seen. This city was far more glorious than any utopia of which philosophers could conceive.

My attention was drawn back to the Highway of Judgment. It seemed to have been the least traveled highway, but now was becoming much more active. I then saw that this was because the other streets and highways all flowed toward this one.

I was then standing in the Great Hall of Judgment, and the Lord began to speak to me.

You have seen My people as My army, My city, and My bride. Now you do not just see these, but you feel them. Only when My truth comes from the heart does it have the power to change men. Living waters must come from the innermost being—the heart. Just as you felt My truth cleansing you, I am making My messengers flames of fire who will speak truth, not to just give understanding, but with the power to change men's hearts. The truth that I am sending will not just convict My people of their sin, but will cleanse them from their sin.

Even as He was speaking, a great zeal rose up in me to do something. Divine strategies I knew could help His people began coming to me. I could not wait to begin. I now believed that even the driest bones were going to become an exceedingly great army! In the Lord's presence, nothing seemed impossible. I had no trouble believing that His church would become a bride without spot or wrinkle, or that His church would become a great city, standing as a fortress of truth for the whole world to behold. I had no doubt that His people, even as weak and defeated as they now seemed, are about to become an army of truth before which no power of darkness can stand. Feeling the power of truth as never before, I knew that His power was much greater than the darkness.

This is our call. To love truth, righteousness, and justice. To do all things for the sake of the gospel. To live no longer for ourselves but for the One who purchased us with His own blood. To challenge the great darkness of our times, and push it back. The power of the truth that has been given to us is greater than any lie. We must never again retreat before the enemies of the cross. By the power given to us through the cross, we must now overcome evil with good. His kingdom is coming, and His will is going to be done, right here on earth as it is in heaven. To proclaim this truth with your life is the reason you are here.

NOTES

CHAPTER 9: BIRTH PANGS AND EARTHQUAKES
1. *The Charlotte Observer*, 4 April 1999, 1.

CHAPTER 10: THE RELIGIOUS SPIRIT
1. Some of the material for this chapter, as well as a few of the test questions, came from Jack Deere's outstanding tape series *Exposing the Religious Spirit*, available through the Tape Catalog of Morning-Star Publications. Catalogs are available free of charge by calling 1-800-542-0278.

About the Author

Rick Joyner is the founder and executive director of MorningStar Publications and Ministries in Charlotte, North Carolina. He has written more than a dozen books, including *The Final Quest*, *The Prophetic Ministry*, *The Harvest*, *There Were Two Trees in the Garden*, and *The Call*.

Rick is also the editor of *The Morning Star Journal* and *The Morning Star Prophetic Bulletin*, and is the director of the MorningStar Fellowship of Ministries and the MorningStar Fellowship of Churches.

Rick lives in North Carolina with his wife, Julie, and their five children. Rick can be contacted by writing c/o MorningStar Ministries, 303 Hollywood Rd., Moravian Falls, NC 28654 or by fax at (336) 838-6380. MorningStar's Web site is located at http://www.eaglestar.org.